BLACK PULP

BLACK PULP

Genre Fiction in the Shadow of Jim Crow

BROOKS E. HEFNER

University of Minnesota Press | Minneapolis | London

Portions of chapters 2, 3, and 4 were published in a different form in "Signifying Genre: George S. Schuyler and the Vagaries of Black Pulp," *Modernism/Modernity* 26, no. 3 (September 2019): 483–504; copyright 2019 The Johns Hopkins University Press. A portion of chapter 3 was published in a different form as "How It Happens Here: Race and American Anti-Fascist Literature," *Los Angeles Review of Books,* November 26, 2016.

Quotation from the correspondence of Will Thomas is reprinted by permission of Anne Wilhelen Smith. Quotation from the correspondence of Carl Murphy is reprinted courtesy of the *AFRO American* Newspapers Archives.

Published by the University of Minnesota Press
111 Third Avenue South, Suite 290
Minneapolis, MN 55401-2520
http://www.upress.umn.edu

ISBN 978-1-5179-1156-0 (hc)
ISBN 978-1-5179-1157-7 (pb)

Library of Congress record available at https://lccn.loc.gov/2021023217

CONTENTS

INTRODUCTION
SIGNIFYING GENRE, ARTICULATING RACE

WHEN NEWS BROKE that Jordan Peele's brilliant 2017 horror film *Get Out* had been nominated for a Golden Globe, fans of Peele's work were no doubt thrilled. Peele's film, one of the most talked-about films of the year, tapped into and transformed long-standing, racist cinematic horror tropes that pitted white minds against Black bodies in a canny updating of body snatching. However, fans were also doubtless perplexed when the film's nomination was for "Best Motion Picture—Musical or Comedy" and its lead, Daniel Kaluuya, was nominated for "Best Performance by an Actor in a Motion Picture—Musical or Comedy." *Get Out* is definitely not a musical, so what exactly was supposed to be so funny about the story of wealthy whites who, attempting to prolong their own lives, murder young, unsuspecting African Americans and transplant their brains into now-mindless Black bodies? Sure, Peele had made a name for himself as comedian, first in *MadTV* and later as the co-creator and costar (with Keegan-Michael Key) of the Comedy Central series *Key and Peele*. But as many commenters noted in praising the film, *Get Out* was a clear departure from this kind of work, taking scenarios that might have served as a premise for a *Key and Peele* sketch and transmuting the uncomfortable humor of interracial interactions into a deep sense of horror and dread and a meditation on the value of Black lives. How, then, did a horror film get so terribly misread?

1

A backlash to this categorization ensued, which prompted Peele to admit that the film's own production companies had submitted *Get Out* under this category, in part because it did not necessarily fit the Golden Globes' idea of drama.[1] In the media junket that followed, Peele took the opportunity to meditate on—and joke about—the intersection of genre and race that occasioned the backlash around *Get Out*'s nomination. In a statement to *Deadline,* Peele admitted:

> When I originally heard the idea of placing it in the comedy category it didn't register to me as an issue. I missed it. There's no category for social thriller. So what? I moved on. I made this movie for the loyal black horror fans who have been underrepresented for years. . . . The reason for the visceral response to this movie being called a comedy is that we are still living in a time in which African American cries for justice aren't being taken seriously.[2]

Peele's contention that social realities actually condition how genre is understood and perceived is a powerful one; it additionally suggests that direct attention to race and racism within the confines of popular genre might offer new ways of seeing. He also indicates that the response highlights a broader cultural inability to read Black genre for its attention to "African American cries for justice." In other words, Black genre and issues of social justice are intertwined in such a way to make them illegible for some audiences. In an interview with Stephen Colbert, Peele riffed on a series of responses to the controversy, joking that he had "submitted it as a documentary" but also admitting that *Get Out* "sort of subverts the idea of genre. . . . But it is the kind of movie that black people can laugh at, but white people, not so much."[3] Peele's clever oscillation between generic definitions—horror, comedy, and documentary—demonstrates just how complex genre can be when discussions of race are at its center.

THE WHITENESS OF THE PULPS

I began work on *Black Pulp* not with the puzzling categorization of *Get Out* in mind but rather with a different but related series of questions. After spending years researching a variety of genres as they were created and developed in the pages of American pulp magazines in the early twentieth century, I found myself asking, where are the Black characters? Where are the Black authors? Where are the Black readers of popular fiction? Pulp magazine horror, like that found in *Weird Tales,* loved to feature intimidating, brown- and black-skinned figures menacing underdressed white women. Pulp adventure stories frequently sent their Anglo-Saxon protagonists to exotic locales where they could subdue vast, nameless hordes of colonized racial others. But African American protagonists were all but invisible across the entire pulp publishing industry. When characters appeared as more than mere stereotypes, it was rare—and usually still unsatisfactory. This was the case when, in 1911, Henry E. Baker and Lloyd Osbourne traded letters in the NAACP organ the *Crisis* over the representation of the African American character Daggancourt in Osbourne's serial "The Kingdoms of the World," published in the pulp *Munsey's Magazine.* Baker saw the representation of this "better educated colored man" as demeaning and humiliating, but Osbourne defended his representation as a kind of incremental progress: "Do you realize that the injustice of our (white) people is so colossal that it is already something for a writer to draw a colored man endowed with such elementary good qualities as affection, trustworthiness, honor, industry, self-respect, etc.?"[4] Osbourne's response here indicates just how far from the norm an African American character with even a modicum of humanity or complexity would fall within the racial politics of the pulp genre system.

Enterprising publishers, engaging what I have elsewhere called genre speculation, could imagine a readership for a magazine like *Zeppelin Stories,* a subgenre of so-called aviation fiction that exclusively published "action stories of lighter than air craft," but the only pulp magazine to engage significantly with African American representation was *Harlem Stories,* which survived for two issues in 1932 under the small and virtually unknown Jaycline Publishing Corporation.[5] Even *Harlem Stories,* a magazine seemingly devoted to depictions of African American life, framed its subject matter from a white point of view. When this magazine was reviewed in the *Baltimore Afro-American,* the anonymous author of the short profile expressed a measured opinion: "The stories, however, for the most part, are written by white writers. This is gleaned from certain glaring errors in the stories that no colored writer with a knowledge of colored America at all could possibly make." The writer continues, "The yarns are . . . written with a degree of sympathy without an overdrawing of either fact or dialect. . . . They tend to make colored folk not monstrosities, but people like one expects to find between the covers of any other magazine."[6] David M. Earle has linked *Harlem Stories* to a subgenre known as the girlie pulps, magazines that featured risqué romance stories often set in entertainment contexts like the theater, something *Harlem Stories* did with its emphasis on cabaret life.[7]

Regardless, a short-lived and likely poorly distributed magazine from a fly-by-night pulp publisher seemed unlikely to attract a broad African American readership, even with its ability to meet the low bar of making "colored folk not monstrosities." It was not the first aborted attempt at a Black pulp. When pulp magazines first started developing genre specializations in the late teens, H. L. Mencken and George Jean Nathan, well-known editors of *The Smart Set,* "toyed with the idea of starting a Negro pulp" to help offset the costs of their more prestigious magazine. In the words of Erin A. Smith, they ultimately "decided there was not enough money in the black community to support one" and instead founded *Black Mask* in 1920. With its introduction of the hard-boiled detective story, this magazine would, after being sold by Mencken and Nathan, go on to become one of the most celebrated magazines of its kind.[8] African American readers were once again denied access to genre fiction that addressed Black experiences or foregrounded Black protagonists.

African American writers were also largely excluded from such venues for popular genres so long as their writing featured prominent racial themes. Nevertheless, many African Americans certainly wrote for pulp magazines, under their own names as well as pseudonyms, but the fiction they published there typically had to ignore race entirely. Will Thomas—discussed in chapter 3—noted that a number of Black writers likely published in the pulps, "but we are not apt to penetrate past their pen names, and so will never suspect their ethnic secret."[9] The key to success in this field, Thomas claimed in "Negro Writers of Pulp Fiction," a 1950 article drawing on his experience making a living at writing for the pulps under unknown pseudonyms, was this reality: "The most frustrating fact a Negro writer has to learn is the reading public—meaning the white public—has rather definite ideas as to what constitutes entertainment, and that the kind of stories and books most of us produce are not in that category."[10] Thomas, who had published his own financially unsuccessful protest novel *God Is for White Folks* (1947), advised readers that the insistence on a racial protest theme would simply not lead to success in the popular writing field. Writers who did not pass by using pseudonyms merely counted on the fact that readers would assume that stories about all white characters were necessarily written by whites. One example of this was *Pittsburgh Courier* columnist Gertrude "Toki" Schalk, discussed in chapter 2, who published stories chronicling the romantic adventures of a cast of exclusively white characters in romance pulps in the 1930s, particularly *Street & Smith's Love Story Magazine, Ainslee's, All-Story Love Stories,* and *Romantic Love Magazine.*

It is difficult to imagine that during this period Black readers and writers were not drawn to the pleasures of popular genre. The first half of the twentieth century was, within the American publishing scene at least, a time during which the pulp genre system essentially invented and developed a host of genres that have exerted a powerful influence on the history of popular fiction and film. Of course, pulp magazines certainly had some degree of Black readership. For example, Shawn Anthony Christian notes that in 1926 Amy Jacques Garvey criticized the presence of pulp magazines (like the girlie pulp *Snappy Stories*) in the reading of "the average Negro": "Rarely one finds a single book of readable worth. Occasionally a detective story, *Snappy Stories,* or *True Romance Magazine,* but how can a young race thrive on such drivel?"[11] Likewise, a rose-tinted 1955 history of the Street & Smith pulp publishers notes that "science-fiction has wide popularity among Negro readers (newsstand sales in Harlem, Chicago's South Side and in many Negro communities in the South show this to be a fact)," attributing this to the idea that "no religious or racial lines [are] drawn in outer space."[12] Critics like John Cheng and John Rieder would certainly disagree with this naive assessment of midcentury science fiction, seeing prominent racial metaphors playing out in stories that valorize plucky whites over decadent and villainous alien races.[13] Science fiction was merely another pulp genre that was, for all intents and purposes, forged in the fires of white supremacy. Longtime pulp editor Harold Hersey put it in no uncertain terms when he (somewhat reluctantly) claimed, "The white man in popular fiction must always triumph in his conquests."[14] Those African

American readers who were reading the pulps were nevertheless trapped in a genre system that valorized whiteness above all else.

In essence, the links between race and genre are potent, and these two concepts are in many respects deeply integrated, as Mark C. Jerng argues in *Racial Worldmaking: The Power of Popular Fiction* (2018). It is not merely that some genres—the plantation romance, the future war story of science fiction—feature racial difference prominently. Instead, he argues that "genre and race should instead be conceptualized as deeply interrelated ways of building-in knowledge in the world" and that they "operate together in making available certain knowledges about and projections of the world."[15] Jerng makes a persuasive case for how race and genre are inextricably interlinked. Even when race is not visually present in popular genres, it nevertheless underscores the generic epistemology that guides and structures these genres' fictional worlds. Jerng's study leaves some room for what he calls "antiracist racial worldmaking," but this is largely confined to late twentieth-century genre revisions that emerged well after the pulp magazines had played out.[16] Jerng's otherwise compelling argument seems to imply that a truly antiracist genre fiction was impossible in the United States in the first half of the twentieth century.

THE ALTERNATIVE SPACE OF BLACK PULP

In pulp magazines, Black readers and writers were not merely denied the pleasures of popular genre fiction—pleasures that might offer escape and imaginary solutions to real problems—but were also usually denied even basic recognition as human beings (and not "monstrosities"). Confronted with the Jim Crow genre fiction of the pulps, they turned their attention to a venue for literary production almost wholly neglected by scholars of African American literary history: the Black newspaper. As I detail in chapter 1, African American newspapers had a long history of publishing fiction and poetry by Black writers, but by and large, until the late 1920s, this output represented what Will Thomas would undoubtedly call protest fiction. However, as pulp magazines gained prominence as legitimate venues for genre experimentation in the 1920s, Black newspapers shifted the kind of fiction they published, becoming in the process a radical space in which Black genre fiction could thrive and reach tens of thousands of African American readers in the process.

My central argument in *Black Pulp* is that attending to the thousands of stories and serial installments published in broadly circulating African American newspapers from the late 1920s through the mid-1950s allows for a recovery of an important and neglected part of African American literary history while simultaneously demonstrating how Black genre fiction disassembles generic formulas saturated with racism and reassembling those genres in the service of racial justice. The *Pittsburgh Courier* and the *Baltimore Afro-American* were the two most prominent venues for the publication of original genre fiction by Black writers, though many other newspapers followed suit. The *Courier* featured this material from roughly 1927 to 1940, with George S. Schuyler single-handedly writing most of the newspaper's genre fiction from 1933 to 1939. The *Afro-American* also began publishing original popular fiction around the same time, but it continued through the mid-1950s, featuring a host of unknown amateur and semiprofessional writers whose names populate this study. Other newspapers across the country entered the fiction business as well, either through the tabloid insert the *Illustrated Feature Section* (discussed in chapter 1) or by editing their own original fiction, often with local interests in mind.

The *Courier* and the *Afro-American* have both received some scholarly attention, though virtually none of this research has seen the literary production in their pages as worthy of more than a casual mention. While early considerations of the Black press, like sociologist E. Franklin Frazier's acerbic *Black Bourgeoisie* (1957), excoriated twentieth-century African American newspapers for creating "a world of make-believe into which the black bourgeoisie can escape from its inferiority and inconsequence in American society," more recent, serious criticism has come to see the Black press as a vibrant part of African American history and print culture.[17] Andrew Buni's *Robert L. Vann of the* Pittsburgh Courier: *Politics and Black Journalism* (1974) and Hayward Farrar's *The Baltimore* Afro-American, *1892–1950* (1998) detail the broad shape of the histories of these important publications, with a strong emphasis on their editorial vision.[18] Mark Whitaker's *Smoketown: The Untold Story of the Other Great Black Renaissance* (2018) features Robert Vann and the *Courier* prominently but focuses almost entirely on the newspaper's sports and arts coverage. Armistead S. Pride and Clint C. Wilson II's valuable survey *A History of the Black Press* (1997) briefly mentions the uplift fiction found in nineteenth-century African American newspapers but essentially ignores the prominence of fiction in these twentieth-century newspapers; Patrick S. Washburn's *The African American Press: Voice of Freedom* (2006) does much the same.[19] Todd Vogel's collection *The Black Press: New Literary and Historical Essays* (2001) devotes only two of its thirteen essays to the early twentieth century, when most major African American newsweeklies were founded or solidified their position in the marketplace.[20]

If the role of major African American newsweeklies as important venues for Black culture in the first half of the twentieth century remains underacknowledged, now is a perfect time to turn our attention to it. This kind of study can benefit from the legacy of rich scholarship on nineteenth-century Black periodicals and popular literary production, from pioneering work by John Ernest, P. Gabrielle Foreman, Frances Smith Foster, Eric Gardner, Elizabeth McHenry, and Carla L. Peterson to more recent interventions by Benjamin Fagan, Katharine Capshaw Smith and Anna Mae Duane, Derrick Spires, and Nazera Sadiq Wright.[21] Likewise, the emergence of projects like Kim Gallon's Black Press Research Collective have made possible new forms of research on twentieth-century African American periodical culture. Meanwhile, the rise of interest in late twentieth-century Black-owned paperback publishers like Holloway House has generated fascinating debates over these cultural producers as forms of Black pulp fiction. Justin Gifford has argued that works by Iceberg Slim and Donald Goines represent "a radical stance against systemic white racism," while Kinohi Nishikawa raises important questions about the problematic "sexual politics" of Holloway House fiction that, drawing on a genealogy he calls "black sleaze," sought an audience primarily of Black men.[22]

Both Gifford and Nishikawa deploy the term "pulp" to describe the literature published by Holloway House; this draws on the vernacular redefinition of the term to characterize virtually any kind of sensational or exploitative fiction. Pocket paperbacks, like those by Iceberg Slim and Goines, are of a piece with the post–World War II paperback publishing landscape, which trafficked in and capitalized on every kind of transgressive subject matter.[23] This commonplace usage masks to a degree the origin of the term, initially used to describe the cheap pulp-wood paper that all-fiction magazines began using around the turn of the twentieth century. These pulp magazines—the print culture phenomenon that gave sensational fiction the nickname "pulp"—remained reasonably conservative in social and political subject matter, in no small part because of their need to travel through the mail (and thereby encounter postal censors). This means that unlike the anything-goes late 1960s and 1970s paperback marketplace that welcomed works like *Trick Baby* (1967) and *Pimp* (1967), African American writers of popular fiction in the early twentieth century would need to use more circuitous paths to offer a form of Black pulp that challenged the hegemony of pulp magazines saturated with racial whiteness. This path would be through the most widely read and widely distributed reading material in Black communities across the United States: the African American newspaper, which served as an alternative pulp space that reached an audience composed almost entirely of middle- and working-class African Americans.

SIGNIFYING/ARTICULATING

In turning its attention to this vast archive of unknown writers and stories, *Black Pulp* intends to do more than merely recover another group of understudied texts. My contention throughout this book is that this group of texts—to my knowledge the largest and most diverse body of Black genre fiction to appear to that point—presents an opportunity for considering the way that genre and race intersect. Any serious attempt to deal with Black genre fiction must deal with the nature of popular genres themselves. Popular genres live and die by repetition and variation. When fictions rely too heavily on convention, they become rote and stale; when they swing too widely away from audience expectations, they run the danger of making a genre obsolete—or creating a new genre entirely. But the repetition—of tropes, themes, scenarios, and settings—quickly creates the building blocks of genre. The field of genre fiction is perhaps the best location to understand what Hans Robert Jauss famously called the "horizon of expectations," which "predisposes its audience to a very specific kind of reception by announcements, overt and covert signals, familiar characteristics, or implicit allusions."[24] In one of the more trenchant theoretical surveys of popular genre, Steve Neale argues that "genres are, nevertheless, best understood as *processes*. These processes may, for sure, be dominated by repetition, but they are also marked fundamentally by difference, variation and change."[25] Far from being mere copies, he notes, "the elements and conventions of a genre are always *in* play rather than being, simply, *re*-played; and any generic corpus is always being expanded."[26]

Neale's sense that genre process are "dominated by repetition, but . . . marked fundamentally by difference, variation and change" sounds a great deal like Henry Louis Gates Jr.'s well-worn definition of the African American cultural practice of "signifyin(g)" as "repetition with a signal difference."[27] For Gates, this act of signifyin(g) forms one of the hallmarks of African American culture, with deep roots in African storytelling practices and a long history of parody and satire deployed under conditions of enslavement and oppression. "Writers Signify upon each other's text by rewriting the received textual tradition," Gates writes. "This can be accomplished by the revision of tropes. This sort of signifyin(g) revision serves, if successful, to create a space for the revising text."[28] Gates acknowledges that the structural and formal revisions associated with signifyin(g), while central to Black cultural practice, have much broader import. "Lest this theory of criticism, however, be thought of as only black," he writes, "let me admit that the implicit premise of this study is that all texts Signify upon other texts, in motivated and unmotivated ways."[29] That all texts implicitly or explicitly refer to other texts has long been a critical commonplace, but it is all the more important in the production of popular genres, where repetition and variation must balance carefully to ensure that new texts are seen as familiar enough to be considered acceptable to readers but different enough to be accorded some semblance of independence from the generic average.

I invoke Gates's notion of signifyin(g) here as a way of thinking about the intersections and overlapping concerns of popular genre production and African American cultural criticism. Gates's framework, along with other works of African American vernacular scholarship that appeared in the 1980s, has fallen out of favor in recent years, as critics have turned toward scholarship that troubles essentialist notions of folk culture.[30] I address this criticism more fully in the conclusion, but signifyin(g) nevertheless remains a touchstone within the critical history of African American literature and popular culture. For the purposes of this study, however, I wish to emphasize this framework's formalist dimension—that is, its emphasis on formal repetition and transformation. For his work, Gates draws strongly on Russian narratologist Mikhail Bakhtin's notion of "double-voiced" discourse, in particular its use of "parodic narration and the hidden, or internal, polemic."[31] For Gates, the African American literary tradition depends on parody and pastiche that fall firmly in line with Bakhtin's theoretical gestures. Bakhtin and other Russian theorists who grew out of the famous Russian formalists of the 1920s—including linguist V. N. Vološinov and Yury Tynyanov— offer much for scholars of form and genre, as well as for scholars working to understand the dynamics of how different literary and representational systems can draw on the same signifiers for different meanings that depend wholly on audience and interpretation, which Vološinov calls "multiaccentuality."[32] This dismantling and deformation of genre systems through forms of signifyin(g) demonstrate the ways that African American newspapers operated as an alternative genre system to that of the pulps. Here I draw on Tynyanov's definition: "A literary system is first of all a *system of the functions of the literary order which are in continual interrelationship with the others.*"[33] Tynyanov's notion of literary systems, constantly in dialogue, wrestling over the meaning of various linguistic and thematic signifiers, offers a way of seeing individual genres as fluid and dynamic, flexible in response to other systems. Signifyin(g) exemplifies this by positing a kind of formal and systemic relationship of "double-voiced discourse," a "multiaccentuality" in which, as Vološinov would have it, "differently oriented accents intersect in every ideological sign. Sign becomes the arena of class struggle."[34]

Another way of characterizing the concerns of signifyin(g) is by framing it as a version of what influential cultural studies theorist Stuart Hall called articulation. "Articulation" is a malleable term that serves a number of purposes across Hall's work. In a 1986 interview, Hall described the function of the term in this way:

> In England, the term has a nice double meaning because "articulate" means to utter, to speak forth, to be articulate. It carries that sense of language-ing, of expressing, etc. But we also speak of an "articulated" lorry (truck): a lorry where the front (cab) and back (trailer) can, but need not necessarily, be connected to one another.

> The two parts are connected to each other, but through a specific linkage, that can be broken. An articulation is thus the form of the connection that *can* make a unity of two different elements, under certain conditions. It is a linkage which is not necessary, determined, absolute and essential for all time.[35]

Thus, articulation carries a meaning that points both to expression and connection. Signifyin(g) is just such a practice: a repetition (connection) with a signal difference (expression). One of Hall's earliest—perhaps his first—uses of the term "articulation," though, will prove even more crucial in understanding the dynamics of the Black newspaper fiction under discussion in *Black Pulp*. In a 1975 study of British youth subculture, Hall and his Birmingham colleagues introduce the term "double articulation." "In what follows," they write, "we shall try to show why this *double articulation* of youth subcultures—first, to their 'parent' culture (e.g. working class culture), second, to the dominant culture—is a necessary way of staging the analysis."[36] This study, entitled *Resistance through Rituals,* charts the ways in which political and class alliances appear in the signifying practices of groups like the Teddy Boys, the Mods, and the Rockers. Such cultural practices negotiate varying alliances and identities, using this double articulation to draw on signifiers from two different locations (working-class culture and hegemonic/dominant culture) while seeking "to modify, negotiate, resist or even overthrow" the structures of power.[37] At the same time, although it remains implicit in the analysis, the subcultures themselves use signifying practices to articulate a relationship/connection—and express a resistance—to the various cultures to which they are articulated.

Hall's model of double articulation dovetails nicely with Gates's signifyin(g): both identify source of connection and friction with "dominant" forms of representation. For the Black pulp at issue in this study, these concepts form a conceptual framework for understanding the sophisticated relationship of genre to race. The writers of the popular genre fictions published in African American newspapers sought to deform and reform popular literary genres in a struggle that was necessarily articulated not only to mainstream generic formulas but also to the emergence of a protocanonical African American literary tradition.[38] Black newspaper fiction represented (and re-presented) virtually every genre associated with the pulps, down to niche genres like aviation fiction. But these genres take on decidedly new forms in African American newspapers; indeed, they represent examples Jerng's antiracist racial world making. Far from being simple examples of repetition and formula, the genres themselves appear to be under assault. Thus, these popular stories and serials become vehicles for understanding how intricately genre and race are woven together in American popular culture.

This articulation of African American genre fiction is thus actually a double articulation, and it offers an important model for understanding the relationship between competing literary systems of the early twentieth century. If the genres of Black newspaper fiction were articulated to the genres of the pulps, if they offered ideological alternatives to the white supremacist formulas found there, then they were also articulated to the emerging African American literary canon—the pioneering work of the New Negro Renaissance and the protocanonical fiction of African American literature. This latter source of connection and friction—which resembles Andreas Huyssen's "great divide" of modernism—is both subtle and profound.[39] The dominant—though not exclusive—mode of the African American canon of the period is one of tragedy: passing narratives end poorly, stories of interracial romance engender tragedy, even stories of personal and professional achievement (such as Walter White's *The Fire in the Flint* [1924]) end catastrophically. This is the foundation of the "racial realism" delineated by Gene Andrew Jarrett.[40] It is also the essence of the "'protest' story" Black pulp writer Will Thomas abandoned to write under pseudonyms.[41] Harlem Renaissance novels rooted in melodrama may find satisfactory solutions, though rarely do they present forms of utopian closure that characterize popular fiction. This tendency toward tragedy and social critique is in many respects the consequence of what James Weldon Johnson called in 1928 "The Dilemma of the Negro Author": The African American writer's audience "is more than a double audience; it is a divided audience made up of two elements with differing and often opposite and antagonistic points of view. His audience is always both white America and black America."[42]

Throughout this study, I will offer many examples of signifyin(g) and articulating practices that characterize what I am calling Black pulp. With the exception of Schuyler, whose outsize presence in the world of

Black pulp makes him inescapable, I have chosen to focus my attention on largely unknown and forgotten writers, for it is these writers who kept the spirit of Black pulp alive for nearly thirty years. These newspapers occasionally published canonical African American writers, but these publications were few and far between.[43] Often these writers would appear at the beginning of their careers, as was the case with Chester Himes, who published in the *Atlanta Daily World,* and Ann Petry, who published (under the names Anna L. Petry and Arnold Petri) in the *Baltimore Afro-American.* Petry's short stories—"Dancer from Harlem" (November 12, 1938), "Marie of the Cabin Club" (August 19, 1939), and "One Night in Harlem" (November 16, 1940)—are interesting in many respects and exploit the strategy of double articulation that governs Black pulp. An approach concerned primarily with Petry's authorship and career could easily identify elements in these texts that Petry develops more fully or richly in her award-winning debut novel, *The Street* (1946). All three of these stories take place in or around jazz clubs and highlight the romantic and sexual potential of this setting. Theresa May, the protagonist in "Dancer from Harlem," must parry the advances of "the sleek owner of the club," who takes her out for drives around uptown Manhattan in his "long shiny car."[44] The cigarette girl protagonist of "Marie of the Cabin Club" falls for a dashing jazz trumpeter, and "One Night in Harlem" finds the romantic couple at its center caught up in a gangland shootout. With Petry as a focus, it would be as easy to see these stories as an example of Petry's "artistic immaturity" as it would to characterize them as trial runs at the theme of nightclub romance that turns out so tragically for Lutie Johnson in *The Street.*[45]

However, foregrounding Petry's authorship of these texts and valuing them solely as a form of juvenilia related to *The Street* does a great disservice to the larger archive of Black pulp. On the one hand, they are articulated to the nightclub atmosphere of Petry's *The Street,* where the tropes and settings conform to the conventions of tragedy in racial realism. On the other hand, they are simultaneously articulated to a tradition of nightclub romance fiction that appeared in the pulps and that was also prominent in a revised Back pulp form almost as soon as African American newspapers began publishing popular genre fiction. I discuss nightclub romance fiction in more detail in chapter 2, but Petry's stories represent a tiny fraction of this fiction as it appeared in the *Courier* and the *Afro-American,* and her stories fulfill many of the generic expectations of Black pulp: Although their protagonists encounter dangers and threats from men who hold power over them, they nevertheless reject tragedy for utopian conclusions and the pleasures of generic satisfaction. And while *The Street* negotiated James Weldon Johnson's divided audience and received critical and popular acclaim, her stories in the *Afro-American* found a vast—and almost entirely African American— readership that was in search of a variety of narrative pleasures decidedly different from the tragic modes of serious African American literature.

PLEASURE, DESIRE, AND BLACK TEXTUALITY

In contrast to the best-known and most celebrated African American texts from this period, African American newspaper fiction offers both the pleasures of genre and the radical challenges to Jim Crow culture to an audience of almost exclusively African American readers. Fredric Jameson has famously argued that mass culture does not merely represent a form of "manipulation" but also features "Utopian impulses" that address "our deepest fantasies about the nature of social life, both as we life it now, and as we feel in our bones it ought rather to be lived."[46] To the degree that such a utopian dimension of African American cultural production has been recognized, it is almost entirely within the realm of vernacular criticism, wresting utopia out of a past, folk community. But the genre fiction that appeared in Black newspapers did not look to the past for such utopian ideals or narrative pleasures; instead, it offered stories that directly addressed racial injustice in the present. Whether in the form of improbable romances or retributive justice, this fiction tapped into the fantasies of its readers, offering solutions to the problems of racial injustices that dominated the news sections of the very same newspapers. In doing so, it moved away from the tragic modes of canonical African American fiction, connecting more directly with readers who sought out fiction as an escape from the realities of American life under Jim Crow. In telling stories of Black life, this fiction articulated itself to the conventions of African American literature; in imbuing its stories with fantasy and utopian hope instead of tragedy, it articulated itself to existing genre systems. Both elements of this double articulation included an implicit critique: It approached elite African American literature with a disdain for fatalism, while it uncovered and restructured the white supremacist underpinnings of popular genre formulas, all while seeking to offer pleasure to its readers.

In the broader study of popular culture, repetition has long served as a focal point for critics concerned with the dangerous intersection of literature and pleasure. Genre fiction represents one of the best examples of this kind intersection: a place where repetition (with slight variations) serves as an endless generator of reading pleasure. Whether under the guise of Freudian wish fulfillment or mass-cultural deception, critiques of this form of reading have been prominent since the early twentieth century after a surge in the production of popular print culture. Following influential scholarship on mass culture by Andreas Huyssen, Laura Frost, in *The Problem with Pleasure* (2013), has charted how this concern with pleasure defined the modernist moment of the early twentieth century.[47] For Frost, "pleasure has a temporary character, followed by renewal and repetition," and modernism offered more complex and difficult pleasures in place of the simple pleasures associated with popular culture.[48] Frost's study includes a number of critics of popular reading, such as Q. D. Leavis, who compared popular novel reading to "a drug habit" and warned against "the cheap and easy pleasures offered by the cinema, the circulating library, the magazine, the newspaper, the dancehall, and the loud-speaker."[49] For Frost, Leavis's cultural conservatism finds its counterpart in the work of Frankfurt School theorists Theodor Adorno and Max Horkheimer, who identified "the reproduction of sameness" as a sinister element of the culture industry's power.[50] For critics from a variety of political perspectives, the market-based leveling of print represented something dangerous: an intoxicating repetition that dulled the senses and hampered critical thinking and aesthetic appreciation.

African American readers of the early twentieth century contended with a similar set of concerns around print, though these featured an added layer of ideological power. From the nineteenth century well into the 1920s, African American print was linked closely to the project of racial uplift. Because literacy itself long held political promise in African American narratives, print took on its own importance in the fight against slavery and Jim Crow. Unlike mainstream white publishers, who began to expand into popular fiction in the mid-nineteenth century, Black publications remained largely focused on serious political and social issues well into the 1920s. This is especially true of the best-known Black print culture venues that began to appear in the late nineteenth and early twentieth centuries. Consider, for example, the editorial statements featured in three of the most prominent and influential African American periodicals of the first three decades of the century. In its February 1900 statement of purpose, the *Colored American* noted, "This magazine shall be devoted to the higher culture of Religion, Literature, Science, Music and Art of the Negro, universally. Acting as a stimulus to old and young, the old to higher achievements, the young to emulate their example."[51] Ten years later, the *Crisis* opened its first editorial in 1910 with the statement, "The object of this publication is to set forth those facts and arguments which show the danger of race prejudice, particularly as manifested to-day toward colored people."[52] And in its second issue (February 1923), Charles S. Johnson's *Opportunity* included in its editorials a section entitled "Why We Are," which claimed that "'Opportunity' hopes to provide a medium of expression for thoughtful studies of Negro life and all other problems in which they are by a circumstance involved, and to make possible thru an emphasis on frank and unbiased presentation of facts and views at least a dependable guide to action."[53]

Orienting their writing to a specific kind of reader, each of these three publications describes its primary purpose as one of uplift, whether that involves a devotion to "higher culture," a commitment to "facts and arguments which show the dangers of race prejudice," or a "frank and unbiased presentations of facts and views" and "a dependable guide to action." Shawn Anthony Christian has delineated the characteristics of the imagined "New Negro reader" that publications like this sought to attract (and even create) with a kind of "pedagogical work . . . to promote as a tradition texts that were both of high literary quality and racially affirming."[54] Part of this, Christian notes, is a set of "progressive reading practices" that encouraged readers to move from lower reading matter like newspapers toward higher forms like cultural and intellectual journals, a movement up the ladder of social class.[55] The reader Christian constructs here is defined by what Kevin K. Gaines calls the "black middle-class ideology" of uplift.[56] As Gaines writes, "Through uplift ideology, elite blacks also devised a *moral economy* of class privilege, distinction, and even domination *within the race,* often drawing on patriarchal gender conventions as a sign of elite status and 'race progress.'"[57]

Conceptualizations of reading practices such as these—or of the literary societies discussed by Elizabeth McHenry—locate literacy in an elite sphere and imagine reading itself as almost entirely connected to the "moral economy" of uplift ideology.[58] There was doubtless a great pleasure in the community fostered in organizations like African American literary societies, but such pleasure was subordinated to the social and political goals of these readers and was only accessible, by and large, to a small group of elites.

By the 1920s, however, the profile of Black readers had begun to shift radically. With literacy on the rise, readers were more abundant, and reading took on more affordances. Census data collected by William J. Collins and Robert A. Margo shows that African American illiteracy declined from 80.8 percent in 1870 to 48.2 percent in 1900 to 14.6 percent in 1930.[59] In real numbers, this meant a growth from just over 932,000 African American readers in 1870 to over ten million in 1930.[60] Alongside this tenfold increase in the number of readers came not only new publications (like many new Black newspapers) but also new readers (not always middle-class) and new purposes for reading (beyond the ideology of racial uplift). One way these desires manifested in the newspapers, Kim Gallon argues in *Pleasure in the News: African American Readership and Sexuality in the Black Press* (2020), was the incorporation of sensationalism in reporting around violence and sexuality.[61] Gallon's work charts the needle these newspapers attempted to thread: "The trick, then, for golden-age black newspapers was to continue to participate in racial uplift and reform while expanding its coverage to engage a mass black readership they imagined found pleasure in reading content about sexuality."[62] Gallon's work implies that the aims of racial uplift and of the experience of textual pleasure remained difficult to reconcile in the early twentieth century, and that newspapers represent a kind of battleground over these concerns.

The question of pleasure has been a difficult one in African American literary and cultural studies. As Ishmael Reed asked in a 1998 essay entitled "Black Pleasure—An Oxymoron," "with the grim statistics confronting African Americans, what is there to take pleasure in?"[63] Reed's question resonates even more loudly in the period of Jim Crow, though he acknowledges certain forms of pleasure in this essay: "One form of black pleasure is that which makes life easier, no matter how difficult the circumstances under which this pleasure is experienced."[64] Nevertheless, the African American canon has been defined by what Claudia Tate calls "the racial protocol," which "has . . . demanded that a black text explicitly represent their lived experiences with racial oppression."[65] Gene Andrew Jarrett describes this hegemonic mode in African American literature as "racial realism," which "pertains to a long history in which authors have sought to re-create a lived or living world according to prevailing ideologies of race or racial difference."[66] African American writers frequently pushed back at these protocols. In 1950, Zora Neale Hurston attributed these restrictions to white publishers in "What White Publishers Won't Print," noting, "This insistence on defeat in a story where upperclass Negroes are portrayed, perhaps says something from the subconscious of the majority. Involved in western culture, the hero or the heroine, or both, must appear frustrated and go down to defeat, somehow."[67] Publishable African American literature, Hurston lamented, must necessarily be tragic and refuse pleasure to its characters. Nevertheless, Tate and Jarrett offer exceptions in the form of what they call anomalies—texts written by African Americans about whites, although their interest in these texts is different. In both cases, however, they highlight the freedom an author feels in rejecting the protocols to write exclusively about racial injustice. An author-centric approach, like that of Tate or Jarrett, necessarily limits its commentary to the intentions, desires, and pleasures of an individual; *Black Pulp* seeks to radically expand this understanding by taking into account the ten million African American readers seeking pleasure in their reading matter.

These pleasures take a number of forms, and they diverge from the racial realism that dominates the African American canon. In certain respects, these narratives resemble what Michael Denning calls the "dream-work of the social" in his study of nineteenth-century dime novels.[68] However, the cultural work performed by Black pulp texts is more direct and immediate than the allegorical reading practices Denning describes. I will use pleasure throughout *Black Pulp* to indicate two particular forms of wish fulfillment associated with popular culture, something that, to echo Reed, "makes life easier." The first is a variation on simple escapism. Genre fiction offers readers the opportunity to escape to another fictional world. In the case of the fiction discussed here, though, this pleasure has a powerful political component. By setting stories in an entirely African American space, some of these texts ask their readers to imagine a world without Jim Crow—a world in which racial injustice simply does not exist and where African American characters can find themselves protagonists in all sorts of narratives. This form of pleasure transcends the simple wish fulfillment so odious to critics of popular fiction; the wishes fulfilled here include—and indeed depend on—radical social and political change. Likewise, the other form of pleasure I identify involves direct confrontation with the structures of white supremacy. If some stories offer a sudden and complete escape from racial injustice, others imagine the pleasure of confronting and eradicating this injustice, in manifestations both small and large. The wishes fulfilled here are also social and political. They allow readers to envision themselves as participants in the struggle for racial justice; they even promote or hypothesize about methods that could lead to a more equitable society. These stories may include cross-racial collaboration or highlight pleasurable, transgressive, and sensational narrative elements like interracial sexual relationships, but they typically deploy these elements in service of a utopian vision of a multiracial American society. This contrasts with canonical African American fiction of the period, which tends to present its characters not as actors in control of the destiny of themselves and the race but rather as objects crushed by the structures of white supremacy.

Whichever form of pleasure these stories activate, these pleasures are almost entirely denied readers of canonical African American literature of this period; they fall outside the racial protocol of serious African American literary production. The cultivation of these pleasures—pleasures manifested most clearly in what I'm calling Black pulp—makes it possible to decouple print from the "black middle-class ideology" of uplift. The transformation is evident in the tone and content of the first editorial (November 1945) of the influential Johnson publication *Ebony:*

> As you can gather, we're rather jolly folks, we *Ebony* editors. We like to look at the zesty side of life. Sure, you can get all hot and bothered about the race question (and don't think we don't) but not enough is said about all the swell things we Negroes can do and will accomplish. *Ebony* will try to mirror the happier side of Negro life—the positive, everyday achievements from Harlem to Hollywood. But when we talk about race as the No. 1 problem of America, we'll talk turkey.[69]

It is difficult to imagine a national magazine like *Ebony* or the short-lived, Los Angeles–based pictorial magazine *Silhouette* (1938–40), both invested in the "zesty side of life," being published during the 1920s.[70] However, the pleasures evident in the zesty side of life—pleasures that stem both from escaping the protocols of a relentless representation of racial injustice and from celebrating triumphs in the face of this injustice—are nurtured and cultivated by the Black pulp texts featured in African American newspapers of the 1920s and 1930s.

Black Pulp tracks the pleasure of these radical revisions across a number of genres that appeared regularly throughout the heyday of twentieth-century African American newspaper fiction, reading them against the pulp genres on which they signify and the cultural forms to which they are articulated. From 1920 through 1955, the *Baltimore Afro-American* and the *Pittsburgh Courier* together published over 2,500 stories and serial installments, a vast archive of genre fiction that has been almost entirely untapped by scholars. For the purposes of my argument in *Black Pulp,* I have focused on the most common genres published in these newspapers and on the examples of this fiction that seemed to mean the most to readers and editors. This kind of importance might be signaled through reader letters, promotion and advertising, prominent editorial placement, repetition of characters and authors, or captivating illustrations. I have also highlighted curious cases of writers moving between Black and white pulp spheres, which helps illuminate the contrast of the two competing genre systems. Most—but not all—of my examples come from serials, which offer lengthier narrative possibilities and a logic that has historically been integral to periodical culture. Beyond the fact that serials simply offer more to work with, the form cannily replicates the publishing context of Black pulp: the newspaper, which reported on the injustices of Jim Crow throughout this period.

Chapter 1 charts the history of a short-lived (1928–32) tabloid insert, the *Illustrated Feature Section,* which boasted of distribution through "thirty-four of America's most prominent colored newspapers," from Baltimore to Portland, Oregon.[71] At its peak, its circulation was close to two hundred thousand copies, not including a substantial pass-along rate. Produced by white advertising agent William B. Ziff but edited by George S. Schuyler, and later lawyer Benjamin J. Davis Jr., this tabloid marked a dramatic shift in fictional content appearing in

African American newspapers. The tendentious and polemical melo-drama that dominated through the early 1920s shifted to a variety of popular genres that engaged, often directly, with pulp magazine formulas. In addition to recovering the history of this influential publication, I also use its contents—including Cora Moten's horror–detective serial, "The Creeping Thing," the first zombie story in African American literary history—to explore how African American authors found ways to upend and transform generic expectations for a national Black audience that had essentially been constituted through the national reach of the *Illustrated Feature Section*. This audience persisted, even after the *IFS* failed, and newspapers from Atlanta to Norfolk to Indianapolis sought to meet new reader desire for popular genre and its radical manifestations, decentering the geographical coordinates of traditional histories of twentieth-century African American literary culture.

Chapter 2 explores variations on one of the most popular genres in both pulp magazines and Black newspapers: the romance tale. I first examine the career of Gertrude Schalk, an African American society columnist who made her living during the 1930s writing about the romantic foibles of all white characters for pulp magazines like *Love Story* and *Ainslee's*. Schalk also contributed fiction to the Black press, including the *Illustrated Feature Section* and George Schuyler's short-lived *National News*, which featured Schalk's "The Yellow Parrot," a complex short story cycle about women working in a Harlem nightclub that explores the boundaries and limits of romance fiction. After detailing Schalk's innovations, the chapter considers a group of stories, published in the *Baltimore Afro-American* in the spring and summer of 1934, that explored one of the most taboo subjects in popular romance: interracial sexuality. These writers did not merely broach the topic; they reveled in it, finding all sorts of interracial and interethnic combinations to entertain readers and test their boiling point on the subject. This summer of interracial love in the *Baltimore Afro-American* points toward the importance of representations of interracial sexuality across Black newspaper fiction, especially when such unions remained illegal in many states. In stories like these, and in serials that Schuyler published in the *Pittsburgh Courier*, writers isolated the fault lines of generic discourse, producing fiction that illuminated the boundaries of romance while offering profound possibilities for genre revision.

Among the most popular fiction published in the newspapers were a handful of speculative fiction serials published in the late 1930s in both the *Pittsburgh Courier* and the *Baltimore Afro-American*. Chapter 3 describes early efforts in speculative fiction that predated and included the *Illustrated Feature Section* before considering the best-known examples of Black newspaper fiction: George S. Schuyler's "The Black Internationale" and its sequel, "Black Empire." I read these serials as fully in dialogue with the tropes and conventions of science fiction, drawing on anxieties about racial conspiracy, racial warfare, and the threat of fascism. However, rather than raise alarms at the presence of a global racial conspiracy, Schuyler explicitly embraces (though somewhat disingenuously) the figure of Fu Manchu–like criminal mastermind Dr. Henry Belsidus, whose superior technology and worldwide network has the potential to eradicate white supremacy. Published in the wake of "The Black Internationale," William Thomas Smith's 1937 serial "The Black Stockings" evokes similar concerns about fascism in presenting a near-future nightmare of the rise of a nativist presidential candidate. Smith's dystopian serial takes as its foil Sinclair Lewis's celebrated 1935 novel *It Can't Happen Here,* levying a powerful critique of the degree to which Lewis underestimates the fascism already inherent in Jim Crow America. Smith's serial is designed as a corrective that imagines a multiracial challenge to the hatred and bigotry that emerge all too easily from an American populace primed for a racially specific American form of fascism.

Chapter 4 outlines the surge in Black heroes in the pages of the *Baltimore Afro-American* in the 1940s and early 1950s, on the cusp of integration and the national civil rights movement. During this time, the *Afro-American* featured heroic series characters in fiction by James H. Hill and H. L. Faggett. Hill's fictional heroes included the Senegalese flying ace Jacques Lenglet, whose exploits involve fighting Germans and American racists in the South, and hard-boiled reporter Jiggs Bennett, who covers and assists antiracist organizations, including the fictional Black Retribution and the very real Mau Mau. These figures offer a violent and legitimized response to the injustices of Jim Crow—holding off a lynch mob with machine-gun fire, sabotaging a bus line that refuses to integrate, exploring the liberatory potential of atomic power—and offer an international dimension to the struggle against white supremacy, as the narratives themselves intersect directly with the *Afro*'s news reporting on prominent civil rights issues. H. L. Faggett's "Black Robin" series turns this vision inward and leavens these stories with a light comedic touch. Traveling undercover, John Robin addresses localized instances of injustice, working to protect Black communities across the South. This series operated in dialogue with readers; the newspaper even solicited ideas from readers based on incidents in their own towns, which made the "Black Robin" series an explicit embodiment of the utopian premises of popular fiction—a fictional solution to the real problems of Jim Crow. While these characters may not exhibit the superpowers of contemporary Black heroes like Black Panther or Luke Cage, they present a stark and inspiring alternative to the contemporaneous tragic figures of the African American canon. Unlike Wright's Bigger Thomas or Ellison's Invisible Man, characters who are acted upon by Jim Crow racism, these figures present active challenges to white supremacy, engaging in the heroic work of battling what one of these texts called "the most ugly facet in America's Hall of 'Shame'—Jim-Crowism!"[72]

In the conclusion, I consider how recentering the understanding of African American literary history around the desires and practices of middle- and working-class Black readers might transform our understanding of the relationship between race and genre. Alongside these suggestions, I examine the rise in historical fiction in the last years that genre fiction appeared in Black newspapers. The Elizabeth O. Hood series, Sultry Sirens: Tan Beauties Who Changed Destinies of Nations, sought to place Black women as protagonists of world history. Finally, the prolific James H. Hill produced a group of short serials that dramatized the lives of figures like Nat Turner but also imagined fictional stories of slave rebellions in a fashion that anticipates the neo–slave narrative of the late twentieth century, working hand in hand with other newspaper features, like J. A. Rogers's series on African American history, to recuperate African American history as a story of individual and collective triumphs in the face of violence and enslavement.

1

BENEATH THE HARLEM RENAISSANCE
THE RISE OF BLACK POPULAR FICTION

AFRICAN AMERICAN WRITERS have been negotiating and signifying on genre conventions since the birth of African American literary production. Whether taking up the conventions of autobiography, melodrama, or the Gothic, writers in the nineteenth century sought to remake these forms in service of new and powerful goals. However, the process of canonization has—as it always does—told one particular story about African American writing and African American readers. This story emphasizes, for the most part, elite literary productions that reached only a handful of Black readers (and likely far more white readers)—that is, literature written by and for the group that W. E. B. Du Bois called the "talented tenth," the "New Negro reader" described by Shawn Anthony Christian.[1] The explosive growth of the Black press in the last decade of the nineteenth century and the first decade of the twentieth century—the founding of nationally distributed weekly newspapers like the *Baltimore Afro-American* (1892), the *Norfolk Journal and Guide* (1901), the *Chicago Defender* (1905), the *Pittsburgh Courier* (1908), and the *New York Amsterdam News* (1909)—was tied to a much different group of readers: working- and middle-class African Americans who were not necessarily the college-educated "race men" (and women) that intellectual journals targeted as their audience. These newspapers, unlike literary and intellectual magazines such as the *Colored American,* the *Crisis,* or the *Messenger,* had a readership that was almost entirely

African American; they constituted the popular reading matter of African America.

These newspapers, however, were more than mere conduits for Black journalism or source material for historical characterizations of African American life under Jim Crow. They also served as literary spaces, albeit largely unacknowledged. They published popular fiction that reached more African American readers than any of the well-documented African American literary journals of the early twentieth century. Central to this untold story of Black popular fiction is a little-known tabloid insert called the *Illustrated Feature Section,* which was included in Black newspapers across the country. This short-lived phenomenon served as a catalyst for Black genre texts, giving writers an opportunity to explore generic formulas and readers the chance to experience the pleasures of genre in an exclusively Black space, away from the gaze of white readers. By turning away from racial realism, literary polemics, and attempts at canonization and instead embracing the pleasures of genre—albeit in some radically transformed ways—the *IFS* changed the course of Black popular fiction and engineered reader demand for new forms of genre fiction that would pave the way for Black popular writing to confront the racial politics of pulp formulas and create revisions that confronted the explicit horrors of Jim Crow and white supremacy.

PRINT CULTURE AND BLACK NEWSPAPER FICTION

By 1928, there could be little doubt that what scholars have come to call the Harlem Renaissance was in full swing. If 1925 saw the declaration of a Negro Renaissance in the pages of the popular press and the publication of Alain Locke's *The New Negro,* by 1928 this surge in African American literary production had become an undeniably significant part of the American publishing scene. As such, as Cary D. Wintz has charted, the year 1928 saw probably the most influential group of novels published by African American writers during the entire decade. The novels published in this year ranged from the vernacular city novels of Claude McKay *(Home to Harlem)* and Rudolph Fisher *(The Walls of Jericho)* to the meditations on color and psychology by Nella Larsen *(Quicksand)* to W. E. B. Du Bois's strange internationalist romance *Dark*

Princess.[2] As a variety of print culture institutions—from presses like Alfred A. Knopf to Black journals like the *Crisis* and the *Messenger*— nurtured African American writers in the first part of the decade, this banner year demonstrated that writers were beginning to explore a wide variety of possibilities for African American fiction.

This was the era, as Langston Hughes has famously characterized it, when "the Negro was in vogue," and with the success of African American writers in prominent magazines like *Atlantic Monthly* and with prominent publishers like Knopf, venues exclusively devoted to African American writing began to evolve as the publishing landscape transformed.[3] Despite a considerable degree of critical success, the publishing institutions that sustained the early years of the Harlem Renaissance found themselves shifting focus near the end of the decade. Jessie Fauset left her influential post as literary editor at the *Crisis* in 1927, and the magazine's investment in literary material sharply decreased after her departure. The National Urban League's magazine *Opportunity* lost editor Charles S. Johnson to Fisk University in 1928, and the magazine similarly shifted its focus away from literature and the arts. And the *Messenger,* A. Philip Randolph and Chandler Owen's socialist-leaning magazine, ceased publication in 1928 after long-standing financial struggles finally caught up with it. Wallace Thurman's short-lived magazines *Fire!!: Devoted to Younger Negro Artists* (1926, one issue) and *Harlem: A Forum of Negro Life* (1928, one issue) tantalize with the possibility of a radically experimental Harlem Renaissance publishing scene, but their failure forces scholars toward more conventional sources to document Black literary output in the final years of the 1920s.

African American newspapers continued a tradition of irregularly publishing a variety of fiction during the 1920s; by and large, however, this fiction tended to be both tendentious and melodramatic. This included the reprinting of protocanonical "race novels" by both white and Black writers, as well as the occasional original story or serial that usually took up a tale of racial injustice and melodramatic redemption. In many respects, this falls firmly in line with the history of literary productions in the Black press. Fiction had appeared in the Black press throughout the nineteenth century and into the twentieth. However, throughout most of this history, the fiction published there was intentionally polemical in its orientation; it served to support the larger ideological goals of racial uplift in the face of enslavement and Jim Crow. This includes not only early entries in the African American canon, like William Wells Brown's *Clotel* (1853; serialized as *Miralda; or, The Beautiful Quadroon* in the *Weekly Anglo-African,* 1860–61) and Martin R. Delany's *Blake; or, The Huts of America* (published in the *Weekly Anglo-African,* 1861–62), but also more propagandistic serials like *The White Man's Burden* by T. Shirby Hodge (a pseudonym of white doctor Roger Sherman Tracy), a futuristic satire on race relations that was advertised for sale regularly in the *Crisis* during the late 1910s.[4] Originally published between covers in 1915, *The White Man's Burden* was serialized in the *Baltimore Afro-American* in 1920–21 with the subtitle "A Story of Africa and the War Predicted by Marcus Garvey." Second serialization—that is, the serialization of a text already published between covers—was common in newspapers like the *Afro-American;* through the early 1920s, the newspaper routinely featured serial reprints of novels with prominent themes of racial injustice. Mary White Ovington's 1920 novel *The Shadow* appeared in the *Afro-American* in 1922, J. A. Rogers's 1917 novel *From Superman to Man* appeared from 1923 to 1924, Joshua Henry Jones's *By Sanction of Law* appeared from 1924 to 1925 (almost simultaneously with its publication between covers), Gertrude Sandborn's 1923 novel *Veiled Aristocrats* appeared in 1925, and a 1922 translation of René Maran's *Batouala* appeared in 1925. Likewise, the *Pittsburgh Courier* also serialized *From Superman to Man* in 1923 and Walter F. White's 1924 novel *Fire in the Flint* in 1926, and the *Chicago Defender* serialized Charles Chesnutt's 1900 novel *The House behind the Cedars* from 1921 to 1922. Reprints like these suggest that during the 1920s, the Black press was engaging in a form of literary canonization, working to distribute important novels from Black writers to a broader readership at a cost more reasonable than that of a novel between covers.

Alongside reprints of more reputable and uplifting race novels, these newspapers featured occasional fiction written especially for the periodicals themselves. Some of these circulated through the networks of African American periodicals, as with the work of Aubrey Bowser, distributed through the Brooklyn-based Kelley Newspaper Feature Service. Bowser, who edited his own short-lived Harlem-based literary weekly entitled *The Rainbow* in 1919–20, published a number of serials both humorous and serious in newspapers through the middle of the 1920s.

Some of these (the serialized passing novel "The Man Who Would Be White" [1922–23] and the melodrama "The Vamp and the Virgin" [1923]) had received prior publication in *The Rainbow,* for which Bowser may have been the sole contributor.[5] Other Bowser publications included the dialect humor series "Toosaynte Le Ovachoo Brown" (published in the *Baltimore Afro-American,* the *Cleveland Call,* and the *Washington Bee*). A figure with strong connections to the African American newspaper industry in New York (he was married to the daughter of T. Thomas Fortune, editor of the *New York Age*), Bowser would later work in the New York City public schools and regularly review books for the *New York Amsterdam News.*[6]

Despite the occasional appearance of original fiction in Black newspapers before 1928, it is clear that this fiction was rarely foregrounded as an important part of these publications. Some readers and editors questioned whether something as trivial as fiction even belonged in the pages of periodicals devoted to the serious business of uplifting the race. A 1915 letter to the editor of the *Washington Sun,* for example, argued that "fiction should have no place in any paper that is published for Afro-American readers. . . . The newspaper that indulges in the publication of what it knows to be untrue is not only striking a blow at its own welfare and existence, but that of the race."[7] While some editors doubtless had a more sympathetic disposition toward fiction and its ability to draw in readers, African American newspapers addressed these concerns through editorial arrangement and page layout. Prominent reprints and serious race novels received more column inches and larger headlines, while occasional examples of original genre fiction and humorous stories were typically buried among news items and appeared with little or no advance announcement. In neither case were these stories and serials illustrated, and the publication of fiction in general was often an irregular occurrence. Editors essentially created different zones of distinction within the newspaper, mediating concerns by readers who saw fiction as striking a blow against political engagement and racial uplift while providing a modicum of genre entertainment.[8]

Things began to change for individual newspapers after the surge in African American literary production associated with the Harlem Renaissance. However, it's hardly fair to associate this movement exclusively with Harlem, given that newspapers across the country began featuring original fiction and taking up the literary space formally occupied by the *Crisis*, the *Messenger*, and *Opportunity*. Even the *Chicago Defender*, which published considerably less original genre fiction than its competitors, experimented with Black genre texts beginning in 1928 and 1929 with serials by Marjorie Damsey Wilson ("Vagrant Love: How Three Men Battled for the Heart of a Pretty Girl," July 14–September 22, 1928), Cora Ball Moten ("Hell," February 16–May 11, 1929), and W. H. A. Moore ("The Danton Mystery," September 28–December 14, 1929). In 1930, the *Defender*, the most thoroughly researched of the Black newsweeklies, essentially stopped featuring original fiction when editor Charles S. Abbott founded *Abbott's Monthly*, an intriguing if short-lived attempt at a middlebrow slick magazine publishing a variety of original fiction and lifestyle articles directed at an African American readership until it ceased publication in late 1933.[9] Through the early 1930s, *Abbott's Monthly* included not only writers who were regularly publishing fiction in the African American newspapers but also featured some of the earliest published fiction by Richard Wright and Chester Himes. Stories like those published in the *Defender* (and later in *Abbott's Monthly*) featured sensational topics, serial cliffhangers, and other trappings of the popular genres that were being nurtured in the pages of pulp magazines. While such serials might incorporate themes of racial injustice, they nevertheless represented a significant shift in Black newspaper fiction: away from politically tendentious melodrama and toward the pleasures of seriality and genre.

"ALL MATTER SHOULD DEAL EXCLUSIVELY WITH NEGRO LIFE": THE *ILLUSTRATED FEATURE SECTION* AND RADICAL GENRE REVISION

The most profound sign of this shift toward genre was the introduction of the *Illustrated Feature Section* in November of 1928. Published by the W. B. Ziff Company, a Chicago-based, white-owned advertising agency that had a long relationship with the Black press, the *Illustrated Feature Section* was a tabloid-size syndicated section that included original genre fiction as well a host of other content, including historical sketches, comic strips, and lifestyle matter.[10] Its first editor was George S. Schuyler, who had spent the previous few years editing the *Messenger* before its final

May–June 1928 issue and moved to Chicago to take up Ziff's new publication. Schuyler would later dismiss the *IFS* as "moron fodder," but Ziff's project was nevertheless an ambitious one, an effort to coordinate publication across a host of Black newspapers nationwide.[11] It was, as an advertisement in the *Houston Informer* claimed, "A New Forward Step in Negro Journalism": "Short Stories and Serial Stories of Negro Life, Special and Exclusive Articles built around interesting, strange and unusual happenings in the Race."[12] The *Norfolk Journal and Guide* advertised it as a "New and Progressive Departure in Negro Journalism," and the *Baltimore Afro-American,* highlighting the forthcoming serial "Chocolate Baby" in the first installment of the *IFS,* noted that "sixteen Associated newspapers cooperate to make this first great magazine venture a hummer."[13] By mid-1929, the *IFS* advertised in one prominent trade journal for writers that it appeared in "thirty-four of America's most prominent colored newspapers"—a number that would remain in promotional material through the section's apparent demise in 1932.[14] Nothing quite like the *IFS* had appeared before. Probably the closest thing to it was the explicitly middlebrow *Half-Century Magazine,* which featured, according to Eurie Dahn, "a mix of household tips, health tips, legal advice, editorials, [and] fashion advice," as well as a variety of "placid domestic fiction" during its 1916–25 run.[15] The Chicago-based *Half-Century* had a reasonable circulation, but it cultivated a specialized audience, using the subtitle "A Colored Magazine for the Home and the Homemaker" from 1921 to 1925.[16]

It's difficult to know exactly how widely distributed the *Illustrated Feature Section* was, but it certainly reached a greater and more varied number of readers than the *Half-Century* had. Haphazard archiving, microfilming, and digitization of African American periodicals mean that supplemental sections like the *IFS* may have been thrown out by librarians or not included when these papers were archived on microfilm before being destroyed. Many Black newspapers (even those from the early twentieth century) survive in incomplete runs, and a significant number of titles from the period were simply not microfilmed at all and have disappeared entirely from the archival record. To make matters more complicated, the newspapers often had some leeway with how they incorporated this syndicated content; some stuck with an identical, stereotyped separate section, while other, larger papers—beginning as early as

Illustrated
FEATURE SECTION
THE AFRO AMERICAN

Interesting,
Entertaining
and
Instructive

Clean,
Wholesome
and
Refreshing

Week Ending November 3, 1928

A DRAMATIC SERIAL

BY SAMUEL I. BROOKS

Chocolate Baby

A STORY OF
AMBITION
DECEPTION
and SUCCESS

DRAWING BY HELEN K. SMITH

GAINESVILLE was proud of Martha Hastings. Beautiful beyond description, her body was as perfect as her deportment was excellent. At high school, where she was finishing her last year, all of the pupils admired and envied her rare intellect. Everybody said she was a credit to the Negro community.

Martha was one of those strikingly handsome girls at whom men glance, not once or twice, but four or five times. Where many of the other girls slouched along and were careless of their dress, Martha bore herself like a blue-blooded lady, and her clothes, though inexpensive, were in the best taste.

Always she looked as if she had just stepped out of a bandbox. People said that her skin was as soft as that of a child, and certainly her gently rounded limbs suggested all that youth has ever stood for. No wonder that men invariably referred to her as "The Chocolate Baby." She was the prize catch of Hainesville and the community waited with baited breath to see who was to be the lucky man.

But Martha, with all of her beauty and shapeliness, with all her fine intelligence, immaculate and tasteful dress and aristocratic carriage, was not thinking of marriage. When she told people this, they would not believe her.

"Why honey!" exclaimed old Mrs. Haverstraw one day as Martha paused to exchange a word with her, "you sure are foolish to be talking like that. Pretty as you are and smart as you are, you can get the best husband in the country. Ain't no rich man but wouldn't be glad to have you for a wife. No sir!"

"But Mrs. Haverstraw," argued Martha, "I'm not ready for marriage yet. You know I am only 16 and when I graduate from high school mother wants me to go to one of the big colleges in the north. Then, too, I think a girl ought to approach marriage very carefully and intelligently these days. I see so many evidences of bad judgment in matrimony that I'm a little scared to give it any thought until I get a little older and have had more experience." As she said this her smooth, dark brown face lost its customary smile and assumed a serious cast.

The truth of the matter was that while Martha had on a few occasions given thought to sex and marriage, they were always fleeting thoughts. She had a veritable horror of making a mistake. True, she would have liked to find a rich husband, if for no other reason than to enable her to care for her widowed mother in her old age. But then, if she married and made a mistake in her choice it would be too late.

The girl knew of the hard struggle her kindly, gray-haired mother had had to keep her neat and clean, send her through high school and try to guide her steps away from the pitfalls that lurk for a beautiful, pure girl, even in small towns such as Hainesville. Bent with toil, Mrs. Hastings continued to cook and wash for the wealthy white families of the town, though she had reached the age when she should have been able to rest.

But rest was a stranger to Mrs. Hastings. Ever since the time, 15 years back, when her husband had been killed in a railroad accident, she had had to struggle along trying to make a living for herself and Martha. The clever railroad lawyers had taken advantage of her ignorance and inexperience so she found herself, after her husband's death, alone and almost penniless.

Like so many other noble colored women, however, she had resolved to struggle on, keep her home together and raise her new-born baby, Martha, as a girl ought to be raised. Living in a small town in the south where everyone knew everyone else, Mrs. Hastings had many friends among the white and colored people. They were more than glad to render assistance to one struggling so nobly to maintain high standards.

Martha was well aware of the struggle her mother had made, and she was very grateful. Knowing her mother's ideals, she strove hard to live up to them in every detail. Aware of the hard years of labor her mother had undergone, she was eager to complete her education, get a good well-paying position and thus be able to give her beloved mother a much-needed rest.

Thus Martha dismissed thought of marriage. Nor did she keep company with any of the scores of young men, old men and boys who ardently paid her suit. Even the boldest were awed by her goodness and innocence, and although she went

Fisk Jubilee Singers In Paris Received By Geo. Clemenceau

France's War Time Premier Autographs Photos For American Singers

PARIS—Thanks to Mr. Sylvestre Dorrian, European manager of the Bell Syndicate and other new services,

I am able to present a stenographic account of the meeting that took place in Paris between M. Clemenceau, the "Tiger of France" and the Fisk Jubilee Singers.

Mr. Dorrian is a native of Virginia and so far as the race question is concerned is just a few hundred years ahead of the average Virginian. He has spent most of his life abroad, and has come in contact with most of the big European personages.

I just him quite by accident, had been invited to dinner by Prince Touvalou at the Coupôle. My Dorrian was at the adjoining table, listening to our conversation, and presently addressed himself to us. He told us that Countee Cullen was on especial friend of his, and asked me if I knew a colored composer who would be willing to set some of Mr. Cullen's poetry to music. He said that he knew several white composers who he could ask but that he preferred to have it done primarily by one of our race.

I mentioned Harry Burleigh, Nathaniel Dett, Clarence Cameron White, Carl Diton and others.

On Majestic

Mr. Dorrian takes a warm interest in the progress of the Negro, and wanted to know what could be done to give the Negro a squarer deal in news articles. He will remain in America on the Majestic November 1 for a few weeks, and plans to confer with two or three colored editors while there as to the best means to bring this about.

Some evenings later Mr. and Mrs. Countee Cullen, Prince Touvalou, Mrs. Roberta Dodds Crawford, and

cer of Chicago, and myself were his guests. He was just kind enough to give me the article above mentioned. The reporter on the occasion was M. Constantine Colas, a personal friend of M. Clemenceau. It is as follows:

Autographs Book

"A room at the Franklin, Paris, Clemenceau's visitors, the Fisk American Jubilee Singers are examining intently a huge autograph book to which are original letters of distinguished people. Marie-Antoinette, Louis XIV, Robespierre, Lafayette, and others. On a horse-shoe table nearby where English translations of many of the 'Tiger' does his writing. In the Clemenceau's works, which M. Constantine Colas, an old journalist-friend of the former premier's, has

1930—began incorporating the *IFS* content into the main sections of their papers, often in a one- or two-page spread. However, there is archival evidence that, at the very least, the *IFS* appeared in the *Atlanta World,* the *Baltimore Afro-American,* the *Houston Informer,* the *Kansas City Call,* the *Norfolk Journal and Guide,* the *Omaha Guide,* the *Pittsburgh Courier,* the Portland, Oregon, *Advocate,* and the *Washington Tribune.* The letterhead for a January 1929 letter from editor Schuyler to Walter F. White lists a number of other titles that the *IFS* was "issued for": the *Arkansas Survey,* the *Atlanta Independent,* the *Birmingham Truth,* the *Cincinnati Union,* the *Cleveland Call-Post,* the *Dallas Express,* the *Dayton Forum,* the *Detroit Independent,* the *Galveston Eagle,* the *Gary Sun,* the *Hartford Pilot,* the *Iowa Bystander,* the *Louisiana Weekly,* the *Memphis Triangle,* the *Nashville Clarion,* the *Newark Herald,* the *New York News,* and the *Register* (possibly the *Southern Register,* based in Jackson, Mississippi).[17] Circulation averages, which are available for fourteen of these twenty-seven newspapers, put the 1929 circulation of the *Illustrated Feature Section* at well over 185,000 for these titles alone.[18] Actual readership was potentially far higher thanks to the high pass-along rates for African American newspapers. Indeed, the *Afro-American Ledger,* the precursor to the *Baltimore Afro-American,* encouraged this activity with the slogan, "When You Have Finished Reading Your *Afro,* Pass It Along to a Friend."[19] And Kim Gallon cites a 1931 master's thesis on the Black press that claims, "In one of the leading Negro colleges, after two days' use every Negro weekly has been so completely thumbed and handled that a fresh issue must be preserved for the rack.'"[20] This means that the fiction published there was easily the most widely distributed African American literature to that point. Also, because readership of Black newspapers had a much higher middle- and working-class African American readership than books or intellectual and literary journals like the *Crisis* or *Opportunity,* this fiction likely had more Black readers than virtually all of the African American canon through at least the middle of the twentieth century.

Ziff's *Illustrated Feature Section* was not without its share of controversy. After all, William B. Ziff was a white businessman who leveraged the power of his advertising agency to get African American newspapers to include the *IFS.* Ziff represents one of the many examples of how the vogue for the Negro during the 1920s was exploited by white interests;

THE OMAHA GUIDE

ALL THE NEWS WHILE IT IS NEWS

Coming Stories by
Edward Worthy
Edward Lawson
Dorothy West

The Finest Writers
Send Their Stories
First to the Illus-
trated Feature
Section

W. B. Ziff Co., 608 Dearborn St., Chicago
Advertising Representatives

ILLUSTRATED FEATURE SECTION— September 3, 1932

BLUE RIBBON FICTION IS FOUND EVERY WEEK IN
THE FEATURE SECTION

ROADHOUSE RACKET

By WILLIAM M. JOHNSON

Pete Wilson, detective, has been given an assignment to clean out the Carlson gang. Fairview's best organized racketeers. Pete, however, finds he is most Sally Wright, soft, and high brown.

Johnson throws together a court detective, a brown girl, and a gang of racketeers, stirs them all up and the result is the exciting—

"ROADHOUSE RACKET"

A low racy roadster slid to an abrupt stop in front of the Hotel Imperial in Fairview and a handsome clean cut young man got out.

A bell boy took his bags and a garage attendant drove off in his car.

Inside the hotel he wrote, "Pete Wilson, Washington, D.C.," on the register in a large masculine scrawl.

"Call me about eight this evening," he instructed the desk man.

"Yes sir, Mr. Wilson," that individual replied in his best hotel manner. "Is that all?"

"Well," Pete favored him with a wide disarming grin, "if you can think of anything else that will help, do that, too."

"Another wise guy," the desk man muttered to himself, watching Pete follow the bell boy to the elevator.

After arranging his things to suit him, Pete poured himself a stiff drink from a choice bottle of Scotch. "The Chief sure gave me a job this time," he mused half aloud, recalling his mission there in Fairview.

"Wilson," the Chief had said, "there's a gang of shady characters working in Fairview. I have reasons to believe that they are run by Paul Carlson, who runs the Black and Tan roadhouse there. Find out their racket. Go about it on your own way, but I want them cleaned out."

So here he was, Pete Wilson, of the International Detective Agency of Washington, D.C., confronted with the task of cleaning out a shady racket. He smiled grimly. "I guess I'm in for some fun—something," he added.

Pete left the hotel about eight-thirty that evening and walked down into the section of the town where the theatres were located.

Since it was rather early yet, he decided to go in one of them.

His eyes fell on a pretty girl in one of the boxes. Now Pete had seen plenty of pretty girls in his life. But never in all his twenty-seven years could he remember having seen a girl like the one he was gazing at now. "Phew!" he exclaimed to himself, "what an angel! I wonder if that's her old man with her?"

Turning to a youth beside him, he asked. "Say, bud, do you know that girl and man up there in the first box?"

"Sure. The girl is Sally Wright and the man is Paul Carlson," the youth replied, turning his attention to the girl on the seat beside him.

"Paul Carlson, eh?" Pete mused. "So that's the guy I'm supposed to get interested in. Well, I don't believe I'm going to like Carlson, but Miss Wright and I should get along fine."

During the rest of the show Pete sat gazing at the girl. He was trying hard to figure out some way of meeting her. At the same time he was telling himself that at last he had found the real answer to all his romantic dreams.

The show ended and he drifted out with the crowd, hoping to catch sight of her again in the lobby.

Finally he saw her. She was standing over in one corner as if she were waiting for someone. Pete began to shove through the crowd in her direction praying fervently

"Well," said Pete to himself, "you sure have gotten yourself into one hell of a fix."

that she wouldn't move away until he got over to her.

The closer he got to her, the prettier she seemed to get. She had a complexion the hue of ripe peach. Her thick black hair seemed to fall all sorts of ways behind her two ears. Pete thought he didn't look as though there was a strand out of place. Her face looked like it might have been a creation of some super portrait artist. What a beauty!

Reaching in his pocket, he pulled out a small lace handkerchief, apparently blessing the female who had put it there and forgotten it. He stooped in front of the girl and arose with the handkerchief in his hand. She was looking straight at him. Something in that look wanted Pete that she knew just what he was up to.

He looked at her for a second and then grinned shamefacedly. "You win," he said, putting the lace handkerchief back in his pocket.

She still looked at him, a half amused expression in her eyes as though she were watching a bashful detective?

"It was a little crude," Pete went on, "but you see I just wanted to meet you."

"Why?" she asked in a voice so soft and sweet that Pete found himself thinking it's ought "to" be

"I'm not trying to be fresh or have always dreamed of finding a anything like that," Pete hastened to assure her. "I'm a stranger here or else I would have had some one to introduce us properly. I'm Pete Wilson."

"Oh!" she exclaimed, a smile lightening her face, making her fairly radiant. "You're the detective, aren't you?"

Pete nodded, too dumbfounded to speak. How did this girl whom he had never seen or heard of before know that he was a detective?

"I'm Sally Wright." The girl went on, extending a small hand which Pete hastily grabbed in hold of his.

"Say, how did you know I was a detective?"

"I saw your picture in the papers when you were working on a case in Pittsburgh last month," she answered, gently disengaging her hand.

"You didn't get a bad impression of me, did you?" Pete asked hopefully.

"Of course not. I thought you were rather nice."

Pete's heart almost skipped a few beats when she said that. "I see we're going to be swell friends," he said softly.

"Well," she smiled mischievously, "maybe."

He pulled the lace handkerchief out of his pocket again. "To not friendship; may it never be blown away. You take it, will you?"

"Uh-huh," she smiled, putting

these lanterns. Above the door was a sign that read:

THE BLACK AND TAN CLUB
P. Carlson, Prop.

"Well, here we are," Carlson said, guiding out and helping Sally out. "What do you think of this place?"

"Ain't bad," Pete replied.

They went inside.

An orchestra sat at one end of the big room. Tables and booths extended around the walls in a horseshoe shape, leaving a fairly large dancing space in the center. Soft colored lights hung from brackets on the walls, giving the room a pleasant blend of coloring. Already there was a fairly large crowd din the room. Blacks, browns, yellows and here and there a white couple sat apparently enjoying themselves as much as their darker brethren and sisters.

Pete followed Sally and Carlson to a booth and seated himself in a chair. The Black and Tan Club, from what he could see, seemed to be a very popular place.

"Well, what'll it be?" Carlson asked, leaning back in his chair and lighting a big black cigar.

"Ginger ale for me," Sally said.

"Milk," Pete said.

"What?" Carlson exclaimed almost falling backward in his chair. The waitress too seemed to be on the verge of a collapse.

Sally was looking wonderingly at Pete, who seemingly unmindful of it all, was gazing innocently at the orchestra.

"What did you say?" Carlson asked again, leaning forward so as to catch every word.

Pete looked at him faintly surprised. "Milk," he replied, "you know, cow fruit."

The waitress giggled.

Carlson pulled out a large silk handkerchief and mopped his brow. "Bring me plenty of rye," he ordered, "and this—see that the gets pile-er-milk."

With their respective drinks before them, they talked on different things in general. But from the way Carlson looked at him every now and then, Pete knew there was something else more important that Carlson wanted to talk about.

Finally Pete asked Sally to dance. He forgot all about Carlson, when he was dancing with her. "You know," he said, "your feet look as though you are the kind of girl that comes to a joint like this often."

"I don't come here often," Sally smiled.

"Good!" Pete said emphatically. "And why do you say that?" she asked looking up in his face.

"You're turning out to be exactly the kind of girl I've been dreaming about."

"You're crazy," Sally said laughingly. But her laugh was a little uncertain.

Back at their table, a big dark heavy set man was sitting talking to Carlson. He was introduced to Pete as being Sam Jones.

Sally excused herself and went to join some friends at another table. Instantly Carlson's oily manner disappeared. "All right, Wilson, what's the game?" he asked abruptly.

"What game?" Pete inquired innocently, sipping his milk.

"C'mon, bo," Jones said, leaning heavily on the table and looking darkly at Pete. "We're wise t' ya."

"Yeah," Carlson added, "we know you're here to try to put something on us. What's it all about?"

"Well," Pete said suddenly, putting his empty glass on the table. "Since you two are so very interest-

white patrons attempted to control writers like Langston Hughes and Zora Neale Hurston, and publishers like Alfred A. Knopf that focused on the white market burnished their credentials by publishing fashionable Black writers. In spring 1929, the *Chicago Whip* spoke out against the *Illustrated Feature Section*'s advertising content, which included suggestive spots for race records and other products. With such "sex and luck advertisements," the *Whip* argued that the *IFS* was "fostering 'the conditions of slavery.'"[21] Schuyler, at this point no longer the editor of the *IFS*, came to its defense in the pages of the *Pittsburgh Courier*, arguing that "the same advertisements have been appearing in all of the Negro newspapers for the past ten years" and that the *Whip*'s "holier-than-thou" attitude was selective and hypocritical.[22] Debates continued on many African American editorial pages throughout the spring, and at a fact-finding conference in Durham, North Carolina, in April, Black banker (and former financial backer of the *Half-Century Magazine*) Anthony Overton claimed that "nine-tenths of the colored weeklies are controlled by whites," highlighting the *Illustrated Feature Section* and charging that it "is also controlled by white people and edited and managed in their interest."[23] Overton quickly came under fire from a variety of sources, and an editorial in the *Norfolk Journal and Guide* noted that "the addition of [the *IFS*] by the weeklies was resorted to purely as an economic defense. It is a measure that promises a considerable increase in volume of advertising."[24]

Debate about the *Illustrated Feature Section*'s advertising content died down shortly thereafter, although troubles with Ziff remained. The *Pittsburgh Courier* had the most contentious relationship with Ziff. A year after the first dustup over white ownership of the *IFS*, the *Courier* issued a notice about ongoing serials from the section: "Due to a misunderstanding with the publishers, the serials, Dark Knight and Mamba's Daughters, are discontinued."[25] The *IFS* would soon return to the pages of the *Courier*, although the paper would intersperse *IFS* content with self-edited fictional content until finally terminating its relationship with the *IFS* in 1931 as the newspaper sought to claim its own space for fiction. Editors were routinely frustrated with Ziff's advertising rates and with the poor quality of his advertisements, which caused so much trouble at the Durham fact-finding conference.[26] Ziff's 1932 promotional booklet, *The Negro Market: Published in the Interest of the Negro Press*, seemingly sought to respond to criticism that Ziff wasn't treating his

Black clients as well as he could by presenting these clients as complex, dynamic, and diverse. In this document, Ziff and his company "endeavored to present herewith to advertisers the salient features of the Negro market which information may give a better idea as to its sales potentialities."[27] Nevertheless, the *Courier* would soon sever its relationship with the company over a couple of issues. Andrew Buni claims that the bold illustrations and photos of "seminude women" "began to offend [publisher Robert L.] Vann's Victorian sensibilities," but there were economic concerns as well.[28] As Vann noted in a letter to another editor, "Ziff could not get us any business except hair straightening and skin whitening copy which I could get myself. I have always wondered why Ziff could not get us some other types of business, and among my new experiences I have found out why; and I cancelled my contract with Ziff."[29]

There is also some evidence that Ziff sought to use the *Illustrated Feature Section* and his power as advertising agent to challenge Claude Barnett's Associated Negro Press.[30] Benjamin J. Davis Jr., a lawyer who followed as editor after Schuyler's brief time at the helm of the *IFS*, resigned his position in 1931 once he realized that the Ziff company was using the *IFS* "to secure a stranglehold on the entire Negro newspaper field" by "establish[ing] a news service, to corner the Negro news market, and then refuse news to any paper that did not retain it as a publisher's representative."[31] Davis, whose father was a lawyer and editor of the *Atlanta Independent,* soon made headlines himself as the criminal defense attorney for communist organizer Angelo Herndon, and later as one of two Communist Party members to be elected to the New York city council. Both Davis and Schuyler went on to have fascinating and wildly divergent political careers, so the mere fact that they both sat in the editor's chair of the *IFS* represents a compelling historical intersection. Little information is available on the section's third editor, Ivy Boone, the longtime secretary to *Baltimore Afro-American* editor Carl Murphy, who took over in mid-1931 after Davis resigned in protest. Although unlike Schuyler and Davis her name never appeared on the masthead, her appointment at the very least demonstrates the strong editorial connection between the *IFS* and the *Afro-American* in the section's final year and half.[32]

Nevertheless, the *Illustrated Feature Section* was, for a brief moment (1928–32), the most widely distributed venue for African American genre fiction. Its national reach made it familiar to Black readers across the country, helping to forge a national Black readership, and its stories and serials forged a largely unexplored path for African American literary production. Rejecting the uplift conventions of fiction that had long been a part of the Black press, the *IFS* specialized in entertaining fiction about Black life, complete with bold illustrations and promotional copy. Its masthead claimed content that was "Interesting, Entertaining and Instructive" as well as "Clean, Wholesome and Refreshing," offering readers a respite from the coverage of Jim Crow America that dominated the pages of the news sections. Indeed, the "entertaining" content featured here focused largely on pleasure—both the pleasure of a thrilling narrative and the vicarious pleasure afforded by genre tales with happy resolutions. African American writers also saw the *IFS* as representing a new kind of pathway for Black readers and writers. In the *Saturday Evening Quill,* a privately printed Boston-based literary magazine, Eugene Gordon quotes a lengthy statement from the *IFS* entitled "Instructions for Contributors":

> Stories must be full of human interest. Short, simple words. No attempt to parade erudition to the bewilderment of the reader. No colloquialisms such as "nigger," "darkey," "coon," etc. Plenty of dialogue, and language that is realistic.
>
> We will not accept any stories that are depressing, saddening, or gloomy. Our people have enough troubles without reading about any. We want them to be interested, cheered, and buoyed up; comforted, gladdened, and made to laugh.
>
> Nothing that casts the least reflection on contemporary moral or sex standards will be allowed. Keep away from the erotic! Contributions must be clean and wholesome.
>
> Everything must be written in that intimate manner that wins the reader's confidence at once and makes him or her feel that what is written is being spoken exclusively to that particular reader.
>
> No attempt should be made to be obviously artistic. Be artistic, of course, but "put it over" on the reader so he or she will be unaware of it.
>
> Stories must be swiftly moving, gripping the interest and sweeping on to a climax. The heroine should always be beautiful and desirable, sincere and virtuous. The hero should be of the he-man type, but not stiff, stereotyped, or vulgar. The villain should

obviously be a villain and of the deepest-dyed variety: crafty, unscrupulous, suave, and resourceful. Above all, however, these characters must live and breathe, and be just ordinary folks such as the reader has met. The heroine should be of the brown-skin type. All matter should deal exclusively with Negro life. Nothing will be permitted that is likely to engender ill feeling between blacks and whites. The color problem is bad enough without adding any fuel to the fire.[33]

Gordon glosses this lengthy quotation in his article "The Negro Fictionist in America" by noting, "Negro fictionists, until recently, busy themselves with damning to perdition all skins that could not be classified as brown or black. Every story contained at least one white villain, and he was rotten all over and right through the middle. The hero was bronze or black, and godly virtue oozed from his manly pores. Right, of course, always triumphed, and black was always right. But now the situation is different."[34] The tendentious melodramatic formula Gordon caricatures here shares a great deal with conventions of Jarrett's racial realism and Claudia Tate's racial protocols, and he celebrates the *IFS* for offering readers something new and less formulaic.

Gordon credits the *IFS* with representing new trends that moved away from fictional polemics associated with racial melodrama toward a more nuanced representation through its emphasis on a wide variety of African American characters. These instructions—such as "be artistic, of course, but 'put it over' on the reader so he or she will be unaware of it"—resemble the kinds of writing advice peddled by trade magazines like *Writer's Digest* for aspiring authors hoping to make it into the pages of the pulps. But other elements, such as the prohibition on "stories that are depressing, saddening, or gloomy," represent a clear articulation both to canonical African American literature and to the protest literature that appeared irregularly in Black newspapers before the introduction of the *IFS*. Instead, the emphasis on pleasure—the pleasure of fiction that could imagine characters living outside the omnipresence of Jim Crow segregation and white supremacy—takes precedence. While many of these rules cited by Gordon held firm in the early days of the *IFS,* the prohibition of stories about the "color problem" would not last long. But when these topics reemerged within Black newspaper fiction, they did so not as a form of propagandistic melodrama or racial tragedy. Rather, they were processed through the recognizable pleasures of genre, offering in the revision and reconstruction of fictional formulas the possibility for radical generic transformations.

This same description of the "Instructions for Contributors" has generated the only critical consideration of the *Illustrated Feature Section* among literary historians. Unlike Eugene Gordon, who saw in the "Instructions" an opening up of possibility for African American writers, Henry Louis Gates Jr. characterized these instructions as "ironclad" and described them as "strictures, widely circulated in those very journals in which black authors could most readily publish, which, along with the extended controversy over black oral forms, enable us to understand the black milieu" that allowed writers like Zora Neale Hurston to define herself as a writer of serious fiction—and a generator of the "speakerly text."[35] Gates's framework replicates the long-standing theoretical dynamic between modernism and mass culture, but, like that well-worn theoretical framework, it ignores many of the actual publishing realities of the period.[36] Hurston herself published with some regularity in the *Pittsburgh Courier,* though her publications bookend the *IFS,* and her slang-laden story "The Book of Harlem" appeared in the newspaper on February 12, 1927.[37] Another Harlem Renaissance writer strongly associated with vernacular language, Rudolph Fisher, published a two-part story ("Common Meter") in the *IFS* in 1930.[38] Like other efforts to disentangle modernism from mass culture and the marketplace, Gates's attempt to isolate—and canonize—Hurston because of her formal opposition to the degraded and compromised form of newspaper fiction obscures the more complex and dynamic print culture at work.

Under the editorship of Schuyler, Davis, and Boone, the *Illustrated Feature Section* published over three hundred stories and serial installments through the end of 1932, the last known issue of the *IFS.*[39] The fiction published there represented a wide variety of genres, and nearly all of it was original fiction, with the single exception being a second serialization of white writer DuBose Heyward's novel *Mamba's Daughters,* his sequel to *Porgy* (1925). The *IFS* featured a number of now-forgotten writers who experimented with a variety of genres. Cora Moten published a fourteen-part romance serial, "Struggling Hearts"; a thirteen-part supernatural detective thriller, "The Creeping Thing"; and a twelve-part weird adventure, "The Black Lily." William Thomas Smith published a twelve-part crime-fighting romance, "The Dark Knight," and a thirteen-part Southern melodrama, "White Laughter." Edward Lawson, who specialized in shorter serials, published sports fiction titles "The Singing Fullback," "The Catfish Kid," "The Harlem Hurricane," "The Pennant Parade," and "Basketball and Brawn," as well as crime fiction serials "The Clinic Murder Mystery" and "The Congressman's Family" and the romance serial "Susan Kane."[40] The *IFS* also featured a short series of science fiction stories ("The Shot into Space," "The Hidden Kingdom," and "Love on Mars") by John P. Moore under the series title Amazing Stories, presumably inspired by the groundbreaking science fiction pulp magazine of the same title. While crime fiction and romance—two of the most popular pulp genres—featured prominently, it was clear that the *IFS* quickly became a venue where African American writers and readers could explore the possible intersections between a wide variety of popular genre formulas and the realities and concerns of African American life.

Cora Moten's "The Creeping Thing" (June 22–September 7, 1929) provides a good example of exactly how these intersections could interrogate the assumptions of formula fiction and offer powerful new ways of understanding the possibilities of Black genre fiction. This serial is ostensibly a detective story, though one with weird overtones, similar to work published in the famous pulp magazine *Weird Tales,* which debuted in 1923. Set in the American South, "The Creeping Thing" concerns the mysterious disappearance of several people from the ominous "octagonal tower" of a house built by Ezra Selwyn, formerly enslaved and later "minister to the black republic of Haiti."[41] The narrator, an African American detective named Tom, returns home to the town at the behest of his friend Alec Jonas to investigate Ezra's disappearance. The serial soon takes on the formulaic quality of a locked-room mystery, as characters who remain alone in the octagonal tower are killed or disappear after the loud and terrifying noise made by the titular "creeping thing." Along the way, the old Haitian servant, Diaron, claims that Selwyn's nephew, the "Haitian dandy" Garland Selwyn, is a "papaloi," killing the victims in order to make zombies out of the corpses.[42] Diaron describes the concept of the zombie in great detail: "Zombies . . . are human corpses without souls, yet living and walking about just as you do. They are usually taken from the graves, monsieur, before the, what

Pittsburgh THE Courier
AMERICA'S BEST WEEKLY

PITTSBURGH, PA., SATURDAY, AUGUST 31, 1929

THE CREEPING THING ·

SYNOPSIS

There have been a number of gruesome murders in Selwyn House. They have occurred in the octagonal tower room, a mysterious addition to the house. It was built by old Ezra Selwyn years before, on his return from a tragic stay in Haiti where his young bride, Mary, has been lost in the voodoo infested jungles. The tragedy has made him an eccentric recluse. He lives in the house alone save for his two Haitian servants, Diaron and his wife, Mena.

Ezra himself is the first one murdered. Each murder is preceded and followed by the sound of some huge reptilian body being dragged over an uneven surface. But there are no entrances to the room large enough to admit such a body and no apparent hiding places.

The bodies have disappeared one by one until the last one, the signalless detective, Alene Hardmore, who is killed in an effort to investigate the mystery. Her body is watched by Detective Tom Frederick and his friend and co-worker, Al Jarton, comes for it.

But—the next day that body is stolen from the undertaking establishment, presumably by Garland Selwyn, a nephew of the elder man, whose mother is a Haitian voodoo priestess.

The bodies have all been scalped; and, after the mysterious disappearance of old Mena's body, an Indian scalping knife is found with a few strands of long black hair attached to its blood-stained blade.

Detective Frederick and Al Jarton subsequently interviewed Diaron, who attributes the Selwyn mystery to Zombies, which he claims are supernatural beings which often act in this manner. Diaron is so sincere in his belief that this will account for the Selwyn house murders, that Detective Frederick and Al Jarton regard the tale very carefully.

In the meantime, it is discovered that Garland Selwyn has suddenly left the Beal House on Maine street, where he has been lodging. Detectives Frederick and Al Jarton then make an appointment with Alec Jones to confer at the Beal House. The three of them meet there in order to find out more about the suspicious movements of Garland Selwyn.

Detective Frederick and his associates find a clue at the Beal House. They also find that Garland Selwyn has left suddenly with an old woman whose identity is unknown.

In the hope that he will discover further clues, Detective Frederick engages Garland Selwyn's empty room.

He then finds a body, strapped and bound mysteriously, in the Beal House. Alec, his companion, drives up in a Ford but disappears mysteriously.

NOW, GO ON WITH THE STORY

For a long moment we stood thus in the silence . . . the inert body supported between us.

limp form of Amanda Beal, I came at length to the threshold.

Mysterious Help

Cautiously and carefully, guided by my dimly-seen companion, I advanced toward the back of the long

you call rot, come. The evil mama—or papa-loi he make magic over the body and the body act and walk as you and me. He make it work in the fields or in the house or maybe do his crime he wish not to do himself. It is very evil practice these Zombie making."[43]

Classical detective fiction—best exemplified by Sir Arthur Conan Doyle's Sherlock Holmes stories—is filled with supernatural red herrings, from ghostly dogs to mysterious speckled bands, but within this tradition, the supernatural suspicions are always superseded by a rational explanation that fundamentally restores order and rationality to the world. Even in hard-boiled detective fiction that draws on weird explanations, these superstitions turn out to be bogus.[44] In his influential 1928 "Twenty Rules for Detective Stories," best-selling mystery novelist S. S. Van Dine suggested that "the problem of the crime must be solved by strictly naturalistic means. Such methods for learning the truth as slate-writing, Ouija boards, mind-reading, spiritualistic séances, crystal gazing, and the like, are taboo. A reader has a chance when matching his wits with a rationalistic detective, but if he must compete with the world of spirits and go chasing about the fourth dimension of metaphysics, he is defeated *ab initio*."[45] In "The Creeping Thing," however, Van Dine's set of naturalistic rules are surprisingly broken. The solution to this mystery actually turns out to be zombies. Garland Selwyn is in fact a papaloi, and he has been turning the victims of his scheme into mindless zombies all along. The noise of the creeping thing is revealed to have a rational explanation (the interior of the room spins mechanically to open a hidden entrance), but the murders themselves represent a violation of the principles of a ratiocinative detective formula—what one character in "The Creeping Thing" calls the misguided "materialist manner"—that rejects supernatural explanations.[46]

Moten's fascinating serial represents an early version of what Stephen F. Soitos has called the blues detective, and its use of zombies as a plot device marks an exciting and revolutionary first for African American literature. Among the characteristics of blues detective fiction, Soitos includes "the presence in the novels of hoodoo practice and hoodoo traditions . . . indigenous, syncretic religions of African Americans in the New World."[47] Moten's "The Creeping Thing" certainly qualifies as a detective text saturated with "hoodoo practice," even more so than a text that has come to exemplify Black detective fiction of this period:

Rudolph Fisher's celebrated Harlem Renaissance novel *The Conjure Man Dies* (1932), in which the solution turns out to be relatively materialist in nature. Publication of Moten's "The Creeping Thing" three years earlier in the *Illustrated Feature Section* is evidence that the elements that Soitos associates with the blues detective had already been widely circulated among African American writers and readers. In fact, the zombies of "The Creeping Thing" appear to be the earliest fictional use of the Haitian zombie in African American literature.[48] As Sarah Juliet Lauro has noted, "The Haitian zombie was formally introduced to the American imagination in 1929 with the publication of William Seabrook's travel narrative, *The Magic Island*."[49] Seabrook popularized the term "zombie"—previously used with a different meaning—to indicate "a soulless human corpse, still dead, but taken from the grave and endowed by sorcery with a mechanical semblance of life."[50] Moten's serial began just months after Seabrook's book appeared; it was already running when Seabury Quinn published "The Corpse-Master" in *Weird Tales* in July 1929, a story credited as being the "first zombie story . . . inspired by *The Magic Island*."[51]

"The Creeping Thing" thus represents a window into the complex importance of the *Illustrated Feature Section* and the authors who published there. The first Haitian zombie story in African American literature, and almost certainly the first Haitian zombie story in all of U.S. literature, the serial was widely circulated and likely had more readers even than Quinn's "Corpse-Master." This places Moten and "The Creeping Thing" at the vanguard of a particular kind of weird horror, and it does so in ways that seem to anticipate a critique of the tradition that would follow it. Popular zombie narratives, especially those transmitted in Hollywood films like *White Zombie* (Victor Halperin, 1932) and *I Walked with a Zombie* (Jacques Tourneur, 1943), are fundamentally invested in perpetuating the white mind/Black body dichotomy that comes under attack in Jordan Peele's 2017 film *Get Out*. These films feature mindless Black bodies controlled by powerful white minds. Under the aegis of the *Illustrated Feature Section*, Moten offers a zombie narrative that does not depend on an explicit racial dichotomy. Because her cast of characters is exclusively Black, she manages to produce a story that avoids the troubling racial politics that have come to characterize the zombie tradition. While the papaloi is a "Haitian dandy," other Haitian characters (like Diaron) serve as valuable sources of information on the figure of the zombie. African American characters include not only the level-headed detective Tom but also some of Garland Selwyn's victims, including Alene Hardmore, "detective extraordinary, and woman hard-boiled."[52] In this case, the *IFS's* instructions to avoid anything "that is likely to engender ill feeling between blacks and whites" allows Moten to present a zombie narrative with a strong sense of ambiguity. It refuses to fall back on simple binary oppositions that demonize racial or ethnic others.

Equally impressive and intriguing here is that both the author and the readers of this early zombie autocritique are radically different from those that scholars typically associate with fiction of this kind. Moten's readers were largely middle- and working-class African Americans scattered across the country, from larger cities like Baltimore and Pittsburgh to smaller and more remote locations like Galveston, Texas, or Des Moines, Iowa, reading the *Illustrated Feature Section* as a part of their locally or regionally distributed African American weekly. Further, as an African American woman writing fiction part time, Cora Moten hardly fits the mold of the canonical figures that literary history celebrates as innovators and pioneers, especially in the genre of weird horror. A native of Quincy, Illinois, Moten was a reasonably successful fiction writer, publishing serials in the *Chicago Defender* and the *Illustrated Feature Section* between 1928 and 1932; she later worked as an editor for the *Los Angeles Sentinel* and as a schoolteacher in the Los Angeles area.[53] Close attention to "The Creeping Thing," then, should alert us to two important considerations. First, genre fiction like that published in the *IFS* is worth considerably more than a footnoted dismissal; this publication's unique position as a venue for Black popular writing by professionals, semiprofessionals, and amateurs allowed for fascinating—sometimes revolutionary—examples of genre fiction that were enjoyed by a significant number of African American readers across the country. And second, to reckon properly with these texts, we must consider unfamiliar names like Moten's rather than seek out and overvalue the occasional appearance of a canonical figure. Most of the contributors to the *IFS* and to other national venues for Black popular fiction were amateur or semiprofessional writers. Many writers we will encounter in *Black Pulp* have similar trajectories; the story of their writing opens up an alternative literary history of African American popular writing.

"The Creeping Thing" encapsulates a number of important dynamics of the genre fiction published in Black newspapers during this period: The most widely read African American literature of the Harlem Renaissance was written by popular but now largely forgotten writers (like Cora Moten), it developed new ways of deploying genre tropes that have often been tied to frameworks of racial difference, and its publishing centers were not necessarily located in the most expected places. Although the *IFS* was initially edited out of Chicago, its premier venues were the nationally distributed *Pittsburgh Courier* and *Baltimore Afro-American,* and it appeared with newspapers from Atlanta to Portland, Oregon. "The Creeping Thing," then, serves as a reminder of just how complex and dynamic African American literary culture of the late 1920s was: Not everyone was in Harlem (or Chicago), and most Black readers who encountered Black-authored fiction did so in newspapers.

Moten's serial is just one of the many productions featured in the *IFS* before it disappeared in 1932. A spotty archival record means that it remains unclear why exactly the *IFS* shut down—or exactly when it did so—but I have been unable to find any evidence of it in extant microfilm after the end of 1932. That year was a busy one for Ziff, who in the spring ran an ill-fated campaign for the Republican nomination for the second congressional district of Illinois.[54] By this time, multiple factors contributed to the end of the *IFS*. Newspaper owners were increasingly frustrated by Ziff's work and were abandoning the section piecemeal, what Ben Davis described as Ziff's attempts to displace the Associated Negro Press had been thwarted, and Ziff himself was on his way to becoming a publishing magnate in his own right, founding the successful magazine house, Ziff-Davis Publishing Company, in 1936. In later histories of the company, as Jason Chambers has noted, he would "refuse to acknowledge" his work for the Black press or credit the *IFS* as playing any important role in his success.[55] By 1935, George Schuyler would refer to the publication as "the ill-starred Illustrated Feature Section of the Negro press" in a column on the importance of J. A. Rogers's contributions on Black history, which also appeared regularly in the *IFS*.[56] However, the section's legacy was more powerful than many have imagined.

DECENTERING AFRICAN AMERICAN LITERARY HISTORY: BALTIMORE, PITTSBURGH, AND BEYOND

Despite its brief run, the *IFS* effectively demonstrated a sincere demand nationwide for Black genre fiction in the pages of African American newspapers. While Black readers seeking the pleasure of genre might find this in the dozens of pulp magazine titles at any newsstand, the stories presented there, as we saw in the introduction, tended either to exclude Black lives entirely or to marshal stereotypes in service of white supremacist formulas. The *IFS*, however, offered an alternative pulp space, one that foregrounded Black experiences and offered versions of genre fiction that elevated Black characters into starring roles. The demise of the *Illustrated Feature Section* would not spell the end of this transformation of genre; indeed, it was only the beginning. The *Pittsburgh Courier*, which finally cut loose Ziff's *IFS* in 1931, had already begun featuring original genre fiction solicited and edited in house, though at first this was somewhat irregular. Examples of this included serials like the sensational twenty-five-part "Bad Girl" by Vina Delmar (1930–31) and Monte King's nine-part crime-fighting mystery "Questionmark" (1932). In March 1933, the first installment of George Schuyler's serial "Sugar Hill" (published under the pseudonym Samuel I. Brooks) appeared in the *Courier*, and after this, Schuyler would have fiction in virtually every issue of the paper through August 1939. Schuyler had already included fiction in his short-lived venture, the *National News*, in 1932, including a story cycle by Gertrude Schalk discussed in chapter 2. The *Baltimore Afro-American*, which shared editorial offices with the *IFS* in its final two years, seamlessly transitioned to publishing many of the same authors who were featured regularly in the *IFS*. In the *Afro-American*, these stories continued to appear in prominent locations in the paper, and with bold, eye-catching illustrations.

The brief and interesting history of the *Illustrated Feature Section* necessarily raises compelling questions about the geographical coordinates of African American literary history. Although its editorial offices were initially in Chicago, they soon moved to Baltimore. The section circulated most widely with the *Baltimore Afro-American* and the *Pittsburgh Courier*, and the newspapers that did include the *IFS* were based in smaller and often more remote locations in the South, Midwest, and

West. The *Chicago Defender* and the *New York Amsterdam News* were not included in the group of "thirty-four of America's most prominent colored newspapers" that featured its content. While the *Defender* saw significant circulation in the 1920s and 1930s, its publication of original fiction essentially dried up when *Abbot's Monthly* appeared in 1930. The *New York Amsterdam News* occasionally featured fiction, but it was always more of a local Harlem paper without broad national distribution. This shift away from New York and Chicago, routinely understood to be the centers of gravity for African American literary culture in the first half of the twentieth century, enables a fuller recognition of the *Illustrated Feature Section*'s influence.

In this way, Baltimore and Pittsburgh become twentieth-century analogs to the "unexpected places" of African American print culture that Eric Gardner describes in his monograph of the same name. Gardner highlights a variety of hubs of African American literary and intellectual life in the nineteenth century, "locations that have often fallen off of our maps of early black culture."[57] While some effort has been made to do the same for twentieth-century African American literature, with a handful of exceptions, the move has not been toward what Gardner describes as a "new regionalism" but rather toward other, international metropolises.[58] Works like Brent Hayes Edwards's *The Practice of Diaspora: Literature, Translation, and the Rise of Black Internationalism* (2003) or Davarian L. Baldwin and Minkah Makalani's edited collection *Escape from New York: The New Negro Renaissance beyond Harlem* (2013) emphasize the rich internationalism of early twentieth-century African American literary cultures but do little to acknowledge those "unexpected places" that nurtured and transmitted African American literary culture in far-flung areas like Houston, Omaha, Des Moines, or Portland, Oregon. Such transnational reconceptualizations of African American literary history have revolutionized the field in many respects, but this approach leaves behind wide swaths of middle- and working-class African American readers across the United States—readers whose interest in and experience of transnational Black culture was felt not only through newspaper reporting but also through a pervasive internationalism mediated by the genre fiction discussed across this study.

Throughout *Black Pulp*, the *Baltimore Afro-American* and the *Pittsburgh Courier* will figure most prominently; after the demise of the

Illustrated Feature Section, these two of the "big four" African American weekly newspapers published fiction with regularity and were distributed widely across the country. By the middle of the twentieth century, they had the largest circulation of all Black newspapers in the country.[59] But an African American literary history that takes into account the legacy of the *Illustrated Feature Section* offers an intriguing oscillation between the national and the local. The section itself was nationally distributed, but mostly through local newspapers. In this sense, it created a national community (even if only an imagined one) of readers of Black popular fiction, offering the "Interesting, Entertaining and Instructive" pleasures of genre featuring African American characters in all sorts of roles. In so doing, the *IFS* whetted readers' appetites and produced a lasting demand for these very pleasures in locations far from Chicago and New York, the traditional centers of African American literary culture. Such demand was in turn met by the local papers themselves, some of which solicited and published genre fiction independently after the demise of the *IFS*. African American readers who saw in these compelling popular stories "just ordinary folks such as the reader has met" (as the *IFS* "Instructions" demanded) would continue to seek and find original genre fiction that could offer them repositories for their own cultural fantasies; these were often fantasies that intersected with their hometown paper's news content, stories both national and local. The "ordinary folks" of these stories, edited by these local papers, often lived in equally "ordinary" places like Pittsburgh, Atlanta, Norfolk, and Indianapolis. If Chicago and Harlem were not the only places that African American literature could be consumed, they were also not necessarily the only proper settings for this literary production. The demand created by the *Illustrated Feature Section* at a national level led to the broader production of fiction, both published and set in "unexpected places."

Consider the *Atlanta World,* initially a weekly that would become the *Atlanta Daily World* in 1932. Founded in 1928 by W. A. Scott II, the *World* carried the *Illustrated Feature Section* for at least some of its early life. Unfortunately, no copies of the *World* containing the *IFS* from this period appear to survive, but by July 1932, the paper could describe the *IFS* as "a supplement formerly used by the World and which now is carried in many of the smaller weeklies."[60] However, the *Atlanta Daily World* would soon begin to feature its own original fiction on an irregular basis. A number of early Chester Himes stories—"The Meanest Cop in the World" (1933), "A Modern Marriage" (1933), and "A Cup of Tea" (1934)—first appeared in the *World,* along with fiction by H. E. Richtersohn, Edward Lawson, Bernard Braxton, Martin Daniel Richardson, and Davis Lee—some of whom had previously published in the *Illustrated Feature Section.* Publication of fiction would be irregular in this daily newspaper, but the paper could easily emphasize its own location in the fiction it did publish. For example, appearing in 1935, "Atlanta After Dark" a "fast-moving, six chapter short short story" by Joseph Stafford (who would later publish fiction in the *Afro-American*), was a hometown tale of "Atlanta's gay night life" and its accompanying crime and romance, proving that compelling African American genre fiction could be set outside the usual environs of major Northern metropolises.[61]

Of course, Harlem and Chicago still loomed large in the collective imaginary of readers, so much of the fiction published across these venues still takes place in these famous locations. But decentering the literary tradition enables a highlighting, for example, of the importance of Pittsburgh's Wylie Avenue in *Pittsburgh Courier* fiction like Monte King's 1932 crime-fighting serial "Questionmark" or the titular setting of Edward Lawson's five-part 1934 romance serial "Miss Norfolk" ("The Story of a Norfolk Girl Whose Strange Beauty Won Her Fame and Happiness"), one of the few examples of fiction that appeared in the *Norfolk Journal and Guide* after the demise of the *Illustrated Feature Section.*[62] The *Journal and Guide,* which only included fiction infrequently after 1932, seemed interested exclusively in genre fiction set in the Black community in the Virginia Tidewater region. Lawson followed up "Miss Norfolk" with two other short serials, "Visiting Nurse" (October 27–November 24, 1934) and "The Morning Star Mystery" (March 9–March 23, 1935), both set in and around Norfolk. During this period, even African American newspapers with small circulations joined the trend. The *Indianapolis Recorder* published a handful of romantic serials set in the Midwest, some of which survive (in part) on microfilm: Marjorie Tucker Brown's "For the Love of Mary" (May 23–July 4, 1931), "The Call of the Blood" (July 11–September 26, 1931), and "Beloved Sinner" (October 29, 1932–February 23, 1933); and Jeanette Bunn's "Her Phantom Lover" (October 3–November 21, 1931) and "For Better, for Worse" (November 28–December 12, 1931). Editorial paratexts around these installments highlight the connection of these writers to Indianapolis and the *Recorder,* calling Brown "our own" and noting that Bunn's "For Better, for Worse" was "written especially for newspaper publication."[63] Even in this small Midwestern paper, which likely did not even carry the section during its run, the *Illustrated Feature Section*'s influence shows through clearly.

It would be an overstatement to claim that the *Illustrated Feature Section* inaugurated the birth of Black genre fiction in the United States; there are plenty of examples that preceded this short-lived tabloid supplement. Earlier examples of genre—like the work of Pauline Hopkins or Oscar Micheaux—found it more difficult to reach a mass Black audience, even if they did represent a growing market for Black genre in multiple forms.[64] However, it is clear that the appearance of the *IFS* was something of a watershed moment in the history of Black popular fiction; it seemingly discovered (and developed) a nationwide appetite and demand for genre fiction by and about African Americans among Black readers. Its influence could be felt across the country, whether in nationally distributed papers like the *Courier* and the *Afro-American,* or in more unexpected places like Norfolk or Indianapolis. The *Amsterdam News,* which never published fiction as regularly as its nationally distributed counterparts, even gave a nod to Ziff's publication with its short-lived *Weekly Magazine and Illustrated Feature Section,* which included two short Schuyler serials, "Flowers of Sin" and "Summer School Idyll," during its brief run in the summer of 1935.[65] If other venues for popular genre—mainstream pulp magazines and Hollywood—ignored these readers, then the pages of the Black press became an alternative pulp space, one that reflected the realities and fantasies of the nation's African American readership. Despite its checkered history, the *Illustrated Feature Section*—owned by Ziff but under the editorial direction of Schuyler, Davis, and Boone—came to represent an exciting possibility in the Black publishing scene: a place where middle- and working-class Black readers could turn for the pleasures of genre, as well as a place where African American writers could begin experimenting with the political and social possibilities of genre fiction outside of the ideologically bounded world of pulp magazines. Its tenure may have been short, but the *IFS* sparked a thriving tradition of Black popular fiction in the decades after its demise.

2

ROMANCING THE RACE
THE POLITICS OF BLACK LOVE STORIES

ALTHOUGH THE TERM "PULP FICTION" has become synonymous with gritty stories of criminals, detectives, and femmes fatales, it wasn't until 1933 that crime fiction became the dominant pulp genre on the newsstands. Before this, the most popular genres in the pulps were westerns and romance, and these two remained among the top four most common genres through the end of the pulp era.[1] Likewise, in the Black press, these genres appeared with some frequency. Westerns were far less common—and they showed up much later alongside other historical fiction discussed in the conclusion—but romance stories were almost certainly the most common genre of stories published across the history of popular fiction that I discuss here. This included fiction published in the *Illustrated Feature Section,* the debut issue of which included the first installment of "Chocolate Baby," "A Story of Ambition[,] Deception[,] and Success" by George Schuyler, publishing under the pseudonym Samuel I. Brooks for the first time.[2] Other fiction appearing in the early issues of the *IFS*—including Caroline Stanwix's "Mississippi Love" (November 10, 1928), Anne Stokes's "Love Wins" (December 8, 1928), A. Aloysius Green's two-part "An Atlanta Romance" (December 15–22, 1928), and Cora Moten's fourteen-part serial "Struggling Hearts" (December 29, 1928–April 13, 1929)—testify to the ubiquity of romance as a genre within the pages of African American newspapers. Even before the debut of the *IFS,* as Black newspapers occasionally tested the waters with original genre fiction in the mid- to late 1920s, the vast majority of stories that appeared could easily be classified as romance fiction.[3] In this respect, the generic distribution within African American newspaper fiction quite explicitly reflects the broader contours of the pulp magazine marketplace.

Nevertheless, romance remains one the most understudied genres of the pulp era. Despite a number of influential texts from the 1980s, romance, in the form of the love story, remains an exceedingly understudied popular genre, especially in the twentieth century. Critics who have examined the genre have often done so with a healthy dose of disdain. Janice Radway's seminal *Reading the Romance,* for example, struggles to comprehend why women, after the emergence of second-wave feminism, might still be drawn to stories that continually reinforce patriarchal power dynamics.[4] Tania Modleski's *Loving with a Vengeance* yokes the nineteenth-century Gothic to late twentieth-century Harlequin romances (leaping over the love pulps of the early twentieth century) in a study that draws heavily on Freudian psychoanalysis.[5] A rich body of American literary scholarship turns to nineteenth-century sentimental literature (the clearest precursor to popular twentieth-century romantic formulas) and what Lauren Berlant called "the unfinished business of sentimentality in American culture."[6] Mass-produced pulp romance fiction of the early twentieth century, however, has not found a comparable scholarly audience.[7] One notable example of early cultural criticism found such stories trite, and these considerations are equally condescending. Stuart Hall and Paddy Whannel, writing about the descendants of the pulps in the mid-1960s, note, "The fiction in women's magazines, the hospital romances and the love comics for teenagers all conform to a quite recognizable pattern. They are all simple *resolution* or *wish-fulfilment* stories."[8] In both these cases, the critics find love stories to be lacking any sort of potential for political or cultural work; tied to patriarchal formulas, romances like these are damned by being simply apolitical versions of Freudian wish fulfillment. Recent scholarship, however, has started to make a case for fiction published in love pulps and romantic confession magazines, but as far as most genre criticism is concerned, romance remains nearly impossible to recuperate in any recognizable cultural studies model.[9]

Attending to the romance fiction published in the Black press, however, can illuminate some of the more powerful cultural work of early twentieth-century romance fiction. This is because even if romance stories in the pulps acted as narrative forms of wish fulfillment, they also described and delineated forms of acceptable behavior, effectively policing the boundaries of reproduction. Readers who encountered romance pulps became instilled with a host of conservative values that ran alongside legal and social prohibitions. For example, representations of interracial or interethnic encounters—a staple of the sensational pocket paperbacks of the late twentieth century—were completely absent in the most popular romance pulp magazines in the first half of the century. At a time when interracial marriage was outlawed in many states, the pulps worked to produce a fictional world in which such encounters were unpresentable because they were unthinkable; wishes like these would never be fulfilled by pulps like the popular *Love Story*. Romance pulps accomplished this by eradicating racial difference almost entirely, presenting readers with fictional worlds of pure whiteness. When romance fiction appears in Black newspapers, this space of pure whiteness is not transformed through a complete reversal, although some stories do take place in exclusively Black spaces. Symptomatic of the more complex articulations of Black pulp, other romance stories represent interracial encounters in both realistic and utopian forms, acknowledging the existence (and the fraught power dynamics) of these relationships rather than simply ignoring them, as the pulps chose to do.

Likewise, the romance fiction discussed in this chapter reveals the way the genre could model acceptable, gendered behavior for its largely female readership. Pulp romance, for example, depended on rivalries between women and typically rewarded the final, generally chaste romantic "clinch" to the most stereotypically moral character in the story. According to pulp editor Harold Hersey, "purity and innocence and naivete are the watchwords of the publishers in this field. . . . They are born housewives."[10] In charting the history the best-selling romance pulp *Love Story Magazine*, Laurie Powers has demonstrated that into the early 1930s, "the stories would always end with a chaste kiss, and there couldn't be any scenes, dialogue, or settings that remotely hinted that the heroine and hero were engaged in pre-marital sex."[11] Pulp romance fiction was not usually the place for stories of moral redemption or second chances; Hall and Whannel note that "if the heroine in the women's magazine story risks social disapproval for a time, this is because she is sure that time will prove her right."[12] By contrast, romance fiction in the *Illustrated Feature Section* and other Black newspaper venues offered a far more morally complex understanding of women's roles. By attending to the realities of Black women's experiences in particular, these romance stories recognized the intersections of race, class, and gender that put these women in circumstances that were a far cry from the fairy tale–like wish fulfillments of romance pulps.

This chapter offers an alternative reading of the interwar love story by foregrounding the peculiar dynamics of this genre as it appeared in African American newspapers. This was a place where writers and readers could encounter realistic alternatives to romance formulas in the pulps while simultaneously enjoying the utopian pleasures of socially progressive romantic fantasies. Central to this argument is the figure of Gertrude Schalk, one of the most intriguing writers to publish in these venues. Schalk wrote fiction for both love pulps and the Black press. On the one hand, in the pulps, her work tracked the romantic foibles of a cast of exclusively white characters. Her work for the Black press, on the other hand, presents a kind of photo negative, a world of Black characters and Black romance, although a decidedly different set of stakes is in operation than her work for the pulps. Like much of the Black newspaper fiction I discuss in this book, Schalk's boundary-crossing work throws into relief the various ideologies embedded within the period's genres. While Schalk's writerly double life demonstrates the possibilities of generic transformation within romance formulas, later writers would continue to perform this work by attacking prohibitions on interracial romance head on. In the spring and summer of 1934, the *Baltimore Afro-American* deployed the presumably apolitical genre of romance to challenge social and legal injustices, including the bans on interracial marriage and sexual double standards confronted by African American women; interracial romance stories would continue to appear as both central narratives and subplots through the 1950s. Both cases demonstrate the kind of radical cultural work that Black romance fiction could perform in its canny articulation to genre conventions and expectations.

GERTRUDE SCHALK'S BOUNDARY CROSSING

Gertrude "Toki" Schalk is an astonishing figure in twentieth-century African American history: a broadly successful writer who has received almost no scholarly attention outside a couple of unpublished dissertations.[13] Born in Boston, she became part of the Black literary society there and published some of her early work in the *Saturday Evening Quill*.[14] Appearing alongside writers like Helene Johnson and Dorothy West, Schalk's work in the *Quill* was well received—her story "Black Madness" received a mention in Edmund O'Brien's *Best Short Stories of 1928*—but not necessarily lucrative (the *Quill* was a coterie publication).[15] Schalk had been contributing short stories to the *Boston Post* since 1925, but her fortunes soon changed when she began selling stories to romance pulps in 1930. Schalk's star rose quickly, with her work appearing in magazines like Street & Smith's *Love Story Magazine* and Munsey's *All-Story Love Story*. After selling her first pulp story, "Moon Magic," to *Love Story Magazine* for $75 in early 1930, Schalk had extraordinary success over the next few years. Publishing both under her own name and under the pseudonym Gerry Ann Hale, Schalk sold regularly to *Love Story*: fifteen stories in 1930, seventeen stories in 1931, thirteen stories in 1932, ten stories in 1933, and nine in 1934. She also published in a variety of other romance pulps. She regularly made over $1,000 a year from her pulp writing—in the depths of the Great Depression.[16] Although she was a regular society columnist for the *Pittsburgh Courier* (contributing "Smart Talk on Society in Boston, by 'Toki'" beginning in 1932, a column that later became "Toki Types"), she actually made most of her income writing for the pulps during this decade, with magazines regularly requesting her work.[17] In a letter written to a close friend in late 1933, she overtly acknowledges this: "I didn't do a col [i.e., column] this week. Was too busy dashing out that yarn All Story called for. Money before charity, y'know."[18] Though Schalk (as Toki Schalk Johnson) would later become a fixture in the Black press—she was one of the first African American inductees into the Women's Press Club of Pittsburgh—at this point in her career she was, like many writers, white and Black, attempting to turn genre fiction writing into a career in the pulp magazines. An African American woman making her living writing about white romance for a largely white readership might seem unusual, even if the presence of African American writers in the pulps is grossly underestimated. How-ever, most pulp readers were likely to presume that Schalk was white, if only because the whiteness of romance pulps was so hegemonic.

Even if readers failed to expect Schalk to be anything other than her white characters, the longtime editor of *Love Story Magazine,* Daisy Bacon, knew better. Schalk and Bacon had a positive personal relation-ship, attested to in Bacon's own *Love Story Writer,* a 1954 guide for "how to write and market the romantic story." In this guide, Bacon singles out Schalk as a potential collaborator on a fascinating project that was never realized. She writes,

> Gertrude Schalk, a Boston girl who was a suburban correspondent for the Boston *Post* and who started writing love story fiction after hearing the broadcasts of our *Love Story* radio program over the Columbia Network, had what seemed like a unique idea for a book on writing. She wanted me to publish the history of her stories which were purchased for *Love Story Magazine*—from the time of each submission and our exchange of letters about the revision until the story was finally accepted and published. After a time, she had a collection of her stories in their different stages between their rewritings and I had her letters accompanying the submitted manuscripts and the carbons of my replies reporting on the story and outlining the revision to be done.[19]

Unfortunately, this project was never completed because the various manuscripts and the correspondence were lost when Street & Smith, publishers of *Love Story Magazine,* relocated their headquarters. Never-theless, the fact that Schalk would have been Bacon's collaborator on an in-depth pulp writers' guide, complete with story drafts and correspon-dence, attests to her success in the field and to the respect Bacon had for her. Even if Bacon obscures Schalk's racial identity in *Love Story Writer,* it is certain that Schalk was not passing in print with Bacon; she met her on a visit to New York in 1930, when the editor took the young writer out to lunch at the Hotel Pennsylvania.[20] Shortly after this, Schalk pub-lished a glowing piece on Bacon, calling her "an excellent example of a modern-day heroine," in the *Boston Sunday Globe.*[21]

Writing for the pulps nevertheless involved a kind of implicit pass-ing in print for Schalk, both because the white readership of the pulps was likely to be wholly ignorant of her stature in the Black press and because her mastery of formulaic love stories featuring the romantic foibles of white protagonists would have been unlikely to raise any doubt in the minds of those readers about Schalk's presumed whiteness. For Schalk, who was deeply embedded in the Black middle-class society of Boston at the time, this was likely the source of some amusement, even as she took the craft of genre fiction writing seriously. Letters to her friend Bernice Dutrieuille Shelton, an African American society columnist in Philadelphia, include witty and self-conscious commentary about the potential awkwardness of the white editor, Daisy Bacon, seeing her off on a trip to Europe in 1931 and suggestions that she might name a protagonist in one of her stories after Bernice, whose relationship with her husband was strained.[22] Schalk herself seemed to have reveled in her many personas: after first publishing under her own name in *Love Story*, she soon adopted the pseudonym Gerry Ann Hale for some of her work in *Love Story* in early 1932. She continued to publish under both names, a common practice that helped editors feign authorial variety with a stable of especially prolific writers. But it was also in early 1932 that she began her "Smart Talk on Society in Boston" column (signed "Toki") in the *Pittsburgh Courier*. This proliferation of names—Gertrude, Gerry, Toki—suggests Schalk's delight in writing for different audiences and embodying different personas. It is possible, however, that some close readers of the pulps might have become aware of Schalk's race when some visual evidence appeared in the pulps. After she had already become quite successful across multiple love pulp titles, her photo appeared alongside an astrological feature in *Ainslee's* in July 1935 (also edited by Bacon at this time), with the caption "Gertrude Schalk, popular young writer, possesses the literary ability of the Gemini native."[23] This issue also featured Schalk's story "Up the Middle-Aisle," profusely illustrated, as usual, with images of glamorous white characters.

Schalk thus provides an intriguing test case for thinking about how genre travels across lines of racial difference. Along with her pulp romance stories and her coterie publications with the *Saturday Evening Quill*, her publications in the Black press to offer an example of a writer using the same genre differently for different audiences. While Schalk published one of her earliest stories in the Schuyler-edited *Illustrated Feature Section*—the romance/thriller "The Sprung Trap" appeared in the

January 19, 1929, issue—her most sustained work of genre fiction for the Black press was solicited by Schuyler for his short-lived *National News,* a New York–based weekly newspaper that lasted only seventeen weeks in early 1932. Compared to the *Afro-American* and the *Pittsburgh Courier,* the *National News* had a miniscule circulation, and it failed to compete with the *Amsterdam News,* which was Schuyler's goal. Nevertheless, Schuyler was not too far removed from his editorship of the *Illustrated Feature Section,* and he saw the inclusion of fiction as essential, even contacting Schalk directly to ask for stories.[24] Schalk's complex eight-part story cycle, "The Yellow Parrot," illustrated by Ollie Harrington, is set in the Harlem nightclub that gives the series its title, and each of the eight stories focuses on the romantic ups and downs of a different dancer employed by club. Representative of Harlem's identity as "the Mecca of the New Negro," the focal character highlighted in the title of nearly every installment evokes stories of migration: "The Kid from Richmond," "The Georgia Peach," "The Boston High-Flyer," "The Chicago Kid," "The California Lemon," "Mississippi Lily," and "The Bronx Baby." Under the wing of Mazie, the oldest and most experienced dancer in the "Yellow Parrot," these young women struggle through competition and jealousy, mutual support and self-defense as they navigate the exciting, but potentially treacherous, world of the Harlem cabaret. The form of the story cycle affords Schalk the opportunity to expand the limits of genre and to offer more than the simple pleasures of the love story.

Schalk had plenty of experience with nightclub romance stories; indeed, this was a prominent setting for many stories in both romance pulps and Black newspaper fiction. Schalk's early "The Sprung Trap" includes a nightclub setting, as does the early work of Ann Petry, discussed in the introduction. Schalk also published a number of stories set in nightclubs and theaters (featuring only white characters) in love pulps. Among these are "Gerry from the Chorus" (*Love Story Magazine,* October 3, 1931), "Stage Romance" (*Love Story Magazine,* December 24, 1932), "Night-Club Romance" (*Love Story Magazine,* March 31, 1934), and "Stardust" (*Love Story Magazine,* May 19, 1934, as Gerry Ann Hale). The nightclub setting offered a number of ideal accouterments for the pulp romance story, in particular glamorous detail and built-in competition for a romantic partner. Whether focusing on stage acts or merely on a dance floor, the nightclub emphasizes visual erotic appeal

Night-club Romance

By

Gertrude Schalk

AS she ducked swiftly out of the swirling snow and into the damp, narrow performer's entrance of the Last Word night club, unbuttoning her heavy sports coat as she ran, Mona blew warmly on icy finger tips and stamped her feet. Down the long passageway, around a corner, through another heavy door, and she finally reached the chorus girls' main dressing room.

She opened the green door, and the glaring babble within struck her like a heavy blow. As usual, Mona shrank just a little from the blare and noise. It seemed that lately everything got on her nerves.

The Last Word itself was all right as night clubs go, catering directly to the moneyed class. The girls had to put up with a lot, however, and lately Mona had found herself forgetting the set smile required of all the girls when a guest wished to buy them supper or a drink. Once she had even "accidentally" shoved aside an overfriendly would-be shiek.

And Hadden, the manager, had given her a long call-down ending up with the usual warning: "There's a hundred girls just waiting to step in your shoes," he had said. And Mona had known sickeningly that he was telling the truth.

But it didn't make the advances of the patrons any easier to take.

There was a tiny ache beginning behind her eyes when Mona slid into the dressing room that night. She was weary; just plain tired out from staying up all night and trying to

First page of Gertrude Schalk, "Night-Club Romance," with illustration, *Street & Smith's Love Story Magazine*, March 31, 1934. Special Collections, Carrier Library, James Madison University.

and the chance encounter; the setting also offers substantial opportunity for rivalry, whether between women or between men (often both).

Schalk's nightclub stories about white characters strongly emphasize the competitive aspect that features prominently across fiction in love pulps. "Night-Club Romance" follows a dancer named Mona, who incurs the wrath of the "star" of the "fan dancers in the city" when she catches the eye of a wealthy man in the club.[25] A conflict develops between the entitled star Fanette and the young Mona over the "millionaire playboy" Cary Talbot.[26] Fanette enlists a reluctant Mona—who believes Cary still has feelings for another woman—into a scheme to entrap a drunk Cary in her apartment, but her plans are foiled when Cary's inebriation turns out to be feigned, and he declares his love to Mona before a final clinch seals their love. This story exemplifies many of the characteristics of Schalk's writing for the pulps and of love story conventions as a whole. The rivalry between Mona and Fanette drives the plot, with each woman fending for herself, and the threat of scandal and immorality (Cary discovered drunk the morning after at Fanette's) remains unrealized as the wholesome romance between Mona and Cary displaces what would otherwise be a shock for the conservative readers of *Love Story*. Schalk's other work for the pulps is along the same lines, emphasizing competition between women over men and teasing readers with the possibility of scandal or serious trouble for her heroines, then resolving the stories in a way that punishes unethical (or sometimes amoral) women and reassures readers that these threats to moral order were never realistic to begin with.[27]

When it came to romance fiction for African American audiences, Schalk imagined both the conditions of romance and the relationships between women in a profoundly different way. These revisions may not necessarily represent a heightened "realism" in her genre fiction, but they acknowledge—in ways her pulp stories do not—real threats faced by women in these erotically charged spaces as well as the necessary bonds between women as essential to survival. In addition, the work of Schalk (and others) in focalizing her narratives through the nightclub or cabaret dancer gives voice to women as "critical modern subjects, citizens of the world," as Jayna Brown describes these real-life performers in *Babylon Girls*.[28] "The Sprung Trap," published by Schuyler in the *Illustrated Feature Section*, bears a number of similarities to the nightclub stories she would later publish in the pulps. This tale is set in the "Club Cleo," a Harlem nightclub, and follows June Kane, "the club's youngest chorus girl," as she initially rebuffs advances from Jimmy Nugent, "chief hoofer," whom June describes as "a immatation *[sic]* of a man" for "prancin' roun' a slippery floor."[29] June is also pursued by "Boots Holmes, Harlem's most notorious banker, gambler, and bootlegger," who pays the club owner $300 to drug June so that Boots may rape her. Jimmy shows up in time to save June, then reveals that he only danced, as he says, "'cause I wanted some extra money. I got a good tailoring business on Eighth avenue that brings me in a nice little bit every month."[30] The story resolves the underlying tension in the main plot by revealing that Jimmy—initially rejected for being a poor and unambitious "hoofer" (male dancer)—is in fact a prosperous small business owner. However, the very real threat of sexual violence that June faces in this story represents a sharp divergence from the conventions Schalk would encounter in the pulp magazines. Romance pulps generally preferred to remain reticent to discuss anything about sexuality; Harold Hersey noted that "the heroines are legless, breastless and brainless."[31] Further, *Love Story,* the pulp where Schalk appeared most frequently, "was considered one of the most conservative of the romance pulps," where, in the words of one trade paper writer, "a heroine is a heroine, and must be good and sweet and darling, if she is to be worthy of the hero's love."[32] "The Sprung Trap," in contrast, foregrounds the threat of sexual violence even in its title, which refers to Boots Holmes's plan to drug and rape June. The fact that Schalk could not only include this terrifying possibility in her story but also make it a central pivot for the plot demonstrates how wildly African American writers could experiment with genre formulas in the pages of Black newspapers, where fiction was not likely to be as monitored by censors in the way it was within pulp magazines. This freedom allowed writers like Schalk to use genre tales like "The Sprung Trap" to detail more explicitly the intersections of sexuality and economics that were necessarily a part of the nightclub atmosphere.

If "The Sprung Trap"—published before Schalk had sold a story to the pulps—offers a variation on the pulp romance formula that paints a more realistic picture of threats of violence and sexual abuse faced by female entertainers, then "The Yellow Parrot" goes much further by depicting a kaleidoscopic array of experiences that push the boundaries

Illustrated FEATURE SECTION
THE AFRO AMERICAN

Interesting, Entertaining and Instructive

Clean, Wholesome and Refreshing

Section 2—Saturday, January 19, 1929

The SPRUNG TRAP by GERTRUDE SCHALK

"WHY don't you gimme a break, Baby?" Jimmy Nugent, chief hoofer at the Club Cleo, leaned over one of the club's small tables, his face carelessly intent as he faced June Kane, the club's youngest chorus girl.

For some reason Jimmy had "taken" to June right off the bat.

Not that June was so beautiful; her bright eyes and black, shiny hair were duplicated at least four times in the club's chorus, while her smooth, brown skin and red mouth were by no means uncommon.

Yet there was something different about June; a freshness, a remoteness from the sordid atmosphere of the club.

Now as she sat there June saw the hot blood surge under the velvety skin, her tiny brown hands clenched themselves fiercely.

"Lissen, I tole yo' befo' I ain't givin' no breaks to nobody."

Her soft southern voice was slightly husky with rising temper.

"How do I know?" taunted Jimmy, grinning suddenly.

"I don' care whether yo' believe me or no," she muttered, and Jimmy laughed aloud.

"Oh, so you're saving the breaks for Boots maybe," there was a keenness in his eyes that belied the raillery in his voice.

JUNE IS INSULTED

June's head jerked up, her black eyes snapped.

"Yo' . . . ."

"Boots sure comes regular every night," Jimmy interrupted June raised her head and, following his nod with her eyes, met the sleepy-eyed gaze of Boots Holmes, Harlem's most notorious banker, gambler and bootlegger.

She shivered suddenly.

"I ain't the only girl in the club," she said, lowering her eyes; "I hate him!"

Jimmy narrowed his eyes, his voice came low and insinuating:

"Or maybe you're saving 'em for Pop, our beloved manager."

June sat erect, two red spots glowing beneath the rouge and powder on her cheeks.

"Pop!" she gasped. "Why, yo' dirty-mouthed hoofer! Pop's ole nuff fo' my pappy!"

"That don't mean a thing," Jimmy leaned across the table. "He takes good care of you. I notice he don't make no date for you like he does the rest of the girls and he don't stand for handling from wise guys," Jimmy held the girl's eyes with his own.

"'Course he looks out fo' me. He knows I ain't the kind-o girl t' get fresh with an' I wouldn't stay here a minute if they was to try it. Pop's been a good, kind fren' t' me ever since I come here, three months ago, an' I ain't goin' to let no two-cent hoofer down him to my face," June's voice was sharp.

JIMMY IS REPULSED

Jimmy lounged back in his chair and shrugged his shoulders carelessly, but there was a satisfied look in his eyes, as if he had found out all he wanted to know.

"Well, I just thought I'd see how the land lay, Baby. Seeing as there ain't any competition, I guess I'll push in my little oar."

"Of all things . . . ." June's eyes opened wide; to sit there and calmly tell her he was going to try to "make" her . . . . "Let me tell yo' one thing, Mr. Hoofer, if there wasn't another man in the whole world but yo' an' I was dying fo' a man I'd drop yo' in the river an' say 'good riddance'."

Jimmy laughed easily; he liked to see June's eyes flash fire.

"An' anyway," went on the girl, angered further by the man's apparent indifference to her

(Continued on Page 4)

Gertrude Schalk, "The Sprung Trap," *Illustrated Feature Section* of the *Baltimore Afro-American*, January 19, 1929. Courtesy of the AFRO Newspaper Archives.

of romance conventions. When Schalk's series "The Yellow Parrot" began to appear in Schuyler's *National News* in March 1932, she had already sold three dozen stories to *Love Story Magazine* and was appearing nearly once a month in the weekly magazine's pages. A successful mainstay in the most established romance pulp title, there is little doubt that Schalk had mastered the magazines' generic formulas by this time. This makes "The Yellow Parrot" an even more interesting and self-conscious development of a romance formula with which Schalk was intimately familiar. "The Yellow Parrot" is structured much like the place-based story cycles (such as Sherwood Anderson's *Winesburg, Ohio* [1919]) that cropped up during the modernist era. Rooted in a distinct setting (the eponymous nightclub), each individual installment tells the story of a single dancer from the nightclub's troupe; the young women represented here are a cross section of the Great Migration. They come from Southern locales like Richmond, Virginia; Georgia; and Mississippi; urban areas like Boston; and far-flung spots like California. These women testify to the appeal of Harlem as a magnetic space for Black entertainment culture—a space that offers the potential for upward social and economic mobility.[33] At the same time, Schalk's "The Yellow Parrot" gives voice to the experience of these dancers as agents within their own narratives rather than as abstract symbols—with what Jayna Brown calls an "iconic status"—of Black modernity and urban sophistication, as is the case in the Harlem Renaissance–era work of Jean Toomer, Langston Hughes, Claude McKay, and others.[34]

The opening installment in this cycle, "The Kid from Richmond," immediately demonstrates Schalk working with far less restriction than she found in the pulps. The protagonist of this installment, Edna May, is described as "the sharpest little brown-skinned girl as ever came out of Virginia," but the narrator notes that "the Edna Mays of this world aren't cut out for school teachers or the regulations that go to the making of them."[35] Unable to conform to the rigid gender roles and expectations that dominate her Southern home, Edna May leaves for Harlem, where she becomes the newest dancer at the Yellow Parrot. Already Schalk has chosen for her protagonist a character that would run afoul of editorial practice in pulp magazines like *Love Story*. If the white protagonists—even the nightclub dancers—of her pulp stories are secretly homemakers in waiting, then Edna May, "The Kid From Richmond," becomes a nightclub dancer precisely because she cannot abide the "regulations" that she would face in her life as a Southern schoolteacher and wife. Edna May is looking for action and adventure; Harlem and the Yellow Parrot will offer her this, but in a way that does anything but assure its readers that everything will work out in the end.

As the newest girl in the club, Edna May experiences some conflict, and her stubborn ways find her rejecting the advice of Mazie, the oldest and most experienced dancer, and welcoming advances from Barney, "a smooth faced brown, dressed neatly in dark blue serge."[36] At first, Barney seems like quite a catch for the newly arrived Edna May: "He had a real estate office on Seventh avenue with two stenographers." Agreeing to go to a party with Barney, and impressed when Barney drops some large bills he calls "small change," they soon run into Barney's associate, Joe, and the setup is clear: Barney plans to sleep with Edna May, then capitalize on her shame to lure her into prostitution. Joe reveals this trafficking plan when he says in a sinister aside to Barney, "They is always yours . . . first." Fortunately for Edna May, Mazie, who has followed her, arrives with two policemen before Barney and Joe can take Edna May inside and pursue their vicious scheme. After Barney exits, Mazie confesses to Edna May that she suffered the same trick from Barney: "Listen, he was run out of Philly for luring country girls into bad houses. I ought to know. . . . I got into one, only the police came an [sic] pulled the joint before anything happened. That's why I warned you about him. You see . . . I fell for that 'small change' line of his too."[37] Mazie, who becomes the de facto guardian angel of the Yellow Parrot, demonstrates her wisdom and experience as Schalk offers a compelling transformation of the pulp romance formulas she knew so well.

While "The Kid from Richmond" does find a resolution that—however temporarily—restores moral order to the story's universe, it does so in an impressive revisionist fashion. Two stark forms of divergence from the pulp conventions raise interesting suggestions about the politics of "The Yellow Parrot." In the first place, the world of romance in this story demonstrates clear and present danger in the form of Barney and Joe. These men are not presented as reformable or as good-hearted characters putting on an act. Joe's line "They is always yours . . . first"—uttered after Barney tries to force himself on Edna May—implies that a disturbing and long-term sexual exploitation is in store for her. These dangerous realities are rarely, if ever, part of romance conventions at the time.[38] This very real threat—one absent in the pulp world—is countered here not by a handsome suitor but by Mazie, the wise and experienced dancer with whom Edna May squabbled early in the story. This evidences the story's second major revision: turning the competitive battles between women of the pulp stories into structures of mutual support and aid. In "The Kid from Richmond," Mazie serves the role of rescuer, one typically held by a potential romantic partner (as was the case in "The Sprung Trap"). Schalk's revision of this trope allows us to see her Black women's romance stories as offering a distinct worldview from the stories she produced about whites. Here women can and will help each other in the face of patriarchal threats. In earlier stories that Schalk published in coterie venues like the *Quill*, this was not the case; Lorraine Elena Roses describes Schalk's female protagonists in these as "women who fail to challenge their exploiters."[39] But in "The Kid from Richmond," Schalk does represent women challenging potential exploitation, and she does so at a time when the genre rarely (if ever) offered an opportunity for true female agency in the face of patriarchy. In this case, pleasure derives from short-circuiting the genre's conventional patriarchal conservatism with a form of feminist solidarity.

"The Kid from Richmond" is certainly one of the most innovative of the installments of "The Yellow Parrot"; some of the other stories feature relatively formulaic romances. "The Georgia Peach" finds its protagonist wanting to snag a rich boyfriend but falling in love with a melancholy youth instead. The "sour" and unromantic Marilee of "The California Lemon" attracts the most desirable patron of the Yellow Parrot and succumbs to his charms while also discovering that he is passing for white downtown as an up-and-coming journalist.[40] And both "The Boston High-Flyer" and "Mississippi Lily" feature female protagonists gravitating toward standard patriarchal fare and conventional romantic coupling. In the former, Bobbie falls for a man who mistakenly kidnaps her (and turns out to be a wealthy foreigner); and in the latter, Lily swoons at a boyfriend's threat of violence against his rivals for her affection. Even the girls' level-headed leader, Mazie, finds romance in the conclusion of the series, "Mazie Hits the Numbers," when the house doctor, treating her for a dangerous illness, proclaims his long-untold love for her.

While Schalk rests on romance conventions for much of the series, two other installments offer curious and unanticipated variations on the romance formula, making this series a rather rich and varied representation of the possibilities for generic revision within the context of the Black press. "The Bronx Baby" follows Mina, a dancer tiring of having "a new guy every night to dance with, a new one every day to eat with," and wary of an ever-nearing future in which "it won't be just dancing and eating with different men. It'll have to be more."[41] The story soon reveals that Mina has a husband and son back in the Bronx. She rushes home after a call, believing Junior to be ill, but instead finds Bob angry at her for abandoning the family. Moved by and attracted to Bob's ferocity, the story ends with a standard clinch. Though the story restores conventional domestic structures at the conclusion, its presentation of a young mother chasing wealth and living the promiscuous life of a Harlem dancer would be enough to get her cut from the pages of a conservative love pulp like *Love Story Magazine*. However, within the pages of the *National News,* Schalk can freely experiment with the myriad possibilities of romantic resolutions offered by the cast of characters in "The Yellow Parrot." Here Mina's independent straying from her family does not disqualify her from returning to domestic security; instead, it seems to strengthen those bonds at the story's conclusion.

The strangest and most radical story in this series is "The Chicago Kid," the fourth installment, appearing at the midpoint of the run of "The Yellow Parrot." When the rich young white man John Martin enters the club, Flora sets her sights on him: "Here was her chance made to order. Other chorus girls landed rich white men, why shouldn't she?"[42] Cozying up to Martin, she receives an invitation to his apartment on Park Avenue and joins him there. When he begins flirting with her, she is surprised how much it resembles the wooing she's experienced with other men ("What was color, money, position when a girl is involved!"). As their flirtation begins to progress to something more serious, a woman—"a tall blonde, rather hard faced, but pretty"—busts into the apartment and declares, "Listen, Harlem. . . . This bozo happens to be my meal ticket and rent money. So lay off, get it? Not that there's much chance of him picking you."[43] When Flora starts to stand up for herself, this woman, Peggy, pulls a gun, and a fight ensues in which Flora beats up Peggy, tears her flashy and expensive evening gown, and

"And let this be a lesson to you—"

Ollie Harrington, illustration for Gertrude Schalk, "The Yellow Parrot, Part 4: The Chicago Kid," *National News*, March 24, 1932. George S. Schuyler Papers, Special Collections Research Center, Syracuse University Libraries.

leaves her sobbing in the corner. At the conclusion, Martin pays Flora and sends her on her way.

This story traces a number of threads that run throughout "The Yellow Parrot" and some of Schalk's other work. Here a competition between women returns—but in an almost phantasmagoric variation, for this version is completely racialized, with Flora and Peggy—both after handsome meal ticket Martin—battling it out in front of him, with Peggy calling Flora "Harlem" (as a kind of slur) and finding it inconceivable that he would choose a Black lover over her, even as Flora has begun to understand that the dynamics of romance and flirtation are the same in any color. Additionally, the story implies that Martin has orchestrated this entire scenario in order to humiliate Peggy, who had clearly been using him as her "meal ticket and rent money" for far too long. After all, as he hands over "a fat wad of bills," he tells Flora, "I've been wanting to do that for months!"[44] In this case, Flora becomes merely a means by which the wealthy Martin, who pays her for her services, can humiliate another woman and restore a kind of patriarchal order in his own world—one upset by the at least temporarily successful gold digger, Peggy. But Flora experiences great pleasure in this outcome: besting an entitled white woman and walking away with a fistful of cash. Granted, as she learns, "millionaires . . . weren't to be had just for the taking, even when they were willing to be taken." Still, her pleasure—and the story's narrative resolution—comes from the comeuppance she is able to deliver to the racist Peggy, and she tells herself, "If I'd known he was going to pay me for beating her up, instead of sending for the cops. . . . I'd have socked her another couple on that skinny nose!"[45] The pleasures of independence and self-defense here far outstrip the conventional pleasures of romance.

Taken as a whole, the installments of Schalk's cycle "The Yellow Parrot" and her contribution to the *Illustrated Feature Section*, "The Sprung Trap," reveal a talented and experienced writer of formulaic pulp romances remaking the narratological and structural conditions of the genre for a Black readership with a less homogenous understanding of romance. Schalk's fictional output for the Black press touches on a number of issues that would have been taboo within the widely read pulps where she made her living: interracial romance, racial passing, prostitution, the very real threat of sexual violence, and the redemption of an absentee wife and mother. Packaged within familiar generic trappings, these variations might go unnoticed, but with an attention to her work's articulation to the contemporary historical manifestation of genre—especially as it appeared in the love pulps—these deviations from formula reveal Schalk to be a canny creator. They also show the readership of the *Illustrated Feature Section* and the *National News* to be more capacious in their understanding of the boundaries of romance. For these readers, the interjection of realistic threats or flexible morality into these stories represented the real conditions imposed on Black sexuality—particularly on Black women's sexuality—under Jim Crow. The women in these nightclub stories represent an ambitious subsection of the Great Migration, and the experiences depicted across the stories prove that the structures of racial capitalism and segregation, along with the patriarchal power dynamics within Harlem, may sometimes prevent a happy-ever-after conclusion. Schalk's broader vision here—when it does find a happy resolution to these stories—ranges much more widely than the ubiquitous romantic clinch, as it does in "The Chicago Kid," where the "happy" ending involves punching a racist white gold digger square on the nose.

BOILING POINT: AMALGAMATED AESTHETICS IN THE *BALTIMORE AFRO-AMERICAN* AND BEYOND

While Gertrude Schalk's experience writing romance fiction for cross-racial audiences in the early 1930s offered her opportunities for levying formal critiques at the genre's building blocks, it also helped her highlight the ways that the narrative resolutions sought by African American readers might differ from those of the largely white readership of the pulps. Romance remained one of the most prominent genres in Black newspaper fiction well into the 1940s and 1950s, after the *Illustrated Feature Section*'s failure opened up opportunities for individual papers to curate their own original fiction. A good number of these relied heavily on stock formulas taken wholesale from pulp and slick romance fiction, often with a kind of local and regional focus, such as Edward Lawson's five-part romance serial, "Miss Norfolk," among others discussed in chapter 1. A number of Schuyler-authored serials in the *Pittsburgh Courier* were love stories, and most of his serials, regardless of genre, included romantic subplots.

The *Baltimore Afro-American* featured its share of conventional love stories, transplanted to Black communities in Baltimore, Washington, and beyond. Writers like Adele Hamlin (who published thirty-one stories between 1931 and 1953), Ted Haviland (who published eight short serials and a number of stories between 1932 and 1939), Lawrence D. Howard (ten stories between 1935 and 1941), Bessie Brent Madison (eighteen stories between 1935 and 1941), Ann Allen Shockley (eight stories between 1950 and 1954), and Bertye Watson (twelve stories between 1935 and 1953) provided *Afro-American* readers with a steady diet of romance fiction, including romantic thrillers, class-crossing relationships, and sentimental stories ending in marital bliss. Many of these stories offered familiar scenarios, such as the setting of the entertainment industry, the rekindling of an old flame, or romantic rivalries. Others, like Adele Hamlin's "Molly Ann: The Love Story of an Unmarried Mother" (March 31, 1934), featured revisions similar to what Gertrude Schalk had offered in her work. Nevertheless, the vast majority of these stories are interesting, if unremarkable, love stories that feature all the conventional trappings of romance fiction of the era, often transplanted into a space free from concerns about Jim Crow segregation.

However, there was at least one way that romance fiction in these newspapers offered an alternative to the formulas codified by magazines like *Love Story:* Black newspaper fiction frequently featured interracial romance at a time when such relationships were simply unthinkable for publication in the pulps—and actually illegal in a substantial number of states. Such representations would have also run afoul of the editorial practice of the *Illustrated Feature Section,* which cautioned prospective contributors that "all matter should deal exclusively with Negro life. Nothing will be permitted that is likely to engender ill feeling between blacks and whites. The color problem is bad enough without adding any fuel to the fire."[46] The *Illustrated Feature Section* had created a venue for Black genre fiction, and in doing so, it gave writers a pathway toward reconceptualizing genre in the service of racial justice. But it was only the demise of the *IFS* in late 1932, when individual newspapers under Black ownership began overseeing the publication of fiction, that the revolutionary potential in such genre revision could be fully realized.

The most powerful example of this change appears in the *Baltimore Afro-American* in the spring and summer of 1934, when the newspaper published interracial romance fiction in sixteen weekly issues over an eighteen-week period, beginning with its April 28 edition. This included ten stories—four of them two-part stories—and one five-part serial highlighting a wide variety of interracial and intercultural romance scenarios. These were Robert Anderson's "Empress" (Black–white, April 28), "Brown Love" (Black–white, May 5–12, 1934), and "Jungle Love" (Javanese–white, May 26, 1934); Harry Winston's "Chinese Love" (Black–East Asian, June 2), "Hotcha Love" (Black–white, June 16), "Cheska" (Black–South Asian, June 23–30), and "Chiquita" (Black–South American, July 14–21); Harriet Wilson's "Ebony Poet" (Black–white, June 9); Bernard Braxton's "Red Love" (Black–white, June 9–16); Gene Davis's "Dusky Flower" (Black–East Asian, August 25); and Ted Haviland's serial "Dixie Belle" (Black–white, July 28–August 25). The publication of these stories followed a direct solicitation to readers, published in the April 7 and April 14 issues of the paper, asking, "Where Is Your Boiling Point on the Race Question: How Much Can You Read about Interracial Love and Sex without Getting Sore?" This question followed the *Afro*'s coverage of the divorce suit of English violinist Albert Sandler from his wife after the discovery of her affair with Clarence Nathaniel Johnstone, an African American singer who had found great success in London.[47] With interracial love in the news, the *Baltimore Afro-American* decided to confront the question of interracial sexuality head on in ways that challenged both pulp romantic formulas and the conventions of African American literature.

Kim Gallon reads these stories as part of "a public discourse where readers deliberated over interracial romantic fiction and enacted a black public sphere where vocalizations of disagreement and opposition occurred over interracial sexuality and its impact on African Americans' quest for racial progress and civil rights."[48] She tracks the eighty-nine letters submitted by *Afro-American* readers and published between April 14 and June 21 as outlining the ongoing debate by "linking [interracial romantic fiction] with ideological and political issues such as race pride, civil rights, and the role of the newspaper itself."[49] This cross section of letters—meditated by editorial choices and placement—did not necessarily, as Gallon argues, represent a scientific poll of attitudes toward interracial romance. Nevertheless, it offered the newspaper as a space for readers with wildly varying opinions to engage with one another and with the fiction about issues that remained at the center of debates about racial justice under the law. Although a small majority of readers, she notes, endorsed the publication of stories like these, 40 percent of the letters opposed them and "correlated the stories with white exploitation and lack of race pride."[50] Such varying responses illuminate the different forms of generic pleasure engendered by these stories. Where some readers saw utopian promise in interracial love stories with a happy ending, others saw an exploitative signal of Jim Crow and preferred a form of Black pulp romance that allowed love to flourish in an all-Black fictional space.

What is notable about this particular moment in the history of Black newspaper fiction is the directness with which the *Afro-American* editors put the question to their readers:

> When stories like the Johnstone-Sandler inter-racial yarn break in the news we are duty-bound to print the facts, but we have been turning down fiction stories dealing with love affairs between the races because we thought our readers did not want their stories too sexy.
>
> We want to know whether you would desire us to change that policy on yarns dealing with black and white love affairs.
>
> The thing that is worrying us is, "CAN YOU TAKE IT?" Tell us how you feel about it. The majority wins. If you say "yes" we'll rake up the snappiest black and tan tales we can find and publish them. If you say "no,' we won't.
>
> SEND IN YOUR ANSWER AT ONCE SO WE CAN PRINT OR REJECT THE STORIES—AFTER ALL, IT'S YOUR PAPER.[51]

The appeal to readers is one that anticipates other dynamic and dialogic practices that would appear throughout the history of Black newspaper fiction, notably around texts like George Schuyler's "The Black Internationale" and H. L. Faggett's "Black Robin" stories (discussed in chapters 3 and 4, respectively). It also resembles the calls that pulp magazine editors made to their trusted readership when they ran "readers' favorite" contests or solicited feedback on magazine contents.[52] Beyond suggesting the intriguing triangulation of reader–writer–editor connections here, this notice reveals that up until this point, the editorial policy for fiction in the *Afro*, like that of the *Illustrated Feature Section* and even the pulp magazines, flatly prohibited the representation of interracial romance.

Such a prohibition may not be all that surprising; after all, interracial marriage was illegal in Maryland and a number of surrounding states when these stories ran in 1934, and would remain so in many of these places (including Maryland) until the late 1960s. These laws remained very much in the public and legislative discourse. In 1935, the year after these stories ran, the Maryland state legislature passed legislation amending the antimiscegenation laws to add prohibitions of marriages between whites and Filipinos.[53] And African American literary models of the era—from the work of Nella Larsen to that of Jessie Fauset—almost invariably presented interracial relationships as tragic or doomed to fail. Even in Fauset's otherwise sunny *Plum Bun* (1929), the protagonist's brief and failed interracial relationship leaves her feeling humiliated and betrayed. Such narratives, situated as they are in the long shadow of the tragic mulatta figure, struggle to imagine any form of interracial love that could transcend the asymmetries of gender and power under racial capitalism. Indeed, these represent what Claudia Tate calls the racial protocols around depictions of interracial sexuality within the African American canon. These power dynamics seem only able to be eclipsed, if only briefly, in a satire like Schuyler's *Black No More* (1931); in traditional romantic fiction and in the romantic structures of African American literature, interracial love was anathema to the very formulas that constituted the genre.

The shift in editorial policy that began at the *Afro* in April 1934 represents an excellent example of Stuart Hall's notion of double articulation, discussed in the introduction. In this case, these interracial love stories function like Hall's definition of a subculture, articulating themselves on the one hand to conventional love stories like those in the pulps and on the other hand to "serious" (and now canonical) African American fiction. This double articulation demonstrates both a borrowing from and a critique of each of these two influential forms. From the pulp formula, these stories take their insistence on narrative resolution and romantic success; from the African American canon, they take a serious concern with the lived realities of racial injustice. But their articulated critiques may be even more important. They take the African American canon to task for its racial realism and gloomy insistence that interracial relationships are doomed to tragedy; such texts lack the imagination to find its way out of present-day injustices. By telling love stories about mixed-race couples, though, the *Afro-American*'s romance fiction pinpoints the most powerful unspoken taboo in the pulps: interracial sexuality. In making this subject the centerpiece of four months' worth of fiction, the *Afro-American* effectively names the unspoken absence around which all conventional pulp romance was necessarily structured. In order to avoid potential boycotts in Southern states or to avoid running afoul of censors and losing mail privileges, romance pulps like *Love Story Magazine* absolutely had to avoid any whiff of racial mixing. In its "boiling point" series of 1934, the *Afro-American* performed its own ideological critique of the genre of romance: offering the very thing that could not be said or represented in the pulps.

Robert Anderson's "Empress" ("A True Love Story of the Love of an Ofay Lad for a Brown Girl") and "Brown Love" ("The True Love Story of an Ofay Girl Who Fell in Love with a House Painter") open the *Afro-American*'s series of stories designed to test its readers' collective boiling point on this question. Intriguingly, both stories are told from the perspective of white characters. The first follows its narrator, Edward, as he courts beautiful singer Evangeline Collins. Edward comes from a small town—likely in Maryland—where African American women were routinely treated as sexual objects by young white men (a trope common in plantation romances); as he notes, "Not a boy of my acquaintance had any aversion to a clandestine affair with the colored girls of our town."[54] He takes an interest in Evangeline, who is visiting from New York, and his initial description of her ("as graceful as a tigress and carried herself like an empress") traffics in racial exoticism. After trying to kiss her and getting a slap in return, he admits an equally troubling consternation: "My Nordic pride battling with my desire for the sepian beauty." Evangeline makes it clear that things have changed in the racial battle of the sexes: "There are no buts about it. You are an intelligent and educated man. You must see that the old order has ceased to obtain. Colored girls no longer think it an honor to be the playthings of white men. I attended summer school in Chicago; I met several really nice white men—but they knew how to treat a respectable girl. We were good friends, and they never got fresh." They begin to see each other on new terms, but after Evangeline leaves for New York, Edward tries to forget her and marries a local white girl. When he meets her eight years later in New York, his passion has not faded, and they go dancing in the liberated space of Harlem, "without fear of being seen." Still unable to imagine a resolution to his interracial desire, Edward proposes keeping two households, which Evangeline rejects. However, upon his return home from Harlem, he discovers his wife in bed with the Black servant "WHO HAD COME FROM HER HOME WITH US WHEN WE WERE MARRIED," the narratively shockingly emphasizes. They are quickly divorced, and Edward and Evangeline marry.

"Empress" rehearses several tropes common to romance fiction of the period, including the long-delayed consummation of a true romance. However, it also highlights a number of key elements that appear throughout interracial romance stories within Black newspapers. In the first place, it acknowledges the troubling double standards surrounding Black women's sexuality, especially in Southern contexts, in which these women were routinely used and abused by white men as "playthings." Edward must work through this exploitative understanding of interracial sexuality and be taught by Evangeline, who—as a successful entertainer on Broadway at the end of the story—is the far more modern and progressive figure in the story. It also highlights the difference between a liberated, Northern urban environment like Harlem (or Chicago) in which such relationships were not only legal but also less likely to be subject to social surveillance, and a Southern town in which sexual power dynamics were forged in the heat of slavery and Jim Crow. These issues come to a head at the conclusion when Edward finds his wife in bed with a servant who had been virtually "inherited" by the couple as if he were enslaved. Edward's earlier failure to read the true nature of this relationship between his wife and the young Black man serves both as a shocking comeuppance of his assumptions about the uniqueness of his own encounters with Evangeline (indicated by the use of all capital letters to reveal his discovery) and a perfect rationale for his divorce (after all, his wife too may be happier in her interracial relationship).

Other stories, like Robert Anderson's "Brown Love," reverse these narrative structures by featuring white female narrators who fall in love with African American men. In "Brown Love," the white narrator, Eugenia, feels "like a slave on the block" when her mother tries to set her up with a wealthy older man.[55] While walking aimlessly, she runs into a "rough-looking character" on the street who tries to force himself on her, and she is saved from this white ruffian by a mysterious Black man. This turns out to be Jimmy, who had strangely thrilled her while working as a house painter in the apartment next to hers. She falls in love almost immediately, and Jimmy warns her that loving him would only bring trouble: "You have never come into contact with race prejudice," Jimmy tells her. "You cannot conceive of its cruelty, its barbarity. The social ostracism that would fall upon you would kill you. As my wife your own race would look upon you as lower in the social scheme than an open prostitute. Nor would you be received with open arms by the people of my race. They would say catty things to you. They would consider you their inferior. You should be a woman without racial identification."[56] Undeterred, Eugenia simply declares, "I have never had the slightest desire for social activities," and they are married and live happily. "Brown Love" introduces a host of alternative frameworks that inform other stories of this type. From a class critique of marriage within the race ("another form of slavery") to the threat posed by dangerous white masculinity in the form of the "rough-looking character" who tries to assault her, the conventions of white heterosexual relationships appear both dangerous and oppressive. For Eugenia, the relationship with Jimmy offers a path out of these terrors and into a world often glamorized in the romance fiction of the era: one of pure love, without need for "social activities." Jimmy's claim that by marrying him she would become "a woman without racial identification" points to a conceivably utopian solution that underlies these stories of interracial love.

In its critique of both the economics of marriage and the problems of racial definition, "Brown Love" hints at the radical political potential of these stories. Bernard Braxton's "Red Love" ("The Story of Intolerant Prejudice of a Southern Girl Who Was Sent to a Northern College") makes this explicit by imagining interracial love and political radicalization to be intertwined and mutually constitutive. Its narrator and protagonist, Julia, an Alabama native and "direct descendant of Jefferson Davis of Civil War fame," begins the story by becoming outraged at the liberal politics and antiracist attitudes of her Northern professor ("He could be nothing but one of those radicals, a Socialist or perhaps a Communist") and urging the dean to fire him for mocking her anxieties about sitting next to a young Black woman in his class.[57] The story quickly shifts to Julia's last year at college, when her friend, Mildred, leaves their sorority house to join the "National Students' League" and advocate for the release of the Scottsboro Boys. Part 2 of this story begins with Julia's driving her friend's "flashy roadster" to visit a sick friend in Chicago.[58] During the trip, she engages in a deeply Freudian fantasy that echoes some of the exoticism present in Anderson's "Empress": "All at once I became strangely afraid of something. If I didn't drive fast something would reach out of the darkness and get me. A man would. A big man. Very dark, and awfully strong and powerful. My imagination ran on. A big fearsome giant. He would sneak out of this thick darkness, stop my car and take me—" When her car breaks down, a young Black man comes to her aid, giving life to her fearful and erotic fantasy. Her anxiety is overcome when she hears his slight Southern accent, and she soon discovers that he is Philip Wilson, brother of the girl she refused to sit next to in her freshman year of college—a girl with whom she has since become friends. She is deeply impressed by his manner, which appears to overcome the dark fantasies that consumed her during her trip west: "The way he said that and gazed down into my eyes! He did it all in a very natural and frank way—as if I weren't a white girl. And I liked him for it. There was nothing in his manner to show that he had any feeling of inferiority. He simply made me feel that I was dealing with a human being like myself—and I was." Their romance moves—as it often does in these short stories—at a rapid pace, and they are married three weeks later, much to the dismay of her Southern parents, whose prejudice she rejects: "So I stood by Philip. I know I'll always stand by him, because I love him and because I truly believe I have found the road to happiness, truth and justice in a cruel world."

By locating Julia's transformation from Southern racist to racial amalgamator alongside a number of signs of radicalization (the battle for academic freedom, the movement for the Scottsboro Boys, her appeal to "truth and justice" at the story's conclusion), Braxton highlights the political potential of these interracial love stories. Unlike the romance fiction of the pulps, which generally sought to avoid social issues at all cost, "Red Love" exhibits a dialogic relationship to a host of current events and to news coverage in the *Afro-American*, which was covering the 1933–34 "Don't Buy Where You Can't Work" campaign in Baltimore and the ongoing case of the Scottsboro Boys, and by 1935 was, in the words of Hayward Farrar, the Black newspaper "most supportive of the Communists."[59] Braxton's story offers a third and more potent revision of the romance formulas: Whereas "Empress" lampooned Edward's anxieties about propriety by showing his wife in bed with the couple's "servant" and "Brown Love" posited the possibility of interracial happiness outside the social realm, "Red Love" figures Julia's choice as explicitly political, to be understood alongside a host of other antiracist acts. She chooses to love Philip, whose treatment of her deracinates her identity ("He did it all in a very natural and frank way—as if I weren't a white girl") and exposes the lie of racial difference that has defined her family's Southern history.

The choice to narrate these three stories from the perspective of white characters also highlights something crucial about the politics of the narrational strategies surrounding interracial romance stories. Most of the Black–white romances published by the *Afro-American* in 1934 (including "Ebony Poet") are narrated by white men and women; only Harry Wilson's "Hotcha Love" features an African American narrator. Nevertheless, these narrative structures allow their authors to deflect the most dangerous stereotypes about Black sexuality, imagining their African American characters not as pursuers but as pursued. Julia's shift in "Red Love" from anxious fantasies of the Black beast presumably intending to rape her to an understanding of the constructedness of race through her sensitive encounter with Philip demonstrates this most explicitly. To focalize these stories through African American perspectives would risk the reaffirmation of sexual stereotypes about voracious Black sexuality and would also limit the texts' potential for character transformation; after all, the opposition to interracial sex originated in the phantasmagoria of white fear.[60] The use of white narrators here differs from the way this strategy crops up in canonical fiction, as Claudia Tate and Stephanie Li have discussed in different ways. This narrative strategy is not about what Tate described as the manifesting of "unconscious desire"; nor is it about legitimizing, as Stephanie Li has argued, "narrative authority."[61] Instead, to the degree that the white narrators of these stories generate pleasure for their Black readers, it is because these readers witness a positive transformation (of characters like Julia) from typical opponents of interracial marriage to advocates for racial equality. The romance formula thus offers not merely the narrative satisfaction of the final clinch but also the promise that romance can lead to a change of heart in white people around issues of racial justice.

Other stories in this cycle differ significantly in that they do not present the Black–white pairing that was subject to the most intense surveillance and litigation in the period. Instead, they dramatize the romance of their Black protagonists with a kaleidoscopic range of characters of various races and from various nations. Freed from the representational land mines of Black–white romance, these stories feature both third-person and first-person narration by African American characters. These stories, almost all of which follow the romantic adventures of a Black female protagonist, also cast a more critical eye at the romantic choices presented to Black women in African American communities. In Harry Winston's "Chinese Love," Janie Wellington chooses a Chinese lover over her overbearing and predatory boss. In Gene Davis's "Dusky Flower" ("A Girl Who Deserted Harlem for Her Oriental Husband"), the relationship of an already married interracial couple is tested when a "dapper" young Harlem businessman begins visiting, though such fears prove to be merely a false alarm.[62] And Winston's "Cheska" ("The Story of a Girl Who Found Romance and Love in India") follows narrator Beryl's desire for Cheska, an Indian classmate at Howard, and the rivalry that ensues when the two of them go to India and are confronted with Cheska's jealous admirer. Each of these stories traffics in its share of orientalism, presenting these interracial matches as exotic opportunities for their female protagonists to escape from the predatory practices of western romance.

As a whole, this series of interracial love stories published in 1934 offers something conspicuously absent from the African American literary canon: a happy resolution to the interracial romance plot. While readers may have eventually tired of the *Afro-American*'s attempts to test their "boiling point" on this question, the 1930s also saw a significant presence of these forms in the *Pittsburgh Courier* serials of George Schuyler. Schuyler's very public interracial marriage to Josephine Cogdell and his contention that "miscegenation is the way—perhaps the only way— the race problem is going to be solved in these United States" meant that these concerns were often central to his genre fiction.[63] A number of Schuyler's *Pittsburgh Courier* serials from this period feature central themes of romance, and two directly confront interracial romance between Black and white characters, doing so in somewhat more sensational terms than the fiction published in the *Afro-American*. "Black Mistress" (November 17, 1934–February 2, 1935) and "A Forbidden Romance" (February 8–July 4, 1936), both published under the name Samuel I. Brooks, are melodramatic love stories that take pulp conventions of cross-class romance and incorporate an interracial dynamic.[64] "Black Mistress" follows Lucy Brown, a Southern transplant new to Harlem, as she wards off advances from a famous preacher, then is finally courted by the aristocratic, white Chester H. Porter. Chester's romantic ideals are explicitly primitivist; he sees Lucy as a figure who can rejuvenate the pale decadence of white society. He tells her, "I think you're beautiful, clean and sweet. And that's something rare in my set. The women I know are pale, anemic, thin, over-sophisticated, spoiled manikins for French dressmakers; you're fresh and strong and naïve. . . . You're not anemic and you haven't been spoiled by governesses and flattery. You are the eternal primitive that periodically saves decadent society."[65] With Chester's money, Lucy attempts to break into Harlem society, though with little success, only to end up the target of blackmail. When her efforts at social climbing fail, Chester finally agrees to marry her and take her to Paris; Lucy agrees, but the serial does not celebrate their union effusively. Even as it endorses interracial marriage—as the *Afro-American* serials had done earlier in 1934—it leaves Lucy unsatisfied at its conclusion.

While "Black Mistress" presents a problematic interracial romance that introduces racial primitivism into the typical cross-class patterns of pulp romance fiction, "Forbidden Romance" presents a more aggressive and positive endorsement of interracial romance, one that owes less to pulp convention and more to Schuyler's radical critique of it.[66] "Forbidden Romance" takes place in the fictional town of Jackmer, Mississippi, and directly addresses links between interracial sexuality and mob violence, as well as the gendered power dynamics and double standards at work in how interracial relationships are viewed in the South. In this serial, the protagonist, Andrew, a Columbia University–educated poet, returns home and ends up helping his mother, a maid for the white Kensington family. The Kensington daughter, Cora, also educated at a Northern college, soon falls for Andrew and his poetic talents. Meanwhile, Cora's brother, Robert, carries on a long-standing affair with Minerva

Satchell, a young "quadroon" and former girlfriend of Andrew's. Andrew and Cora's relationship quickly develops under the threat of mob violence, and the serial concludes with the couple escaping from Mississippi on a train and being married at the first opportunity north of the Mason-Dixon Line to avoid any further legal entanglements. On the one hand, "Forbidden Romance" deploys a familiar convention of pulp romance: cross-class encounters that uncover a sensitive and cultured figure in servant's clothes. However, injecting Southern racial injustice into this story line serves to reject the primitivist fantasies (of, for example, "Black Mistress") and force a reckoning with prohibitions against miscegenation. The critiques multiply here. The Andrew–Cora relationship highlights the threat of mob violence as punishment for interracial sexual encounters, while the exploitative relationship between Robert Kensington and Minerva Satchell demonstrates the wrongs suffered by Black women as a result of Southern double standards about interracial sexuality—a theme Schuyler returns to in a number of other serials set in the South.

The racial politics of romance fiction have remained a thorny issue well into the twenty-first century. In 2019, for example, the Romance Writers of America experienced an online dustup when a former board member criticized a recently published novel as a "racist mess," and was censured by the RWA for her comments.[67] Anxieties about an overwhelmingly white readership and long-standing issues with racial exoticism make even contemporary discussions of romance highly fraught. These current dynamics, however, serve to highlight the degree to which the Black pulp romances of the 1930s featured across numerous African American newspapers acutely understood the problems inherent in the very formula of romance. In stories like those discussed here, writers and readers found a place where the racial politics of romance fiction could be leveraged not merely in service of the wish fulfillment of individual readers but—more importantly—in service of a set of socially and politically charged goals. In their reconstruction of these formulas, these stories dismantled patriarchal fantasies about women's roles in romantic encounters, and they sought to imagine the utopian potential that romance could offer in the drive toward racial justice. Here the pleasures are multifold.

The stories provide not only the narrative satisfaction of a final clinch between lovers but also depictions of African American women's romantic autonomy and the radical rejection of prohibitions against interracial marriage that characterized Jim Crow white supremacy.

Of course, the stories discussed in this chapter represent the most transformative challenges to patriarchy and Jim Crow; not all romance fiction in the African American newspapers offered such radical visions. Three months after the "boiling point" summer, for example, the Black pulp genre system demonstrated the way it could police its own sexual boundaries. Ralph Matthews's two-part story "She Wolf" (November 17–24, 1934) offers a homophobic take on the nightclub formula. With the tag line "She had charm and beauty . . . but she preyed on her own sex," "She Wolf" tells the story an older lesbian pursuing a young Harlem dancer, eventually taking her to an all-female gathering where the partygoers seem to transform into a literal "den of wolves" at the moment

Ralph Matthews, "She Wolf, Part 2," *Baltimore Afro-American*, November 24, 1934. Courtesy of the AFRO Newspaper Archives.

the young protagonist realizes she is being courted by a lesbian.[68] Matthews also served as a reporter and sometimes contributed to what Kim Gallon has called the *Afro*'s "pansy-beat," reporting "on a general range of topics and events relating to gender-nonconforming dress and homosexuality among Black men."[69] Because of his regular association with queer men, it might seem curious that Matthews would pen such a vicious story about predatory lesbians. However, stories like "She Wolf" serve as reminders that even within the often radical world of Black pulp, residual conservative ideas could remain powerful components, demarcating and delimiting the possibilities of genre revision.

In the twenty years that followed the "boiling point" summer, the majority of romance fiction published in the *Afro-American* featured exclusively intraracial romance. In this respect, it might seem that the genre's boiling point had been reached after that kaleidoscopic summer of interracial love. However, the legacy of these stories more often manifested in the romantic subplots of all variety of popular genres featured in the *Afro* and the *Courier*. Indeed, interracial relationships are common across Schuyler's science fiction, the hero fiction of James H. Hill and H. L. Faggett, and even in the historical fictions of Hill and Elizabeth O. Hood, all discussed in this book. In this respect, interracial romance became less of a central organizing theme or thesis of Black pulp after 1934. Instead, it became a somewhat more understood background for the action of another story. This shift diminished the utopian element that featured strongly in the "boiling point" summer fiction, replacing this with a more measured understanding of the sacrifices and challenges that these relationships could place on both parties in the era of Jim Crow. James Hill's four-part romance serial "Kitty Lane" (August 30–September 20, 1947) perhaps best represents this new complexity. This story describes the doomed love affair between a white lawyer and politician and the NAACP field agent who helps him win a career-making housing discrimination case. Just as the lawyer is on the verge of being elected to Congress, Kitty Lane ends their romantic relationship because "she couldn't bear another assault on George, scorn and derision directed at their children, her father's hatred and scorn, the ever-present possibility of sudden death for the uninhibited crusader."[70] This melancholy realism is tempered, however. The serial teases with a possible reunion in Washington when Kitty receives an appointment as the newly minted congressman's advisor on race relations, but the optimistic sensibilities that governed the romance stories of the mid-1930s are significantly muted by concerns about safety and the future. The aggressive utopian pursuit of romance without racial barriers subsided soon after it burst on the scene in the mid-1930s. However, fiction in the African American newspapers of the late 1930s sought to understand and articulate a different textual relationship to utopia—and dystopia—in spectacular ways and through other generic means, such as the mode of speculative fiction.

3

NEWS FROM ELSEWHERE
SPECULATIVE FICTION
IN THE BLACK PRESS

"For better or for worse," Samuel R. Delany wrote in 1999, "I am often spoken of as the first African-American science-fiction writer."[1] Following this statement, Delany quickly described the long history of African American speculative fiction that preceded his. The collection in which this was published, Sheree R. Thomas's *Dark Matter,* brings together a host of work from the African diaspora that would help to set in motion the broader understanding of what today is understood as Afrofuturism. Delany's brief history acknowledges a number of vital texts: Martin R. Delany's *Blake* and Sutton E. Griggs's *Imperium in Imperio* (1899), as well as the work of George Schuyler, including both his celebrated Harlem Renaissance satire *Black No More* and his serials published in the *Pittsburgh Courier.* Delany even acknowledges the likelihood of speculative fiction writers passing under pseudonyms in the pages of the pulps. These writers "conducted their careers entirely by mail in a field and during an era when pen names were the rule rather than the exception. Among the 'Remington C. Scotts' and the 'Frank Jonses' who litter the contents pages of the early pulps, we simply have no way of knowing if one, three, or seven of them—or even more—were blacks, Hispanics, women, Native Americans, Asians, or whatever."[2] As we have already seen in *Black Pulp,* African American writers like Will Thomas and Gertrude Schalk were among those made their living writing for the pulps in the 1930s and 1940s, effectively passing in print.

Delany's discussion of Schuyler's *Courier* serials is brief and dismissive; he seems more interested in how these relate to Schuyler's later archconservatism than in how they represent a particular moment for Black speculative fiction. Delany is not alone in this; few scholars have taken these works (collected between covers in 1991 as *Black Empire*) seriously as speculative fiction, and those that have considered Schuyler's work in detail have examined precious little of the publishing context surrounding these texts. Schuyler's serials were not the first or only speculative fiction that appeared in African American newspapers in the twentieth century. While this genre only occasionally appeared in venues like the *Illustrated Feature Section* and later in the *Courier* and *Afro-American,* it nevertheless offered a host of possibilities for social and political revision of existing genre formulas aligned with other genres. Indeed, the pleasures engendered by all genres of Black pulp are, at some level at least, speculative in nature. As I note in the introduction, Black pulp routinely sought to imagine a world outside of Jim Crow segregation or one in which direct action against white supremacy takes on large and symbolic forms. However, more conventional examples of speculative fiction serials in the *Courier* and the *Afro-American* represented, in the 1930s especially, the most prominently featured and aggressively advertised fiction published by these newspapers, suggesting a heavy investment in this genre by both editors and readers.

Schuyler's thirty-three-part serial "The Black Internationale: Story of Black Genius against the World" (November 21, 1936–July 3,1937) and its twenty-nine-part sequel "Black Empire: An Imaginative Story of a Great New Civilization in Modern Africa" (October 2, 1937–April 16, 1938) unquestionably represent one of the high points of African American newspaper fiction.[3] Doubtless assisted by Schuyler's status as a canonical figure and their 1991 republication as *Black Empire,* these represent the only Black newspaper fiction that has generated any significant attention in African American literary and cultural studies. They were the most aggressively promoted and successful serials ever published by the *Pittsburgh Courier;* supported by promotional flyers, the newspaper's circulation manager W. G. Nunn wrote to Schuyler that the first of these two was "the answer to a circulation man's prayers," and it likely contributed to the newspaper's rise in circulation in the late 1930s.[4] These texts take part in a transformation of speculative fiction in the 1930s, away from the hard science fiction of Hugo Gernsback's *Amazing Stories* and toward a more socially engaged form of science fiction that used the form to work out social and political thought experiments.[5] In the case of Schuyler, these serials do draw on some Gernsbackian conventions, but they are far more concerned with notions of Afrocentric utopian and dystopian forms. Like Schuyler's "Black Empire" serials, William Thomas Smith's twelve-part serial "The Black Stockings" (June 5–August 21, 1937), likely inspired by the success of Schuyler's serials in the *Courier,* brought similar concerns to the pages of the *Afro-American,* using the genre of speculative fiction to imagine the rise of a nativist and fascist presidential candidate in the United States. And again, like Schuyler's "Black Empire" serials, Smith's work was forcefully advertised. In the tradition of the *Afro's* genre fiction, it also featured lavish illustrations, and its text covered virtually the entire back page of the *Courier* during its run—a prominent spot that had never before been used for fiction in the *Afro-American.* Each of these works investigates the intersection of Afrofuturity and the rise of fascism in the 1930s. They provide complementary visions of utopia and dystopia—both problematized—that are firmly engaged with evolving trends of the genre in the 1930s, and they demonstrate vital and influential paths forward for Black speculative fiction.

"YOU HAVE INTERFERED WITH SCIENCE": RACE AGAINST EARLY SCIENCE FICTION FORMULAS

At the time of the publication of the serials by Schuyler and Smith in the late 1930s, speculative fiction was by no means unknown in African American newspaper fiction, although it had come in and out of fashion over time. Some of the earliest serialized fiction in the *Baltimore Afro-American,* for example, was in this mode. "The White Man's Burden: A Satirical Forecast," written by white doctor Roger Sherman Tracy and published under the pseudonym T. Shirby Hodge, appeared between covers in 1915 and was serialized in the *Afro-American* from 1920 to 1921. This futuristic Rip Van Winkle–style tale finds its white narrator suddenly awakening in an anarchist African utopia in the year 5027.[6] Superior technological advancements in harnessing magnetic energy developed by an African American scientist in the late twentieth century are dismissed by racist whites, and these become the basis for the development of a vastly superior society on the African continent, while geopolitical shifts see Asian nations conquering Europe and Europeans being forced to the Americas and living in a state of near barbarity. Recommended by Du Bois and advertised for sale in the pages of the *Crisis* alongside works by Du Bois, Booker T. Washington, Paul Laurence Dunbar, Alice Dunbar Nelson, James Weldon Johnson, and Mary White Ovington, this text represents an early use of speculative fiction in an ideologically charged model that found favor with editors of the *Crisis*.[7] With the exception of its speculative premise, its activist, tendentious orientation falls much in line with other fiction published in African American newspapers before the late 1920s.

The *Illustrated Feature Section* also included its share of speculative fiction. It published Cora Moten's fantasy romance "The Black Lily" (1930–31) and featured a cluster of stories in late 1930 by John P. Moore under the heading "Amazing Stories," almost certainly inspired by the celebrated Hugo Gernsback–edited pulp magazine of the same title. These stories—"The Shot into Space," "The Hidden Kingdom," and "Love on Mars"—form a loosely organized serial about a group of "eminent Negro scientists" traveling to Mars in the year 2030.[8] The narrator of these stories, "bachelor writer" S. Q. Brent, reflects on the expedition, the "beautifully dark women" of Mars, and the unlikely romance between a Martian woman, "Ioane the Man-hater," and Brent's friend, Captain Sto.[9] Moore's adventure tale, set one hundred years in the future, works to emphasize a future for Black excellence (in the form of the "eminent Negro scientists") and the ubiquity and beauty of dark skin: The background of Sto and Ioane's romance is a war between "the two great black Martian kingdoms."[10] Moore's reference point here appears to be Edgar Rice Burroughs's series of John Carter novels, beginning with *A Princess of Mars* (1912), which used a Confederate soldier as a protagonist and projected a form of race war onto the Martian landscape.[11] Moore's reconfiguration of Burroughs's Mars erases whiteness from this planet in favor of two different Black empires battling over control.

Nevertheless, the prevalent background of race war in speculative fiction represented a significant hurdle for African American writers of this early period. Pulp science fiction stories depicting racial conspiracies and celebrating white ingenuity in the face of racial threats are regularly found in the pages of the pulps *Amazing Stories, Astounding Stories,* and *Weird Tales*—magazines that would help shape and define mainstream science fiction as the genre consolidated in the 1920s and 1930s. Notable among these early representations are Philip Francis Nowlan's two *Amazing Stories* contributions, where an early version of Buck Rogers leads a plucky band of white Americans against the technologically advanced but physically degenerate Han empire, a group of Mongolians described as "hereditary enemies . . . of the White Race."[12] Futuristic race war stories like these featured villains who were, as John Cheng has described, "neither simply Asian nor alien but both."[13] These race war stories offered white racial fantasies that dramatized victory over what racist pseudoscientists of the era like Lothrop Stoddard characterized as *The Rising Tide of Color* (1921) and *The Revolt against Civilization: The Menace of the Under Man* (1922).

Other early pulp science fiction authors conceived of race war in the Black and white terms that echoed and informed work by writers like George S. Schuyler. Science fiction scholars have, for example, seen a potential source for both Schuyler's *Black No More* and *Black Empire* in David H. Keller's "The Menace" (*Amazing Stories Quarterly,* summer 1928).[14] As in Schuyler's *Black No More,* "The Menace" features a revolutionary race-changing technology. In "The Menace," however, this technology is deployed as part of a secret racial conspiracy: "Once these millions of negroes are made white, we will start them in business. With white skins, unlimited capital and boundless ambition, they will easily secure control of the commerce of the nation. We will fill Congress with them. The whites will elect a President, a white President, but he will be one of our race. . . . With the States in our control, we will go on and conquer the world."[15] Confronting this "menace" is a white detective, Taine, who tells the organization's "jet black" leader, Ebony Kate, "Your race can change the color of their skins but they cannot change the color of their souls. No matter how white they may become, they will always remain black inside."[16] The intertwining of an insidious racial essentialism with the fears of a powerful, nonwhite racial conspiracy formed a foundational axis for early pulp science fiction, a tendency outlined by Edward James in his foundational 1990 essay "Yellow, Black, Metal and Tentacled: The Race Question in American Science Fiction."[17]

Of all the contributors of fiction to the African American news-papers, Schuyler seemed the most consistently interested in science fiction formulas. This is most evident in his unpublished notes and story ideas, held at the Schomburg Center for Research in Black Culture. These notes suggest Schuyler's constant engagement with and transformation of pulp tropes. Schuyler wrote out many brief story ideas on undated three-by-five index cards; virtually none of these was executed, but they reveal Schuyler's intense interest in the building blocks of genre fiction. In some cases, these ideas seem merely to replicate pulp conventions verbatim. This is the case for his rough notes on an idea called "The Insect War": "a sensational 'terror' novel about a scientist who in experimentation creates a gigantic species of insect that is able to procreate its kind. It overruns the world which at that time 1970 through technocracy is almost a utopia thanks to Science. After horrible devastation the insects are at last vanquished by a death ray. Man is again triumphant. Bring in love interest. Politics, etc."[18] Here Schuyler demonstrates his awareness of the conventions of early science fiction pulp magazines, which often featured the so-called bug-eyed monster on the cover. This genre trope was so common that a 1930 *Author and Journalist* feature on how to write for the early science fiction magazines listed "The Giant Insect Tale" as one of the "four grand divisions" of the genre.[19] The author's characterization of this kind of story bears striking similarity to Schuyler's notes: "First—a scientist, experimenting on beetles, grasshoppers, etc. discovers a means of making them grow rapidly. . . . Unfortunately, however, the insects grow a lot too rapidly until, attaining gigantic proportions, they 'burst from their cell with a helluva yell' and proceed to terrorize humanity until squelched by an invention of the hero."[20]

Other Schuyler note cards feature shorter plot ideas but show a clearer sense of how to inject a progressive treatment of race into pulp genres, with a particular interest in science fiction. "The Sinister Physician," for example, would have featured a protagonist "who decides to avenge treatment of Negroes by blowing up public buildings, setting one faction against another. Starts Civil War."[21] Another idea, entitled "The Land under the Ice," echoes the technological fascinations of the "Black Empire" serials (as well as Pauline Hopkins's speculative fiction novel *Of One Blood* [1902–3] and T. Shirby Hodge's *The White Man's Burden*) as it would have charted the discovery of "a country where civilization has existed for millions of years; where black men have conquered telepathy, atomic energy."[22] These note cards also feature story ideas that thematize Schuyler's ideas about race and racial amalgamation. He describes "The Last White Man" as "a satire dealing with the results of birth control, abortion, late marriages, etc. Yellow and Black races take earth. Last White man born in North Arkansas Hills—his adventures in mulatto America."[23] The variety of note cards in the archive shows Schuyler to be performing an act of signifying genre: his mastery of genre tropes is quickly overtaken by his satiric and ideological deformation of those very tropes. White fantasies of scientific superiority are wholly inverted, and futuristic race war tales become fodder for satire about misguided racial purity.

The fact that none of these were executed, however, suggests either that Schuyler wasn't interested in submitting to the science fiction pulps or that he saw little potential for them in the *Pittsburgh Courier,* where he would regularly publish romance, crime, and adventure fiction serials throughout the 1930s. The fantasies of scientific advancement and futuristic utopias may have been difficult to square with the Jim Crow–era news that accompanied this fiction. Early in the decade, when science fiction appeared less frequently in the Black newspapers, Schulyer produced a crime serial that demonstrated the acute anxiety around the intersection of utopian science and racial fantasy that characterized much of early pulp science fiction. The 1934 serial "The Beast of Bradhurst Avenue" (published under the pseudonym Samuel I. Brooks) is ostensibly a mystery story. It follows the investigation of a series of brutal murders of women in Harlem. Their corpses are discovered beheaded, and the investigation fixates on an interracial romance between Gure African princess Mbula and her white lover, Ronald Dane, that may have violated tribal conventions and resulted in severe punishment. This line of investigation, while certainly exotic and titillating, proves to be incorrect, and the serial's swift resolution turns up a kind of photo negative of utopian science: Grausmann, a murderous German scientist living in Harlem, is killing Black women and attempting to graft their heads onto the bodies of dogs. Upon discovery, he exclaims, "You have interfered with science. You have stopped my life's work with your damned meddling!" However, his notion of scientific discovery seems predicated on racial violence: "To transplant a living human brain to the skull of a great dog. It would have been remarkable, revolutionary! . . . The female Negro brain because of its small size was best adapted for my purpose."[24] In "The Beast of Bradhurst Avenue," the representative of scientific advancement is a brutal racist whose entire scientific project reinforces the structures of white supremacy. Here science and experimentation, often figured as heroic in early science fiction pulps like *Amazing Stories,* are associated with eugenics and racial extermination—an ominous note for a serial published in the year after the Nazis rose to power in Germany.

"The Beast of Bradhurst Avenue" suggests a deep suspicion that the utopian promises of science were in fact a cover for white supremacist violence; the valorization of scientific advancement was not enough to make science fiction a viable genre for readers of the *Pittsburgh Courier* or the *Baltimore Afro-American.* Indeed, the lingering influence of the racist pseudoscience of influential writers like Madison Grant and Lothrop Stoddard, combined with the rise of fascism in Europe, hardly made the forces of scientific advancement an easy fit for generic revisions in the direction of racial justice. Schuyler had successfully lampooned race distinctions and the pseudoscience behind them in his novel *Black No More,* and race-swapping science topics popped up—with less comic overtones—elsewhere in African American newspaper fiction, as in Nick Lewis's four-part serial, "The Baron of Harlem" (1933).[25] But when Schuyler attempted to extend his satire of these pseudoscientific concepts—as he did in the unpublished summary "Ape Carver"—he found it difficult to avoid dangerous forms of stereotypical representation.[26] Nevertheless, while science alone was insufficient for Schuyler and other writers to deploy speculative fiction as a means of racial critique, futuristic utopian and dystopian fiction provided Schuyler and career pulp writer William Thomas Smith opportunities to reconceptualize the possibilities for Black speculative fiction and to imagine futures both dangerous and liberatory.

"BLACK GENIUS AGAINST THE WORLD": BETWEEN UTOPIA AND DYSTOPIA IN SCHUYLER'S SPECULATIVE WORLDS

Schuyler's two speculative fiction serials, collected in 1991 in the volume *Black Empire,* have received considerable attention and posed a number of problems with readers and critics since their recovery and republication. These serials follow the global ambitions of Dr. Henry Belsidus, a scientific genius who assembles a worldwide organization called the Black Internationale in an effort to wrest control of the African continent from European imperial powers. Using methods both highly technological and unwaveringly criminal, Belsidus and his organization succeed in developing scientific marvels like hydroponic farms and solar energy—and in reconquering Africa through terrorist acts and traditional warfare with the countries of Europe. After gaining control of the continent in the first serial, "The Black Internationale," Belsidus successfully struggles to maintain it in its sequel, "Black Empire." Critics have attempted to reconcile the violent and visionary pan-Africanism of these serials with Schuyler's later conservatism; by the early 1960s, Schuyler had become an archconservative anticommunist infamous for denouncing civil rights leaders.[27] However, reading Schuyler's genre fiction as a kind of intellectual biography—even an incoherent one—is dangerous for any number of reasons, and it does a disservice to the texts, which seemed to have meant far more to readers of the *Courier* than they did to Schuyler himself. As with his other fiction in the *Courier,* in the "Black Empire" serials, Schuyler is less interested in producing an intellectual manifesto or autobiography and more interested in experimenting with an inversion and transformation of the repeatedly invoked tropes of pulp genre.

"The Black Internationale" and "Black Empire" appeared in the *Courier* in the midst of a mid-1930s surge in the so-called hero pulps. These titles had a less successful, though curiously complementary, genre focused on villains. Particularly interesting in this respect are the short-lived Sinophobic titles *The Mysterious Wu Fang* (1935–36) and *Dr. Yen Sen* (1936), which sought to capitalize on the immense popularity of Sax Rohmer's Fu Manchu series. Rohmer's criminal mastermind originally appeared in three titles from 1913 to 1917 but was soon resuscitated in a series of films (1929–32) and novels (1931–41). In a study charting the power of Fu Manchu as a serial figure and a "the yellow peril incarnate in one man," Ruth Mayer describes this criminal mastermind as

> an ingenious scientist and linguist, with a commanding knowledge base that encompasses obscure necromantic traditions and cutting-edge biochemical research and an intimate familiarity with

innovations in military and communication technologies. From the beginning, he is determined to rule the world, but he is always also strangely disinterested in political or economic power. His incentives are never entirely clear. Fu Manchu is the head of a huge and intricate secret oriental organization, the Si-Fan, whose agenda is equally obscure.[28]

A powerful foreign genius with a worldwide organization, Fu Manchu is the ideological inversion of the pulp hero, a worthy opponent of a white scientist/adventurer like hero pulp regular Doc Savage. Rohmer's Sinophobic Fu Manchu stories share a great deal with the nativist and xenophobic rhetoric of early science fiction pulps, in which sinister racial conspiracies, often Asian in origin, are challenged by muscular white science and ingenuity.

Schuyler's "The Black Internationale," as its revolutionary title might suggest, explicitly features a racial conspiracy, one that bears a striking similarity to that of Fu Manchu's Si-Fan secret society and the science fiction dystopias of Philip Francis Nowlan and David H. Keller. Brilliant and talented Belsidus leads the shadowy organization of the title, the mission of which recalls the ambitions of Fu Manchu: to amass great wealth through a combination of criminal enterprise and superior technologies in order to build a military force that can retake the continent of Africa from the European colonial powers. Advertised by the *Courier* as "an amazing serial story of black genius against the world," "The Black Internationale" directly confronts the sinister, racist insinuations of pulp science fiction by insisting that, yes, there is a racial conspiracy afoot. This conspiracy features an army of African American scientists and technicians developing superior technology—including "solar engines" that harness the power of the sun for steam power and electricity, and vast hydroponic farms for cornering the food market—as an economic basis for a powerful international movement to reconquer the African continent.[29] Rather than follow the adventures of a white hero challenging this "terrifying" possibility, Schuyler has positioned readers to identify with the largely amoral genius and criminal mastermind Belsidus and to support these efforts. Fu Manchu may have captivated readers, but he was never meant as a figure of identification or idealization. Schuyler's radical revision of this pulp figure asks readers to sympathize with and

Thrills - Punch - Mystery - Sales !!

Now Running Each Week

Nothing Like It In
The History of

Negro Fiction

A Heart-gripping

Breathtaker,

Packing Plenty of

Punches

In Every Paragraph

One of Those "Must" Stories That Send The Fiction Fans Rushing To The Newsstands.

It "Sends" Them Like Nobody's Business, And They Come Back Each Week for More.

(OVER)

"The Black Internationale" insert, *Pittsburgh Courier*, 1937. George S. Schuyler Papers, Special Collections Research Center, Syracuse Universities Library, New York.

cheer on a criminal mastermind whose scientific skill and antiracist goals are, from the perspective of the African American readers of the *Courier,* not the elements of a vast criminal conspiracy but the glimmerings of a utopian future without white supremacy.

In "The Black Internationale," journalist and narrator Carl Slater receives an education in the utopian science of Belsidus by Patricia (Pat) Givens, head of the Black Internationale's air force, and soon to be Slater's love interest. As Patricia tells him, "It is the skilled technician, the scientist, who wins modern wars, and we are mobilizing the black scientists of the world. Our professors, our orators, our politicians have failed us. Our technicians will not."[30] The movement's faith in science echoes Hodge's "satirical forecast" *The White Man's Burden* and strongly resembles the ideology that dominated the Hugo Gernsback–edited *Amazing Stories* in the late 1920s. His editorial introducing the magazine in April 1926 noted that a story of "scientifiction," as Gernsback termed it, should be "a charming romance intermingled with scientific fact and prophetic vision," and "new inventions pictured for us in the scientifiction of today are not at all impossible of realization tomorrow."[31] Like other early science fiction, Gernsback's magazine promoted "optimistic claims to progress and purpose" and an "exuberant, electric faith . . . [in] what he called the 'gospel of science.'"[32] As such, stories in early issues of *Amazing Stories* routinely featured tours of laboratories and lengthy descriptions of scientific inventions and processes, often at the expense of narrative progression.[33]

Patricia's tour of the Black Internationale operations would certainly qualify under Gernsback's guidelines. In what the chapter title calls the "greatest farm in [the] world, with science at controls," Carl encounters a massive hydroponic farming operation. Engineered by Sam Hamilton (whom Belsidus calls "one of the outstanding chemists in the United States"), this south Jersey farm produces nearly perfect produce, without disease or "poor distribution of food elements," including strawberries that Carl describes as "fully as large as full-grown plums, bright red and as luscious as I've ever witnessed."[34] Catherine Keyser has linked these preternaturally luscious fruits—and the beautiful Pat who eats them—to Schuyler's own interest in "rational breeding and scientific nutrition," which "promise a better future for black people—one of prosperity and fertility."[35] Hamilton's superior scientific knowledge serves multiple purposes in Schuyler's adaptation of these science fiction formulas. Despite his skills, Belsidus tells Carl, "the white people won't give him a break," so Sam's success helps to promote a vision of Black scientific excellence that far surpasses that of white American scientists, who have rejected him out of pure prejudice.[36] At the same time, the farm, with its highly efficient methods of cultivation and superior product, sends its goods to market to fund Belsidus's worldwide activities.

But Sam Hamilton's hydroponic farm is only successful because of another scientific marvel developed under the auspices of the Black Internationale: Al Fortune's "sun engine," what Sam describes as "probably the most revolutionary invention in the past thousand years. Men have been trying for a century to invent a cheap sun-harnesser which will cheapen sun power below the cost of coal power. Now, a Negro has done it. There have been other solar engines, but this surpasses them all."[37] The serial pauses to explain in detail the process behind this solar powerhouse, listing exact pressure measurements and construction components of this new discovery, signifying on the conventions of early science fiction pulps, which considered "scientific accuracy . . . a stylistic prerequisite."[38] The narrative reveals these technical details as if providing a blueprint for readers to construct their own world-changing technology. The solar powerhouse heats the hydroponic farm for no cost at all, ensuring that the profitability of the entire operation is extraordinarily high. As such, Schuyler's "Black Internationale," its name clearly a nod to global communism, has developed scientific advancements that allow it to corner and exploit the capitalist market in service of the destruction of European and North American imperialism.

While Belsidus's organization relies on—and Schuyler's narrative dwells on—forms of Black achievement through scientific advancement, "The Black Internationale" does not shy away from representations of antiracist and anticolonial violence and struggle. After reports of the gruesome lynching of a Black man in Mississippi, Pat and Carl fly to the offending town and drop bombs on it, killing two hundred residents in retribution for the lynching. This echoes the thwarted bombing of the Klan special train in W. E. B. Du Bois's international romance *Dark Princess* (1928), but it also draws on earlier work by Schuyler himself, in particular the twelve-part 1933 serial "Georgia Terror," which Schuyler published in the *Courier* under his own name. This serial follows the investigation of the systematic assassination of the men who lynched an African American labor organizer by a revolutionary group called the Merciless Avengers. The group's leader makes their goals clear: "Our group is also determined to put an end to lynching in the only way it can be ended: by taking the life of every white man who participates in a lynching."[39] At the conclusion, the Avengers escape punishment in an airplane, flying off into the sunset after achieving their goal of revenge. When Patricia describes the rationale of the attack to Carl in "The Black Internationale," she uses virtually the same language as the Merciless Avengers, demonstrating a strong continuity between these two Schuyler texts. Adding complexity to the Belsidus methods, however, is the fact that Patricia and Carl drop leaflets signed by "The Sons of Christ," a supposed Catholic organization claiming responsibility for the attack. Carl puzzles over this "deep-dyed, villainous scheme" of misdirection, but the approach of sowing discord between whites becomes, as the narrative moves forward, one of the central strategies of Belsidus's master plan.[40]

As Carl's language about the "deep-dyed, villainous scheme" suggests, the methods of Belsidus and the Black Internationale raise a number of questions about reader identification. The political movement consolidates its power through the "Church of Love," a synthetic religion described as "something spectacular and colorful, with gorgeous raiment, pageantry and music, all based on Negro motifs and psychology."[41] The church also doubles as "a center for propaganda," suggesting the Internationale's more sinister forays into ideological mind control. "We're not worried about the masses," one character opines. "The masses always believe what they are told often and loud enough. We will recondition the Negro masses in accordance with the most approved behavioristic methods."[42] Such comments, inspired by Schuyler's interest in the behaviorism of psychologist John B. Watson, echo familiar critiques of popular fiction as an insidious culture industry, and the Church of Love's manipulative ideological methods operate as an analog to Schuyler's own critique of his genre fiction and its readers. Schuyler himself considered "The Black Internationale," his most popular story, "hokum and hack work of the purest vein."[43] Schuyler's low opinion of these stories, found in private correspondence with *Courier* staff member P. L. Prattis, stemmed from what appears to be his own sense of the bankruptcy of the pan-Africanist ideology expressed in them: "I deliberately set out to crowd as much race chauvinism and sheer improbability into it as my fertile imagination could conjure. The result vindicates my low opinion of the human race."[44] But reader interest in Schuyler's serial was impressive; the *Courier* published multiple letters from readers about the serial, likely selecting (or even fabricating) particular kinds of letters to boost awareness, a common practice in pulp magazines. Some letters asked if Carl Slater's narrative was true—a perfectly reasonable question given the serial's context and other coverage of the *Courier*. Harry Louis Cannady's letter, published May 8, 1937, said, "I was a member of the 367th Infantry regiment in the World war and if the Black Internationale is a real organization, I want to join it."[45] Another reader from Gary, Indiana, claimed, "If the story of Dr. Belsidus is true, I am sure that he can line up more than 1,000 persons in this town right away."[46]

While Schuyler may have dismissed his own work, reader enthusiasm and the ultimate narrative direction of the "Black Empire" serials represent a complex relationship to both race chauvinism and genre conventions. Told through the point of view of Carl Slater, a journalist who, after being kidnapped by Belsidus, becomes Belsidus's loyal private secretary, these serials oscillate between a deep sympathy for Belsidus's goal of uniting Africa and destroying white supremacy, and a kind of terror over the ruthless methods he employs. These methods become increasingly more brutal as the two serials wear on. The opening of "The Black Internationale" has Belsidus himself murder a "charming, young, blonde white girl swathed in a gorgeous fur coat" in a darkened Harlem doorway—certainly an image designed to emphasize the serial's sensational quality.[47] In "The Black Internationale," however, the focus generally remains on the utopian promises of science, calibrated acts of revenge against racial violence, and the establishment of an African empire. While these elements may feature some unsavory violence or hints of a "deep-dyed villainous scheme," readers nonetheless saw Belsidus as a heroic anticolonial and antiracist figure; the subtitle of "The Black Internationale," after all, was a "Story of Black Genius against the World." Promotional copy prepared by the *Courier* emphasized Belsidus's role as a "black genius" and mastermind of the Black Internationale; the newspaper, riding high on the circulation boost the serial had engendered, sent out twenty-five thousand inserts advertising "The Black

Internationale."[48] These inserts highlighted the generic conventions of Belsidus's genius and his organizational mastery, and emphasized the serial's political radicalism and its complicated use of cruelty and violence:

> It is not a story exclusively about American Negroes, but a story about Negroes everywhere, united by a common bond of hatred of white exploitation, persecution and ostracism.
>
> One determined black man, educated, suave, immaculate, cruel (at times) and unmoral, gathers around him the genius of the Negro world, and using every device imaginable, organizes the greatest conspiracy in history against White Supremacy!
>
> Agents' Sales Soar When agents call their customers' attention to these gripping Courier serials that appeal to REAL RED-BLOODED Negroes on four Continents.[49]

Schuyler's canny use of the tropes of the genius and the criminal mastermind as a figure of identification offer yet another way of challenging the pulp conventions that figure heroes as white individuals and villains as shadowy nonwhite conspiracies. By embracing the Fu Manchu–like villain of the pulp imagination and transforming this figure into a cruel (and admittedly amoral) crusader for racial justice, the "Black Empire" serials represent one of the most radical genre critiques to appear in the African American newspapers. These wildly popular stories attest to Schuyler's work as a kind of antipulp, reveling in its inversions and perversions of the systems of genre that characterized most pulp production.

It's unclear whether Schuyler had always planned a sequel to "The Black Internationale." After completing this first serial, he immediately turned his attention to "Midsummer Madness," a romance serial for the *Courier* about the infidelities of the young wife of a wealthy middle-aged man, published under the pseudonym Rachel Call. But perhaps the overwhelmingly positive responses to "The Black Internationale" and the character of Belsidus may have given Schuyler pause. In the sequel, "Black Empire," the elements are twisted into a form that makes it more difficult to sympathize with his methods and goals. As Belsidus's plans move forward, the scale of destruction grows exponentially, and in "Black Empire," these brutal acts include spreading typhus, cholera, and bubonic plague across Europe as well as killing fifteen thousand British machinists and technicians with a poison gas in an effort to bring European military development to a halt. In the sequel, technology loses its utopian function: no longer is the focus on growing delicious and profitable strawberries and generating solar power in a Gernsback-ian mode of demonstrating Black scientific excellence. Instead, technical expertise has been turned toward technologies of war, with "stratosphere planes" that deliver typhoid-ridden rats to European cities; a poison gas ("it surpassed anything the white chemists had been able to produce for speedy asphyxiation"); and an "infernal machine," a weapon that can "disintegrate any metal."[50] Technology here has transformed from a progressive and liberatory function into one designed almost exclusively for destruction. As such, the move between "The Black Internationale" and "Black Empire" is akin to the shift from utopia to dystopia. If Schuyler had built up Belsidus as an antiracist hero (if also a dangerous authoritarian) in "The Black Internationale," he chose to transform him into a more ruthless villain in "Black Empire."

Despite this change, Schuyler's text retains an ambivalence about identification with Belsidus. The narrator, Slater, clearly the reader's agent in the text, tires of what he calls "this cruelty, this cold and calculating killing," but he ultimately reconciles himself to Belsidus's methods, asking, "What omelet was ever made without breaking eggs? How had Africa been enslaved except through murder?"[51] Here Slater acknowledges the tropes and conventions of the classic exotic adventure stories prevalent in the pulps—stories that built their appeal (and their white heroes) on the very murder that Slater describes, even as he registers concern about the authoritarian qualities of Belsidus's leadership and the violent methods he uses. "Black Empire" even signifies on these adventure serials in a sequence that finds Carl, Patricia, and others in the movement captured and nearly killed by "cannibals" somewhere near "Northern Sierra Leone." In the mode of a true pulp adventure, the heroes are rescued just in time from a group of "angry brown men, naked except for breech cloths, and brandishing bush knives, spears and old rusty rifles" with "teeth . . . filed to sharp points."[52] These exotic and stereotypical "savage" African villains that appear in the sequel serve as a strong counterweight to the more complex political vision of "The Black Internationale." The first serial does show a group of African chiefs prostrating themselves before Belsidus, who calls himself "the King of Kings" as he builds his anticolonial coalition, but the staged pageantry of this scene is far less problematic than Schuyler's uncritical use of African cannibals as a sensational narrative device in "Black Empire."[53]

Even with the increasing intensity of Belsidus's despotic violence and Schuyler's attempts to complicate reader identification, the "Black Empire" serials nevertheless retain a strong focus on Belsidus as an important, if deeply flawed, leader with a laudable goal. Delany, in his brief consideration of these works in "Racism and Science Fiction," claims that "Black Empire" "remained unfinished," though there is little to suggest that is the case.[54] These comments may stem from the curiously ambivalent, bittersweet ending of "Black Empire." Having used their advanced technology to destroy "Mussolini's air fleet" outside of Benghazi in the "last decisive battle for the Dark Continent," Belsidus claims victory.[55] In a speech to delegates, he tells those gathered, "You must banish race hatred from your hearts, now that you have your own land, but you must remain ever vigilant to defend this continent which is rightfully ours. . . . Through your brains, your labors and your sacrifices, Africa has been redeemed. The shackles have been struck off, we are free and our children shall be free forever. Go forth, my comrades, and imbue your followers with the determination to remain forever free!"[56] After this rousing speech, Patricia and Carl exchange a tender moment, but the narrative concludes with an image of Martha Gaskin, Belsidus's white mistress from the start of the first serial and a ruthless and effective undercover agent for his revolutionary group throughout the two serials. In the final sentences of "Black Empire," Carl looks "down from the front row to where Martha Gaskin sat, her blonde hair looking odd among those Negroes. She was twisting her tiny handkerchief in her hands, while a pair of tears coursed unnoticed down her cheeks."[57] This arresting final image of white tears (of pain? joy? regret? relief?) naturally echoes the first scene in "The Black Internationale," in which Carl witnesses Belsidus murdering "a charming, young, blonde white girl" in a dark Harlem doorway, but its final undecipherability may also leave readers unsure how best to understand the nature of Belsidus's victory.[58]

Schuyler's radical inversion of the pulp trope of the criminal mastermind is an important part of what makes the "Black Empire" serials so successful, even as the sequel ends on a note of ambiguity. This inversion is a powerful example of Schuyler's signifying on and articulation to pulp conventions of racial conspiracy and futuristic race war that appeared with frequency through the 1920s and 1930s in magazines like *Amazing Stories* and *Astounding Stories*. In reconceptualizing this trope not as a (doomed) sinister threat to white global order but as a (successful) movement to end global white supremacy, he activated reader imagination and imagined a form of Black science fiction that could see scientific advancement not as a weaponized tool of racial injustice but as a path for Black liberation. Use of pulp conventions against the ideological underpinnings of the pulp genre system in "Black Empire" represents Schuyler's most effective innovations, though other work discussed across *Black Pulp* shows similar moves in genres like romance and adventure fiction.

IT CAN HAPPEN HERE: WILLIAM THOMAS SMITH'S "THE BLACK STOCKINGS"

In the shift between "The Black Internationale" and "Black Empire," Schuyler appeared determined to raise more questions about Belsidus's authoritarianism, to render it in a form less sympathetic to readers. The question of authoritarianism doubtless loomed large in the minds of both Schuyler and his readers in 1937, between the two serials. In Europe, Adolf Hitler had been in power in Germany since 1933 and Benito Mussolini in Italy since 1922. Meanwhile, Francisco Franco was leading fascist military forces (supported by Hitler and Mussolini) against the Republican loyalists in Spain as Schuyler's serials were being published. Schuyler dealt more directly with Italian fascism in two serials that took up Italy's imperialist reconquest of Ethiopia in the Italo-Ethiopian war of 1935–36: "The Ethiopian Murder Mystery" (October 5, 1935–February 1, 1936) and "Revolt in Ethiopia: A Tale of Black Insurrection against Italian Imperialism" (July 16, 1938–January 21, 1939).[59] In this evolving geopolitical climate, it was more difficult to imagine authoritarian leadership as a solution to the problem of colonialism and white supremacy by the time Schuyler started his second Belsidus serial.

Another factor may have intervened, however. With the wild success of "The Black Internationale" for the *Pittsburgh Courier*, the *Baltimore Afro-American* began its own speculative fiction serial in the summer of 1937, before Schuyler's first Belsidus serial had even concluded. The first installment of this twelve-part serial, "The Black Stockings," covered

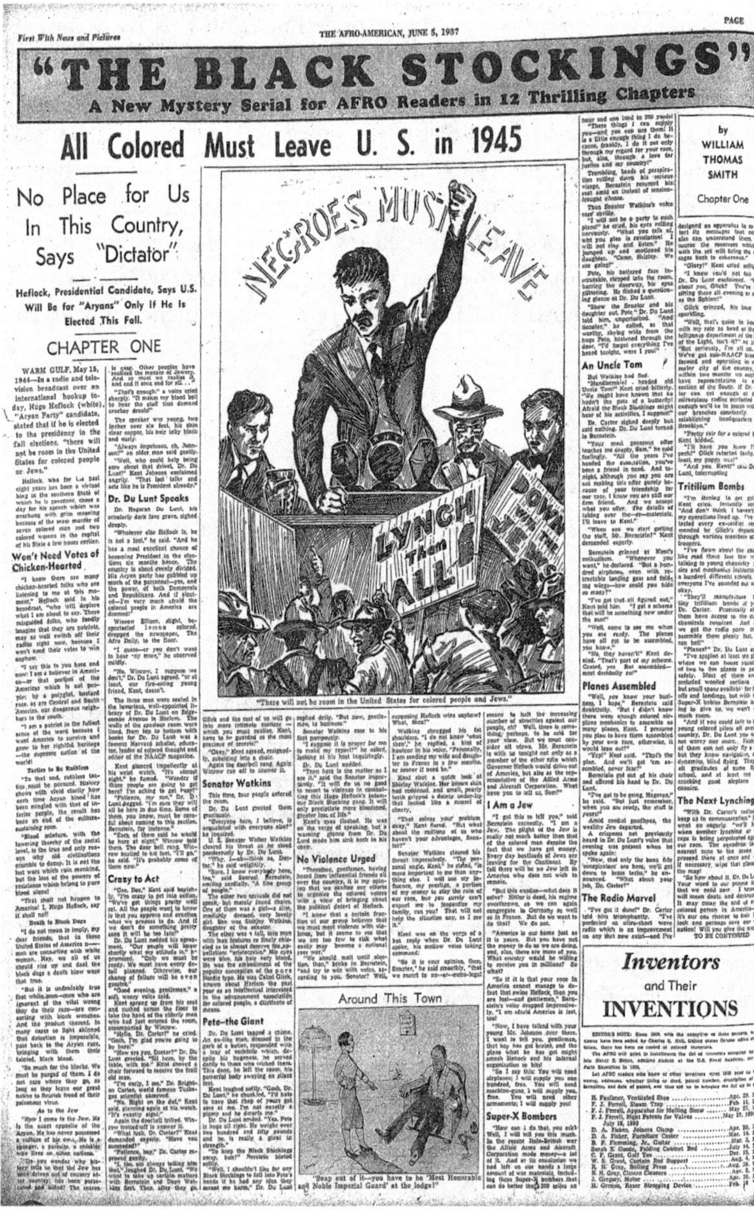
First With News and Pictures

THE AFRO-AMERICAN, JUNE 5, 1937

PAGE

"THE BLACK STOCKINGS"

A New Mystery Serial for AFRO Readers in 12 Thrilling Chapters

All Colored Must Leave U. S. in 1945

No Place for Us In This Country, Says "Dictator"

Heflock, Presidential Candidate, Says U.S. Will Be for "Aryans" Only If He Is Elected This Fall.

CHAPTER ONE

by WILLIAM THOMAS SMITH

Chapter One

Won't Need Votes of Chicken-Hearted

Dr. Du Lunt Speaks

Crazy to Act

Senator Watkins

No Violence Urged

Pete—the Giant

I Am a Jew

Super-X Bombers

An Uncle Tom

Planes Assembled

The Radio Marvel

Tritilium Bombs

The Next Lynching

TO BE CONTINUED

"There will not be room in the United States for colored people and Jews."

Around This Town

"Snap out of it—you have to be 'Most Honorable and Noble Imperial Guard' at the lodge!"

Inventors and Their INVENTIONS

William Thomas Smith, "The Black Stockings," chapter 1, *Baltimore Afro-American,* June 5, 1937. Courtesy of the AFRO Newspaper Archives.

the entire back page of the *Afro-American* on June 5, 1937, with a bold illustration by the newspaper's celebrated illustrator and cartoonist, Francis Yancey. Under the serial's title appeared a shocking headline—"All Colored Must Leave U.S. in 1945"—and below this two subheads, "No Place for Us in This Country, Says 'Dictator'" and "Heflock, Presidential Candidate, Says U.S. Will Be for 'Aryans' Only If He Is Elected This Fall."[60] Yancey's accompanying illustration shows the candidate, Hugo Heflock, delivering a speech with fist raised. Behind him are the words "Negroes Must Leave," and the crowd gathered in front carries signs reading "Lynch Them All" and "Down with the Jews." The layout and presentation of this first serial is shocking; its prominent placement on the newspaper's back page and its pseudojournalistic headlines carry a seriousness and verisimilitude that could easily make readers wonder if this presidential campaign is real and if this feature is simply covering the latest incarnation of white supremacist political rhetoric. The fictional installment even opens with a dateline ("WARM GULF, May 15, 1944"), and its first few paragraphs report on the elections and Heflock's speech in a manner that evokes the *Afro-American*'s regular reporting. If the wishful thinking of the *Pittsburgh Courier*'s readers could imagine that Belsidus's global anti-imperialist movement was real, then the *Baltimore Afro-American* sought to make blurring the boundaries between its near-future dystopian serial and its news coverage a central feature of "The Black Stockings."

"The Black Stockings" received the most prominent placement of any fiction published in the *Afro-American* and was advertised in advance by a full-page ad calling it "the biggest mystery serial ever presented to *AFRO* readers"; it also featured an author who had not published regularly in the Black press since the days of the *Illustrated Feature Section*.[61] This was William Thomas Smith, who, under the name Will Thomas, published the article "Negro Writers of Pulp Fiction" in *Negro Digest* in 1950 (discussed in the introduction) and wrote two other significant works, the 1947 passing novel *God Is for White Folks* and *The Seeking*, a 1953 memoir of his family's life in an all-white small town in Vermont. Judging from his own words about his life and career, Smith (as I will refer to him here) made much of his living during the 1930s and 1940s writing under a number of unknown pseudonyms for "the love and adventure type pulp magazines."[62] Smith does not mention

"The Black Stockings" in his memoir, though he does mention writing fiction for the *Illustrated Feature Section*.[63] As such, it is unclear why he might have returned to the Black press to publish this one highly publicized serial, his last appearance (under any of his known bylines) as a writer of fiction for the Black press. One possibility is his own fascination with and interest in responding to the work of Sinclair Lewis, whose *It Can't Happen Here* had been published just two years earlier. Understood in this light, "The Black Stockings" represents a powerful act of signifying on Lewis's famous cautionary tale about the potential for fascism to rise in the United States.

Lewis's *It Can't Happen Here*, published in October 1935, was a popular literary sensation, and it remains the most famous fictional thought experiment to imagine the rise of an American fascist government. Despite its only being in print for the final two and half months of 1935, it was nevertheless the fourth-highest-selling fiction title of the year, and it remained on the *New York Times* best-seller lists into June 1936.[64] The novel describes the rise of a fascist presidential candidate, Buzz Windrip, as focalized through the perspective of an incredulous liberal Vermont journalist, Doremus Jessup. While the novel features brief moments of racial animosity, it saves much of its drama for the conflict between Jessup and his former hired man, Shad Ledue. *It Can't Happen Here* ultimately imagines the potential rise of fascism in the United States as built from the combination of ignorance and resentment of working-class whites and the appearance of a populist presidential candidate who appeals to the nation's disaffected voters with bombastic rhetoric and nationalist demagoguery.

Lewis's novel was hailed in the Black press, even if some critics raised questions about how well Lewis had articulated the racial dynamics of a potential American fascist state. While W. E. B. Du Bois recommended it in his column in the *Pittsburgh Courier*, Ted Poston of the *New York Amsterdam News* suggested that the novel failed to fully articulate the implications of fascism for African Americans: "The Negro's position under the American dictatorship is touched on frequently by Mr. Lewis, but it is this reviewer's opinion that Buzz Windrip is not half as harsh with this oppressed group as an actual Fascist dictator would be forced to be."[65] A few months later, writing about his own summer reading choices in the *Amsterdam News*, civil rights leader and future congressman Adam

Advertisement for William Thomas Smith, "The Black Stockings," *Baltimore Afro-American*, May 29, 1937. Courtesy of the AFRO Newspaper Archives.

Clayton Powell Jr. succinctly addressed *It Can't Happen Here*'s short-comings in understanding the racial dynamics of fascism and articulated the latent fascism of American Jim Crow. As he noted, "Fascism is here and has been, as far as the Negro is concerned, for some time."[66]

The *Baltimore Afro-American* never formally reviewed Lewis's novel, and it received just a couple of mentions in passing in the newspaper in the year after its publication; however, Smith's "The Black Stockings"— which began serialization in the *Afro-American* about a year after Powell highlighted the fascism integral to American Jim Crow—serves as review, critique, and radical transformation of Lewis's best-selling novel. It's clear that Smith knew *It Can't Happen Here* and had followed Sinclair Lewis. Letters to Vermont writer Bradford Smith (no relation) in the late 1940s suggest that Smith had tried to enlist Lewis's help with an unpublished novel manuscript.[67] Further, in his 1953 memoir, *The Seeking*, he references *It Can't Happen Here* directly, referring to "a statement attributed to the late Sinclair Lewis, the famed writer, that there was as much native fascism in Vermont as anywhere in Europe"—which is, in effect, the thesis of Lewis's dystopian novel.[68] Although his memoir ultimately moderates this statement and celebrates the democratic spirit of acceptance that Smith encountered in Vermont, the much earlier publication "The Black Stockings" falls more firmly in line with the reaction of the Black press, implicitly critiquing Lewis for underestimating the racial dynamic of any potential American fascism and locating the source of any fascist movement not in white working-class resentment but in the racial capitalism of Jim Crow segregation and white supremacy.

Smith seeks to make these connections clear in the opening installment of the serial in the form of the journalistic report on Heflock's campaign rally. Following the futuristic dateline, the serial continues: "In a radio and television broadcast over an international hookup today, Hugo Heflock (white), 'Aryan Party' candidate, stated that if he is elected to the presidency in the fall elections, 'there will not be room in the United States for colored people or Jews.'" What follows is a lengthy quotation of Heflock's speech, a host of stock nativist rhetoric. Heflock emphasizes an American purity: "I am a believer in America—or that portion of the Americas which is not peopled by a polyglot, bastard race, as are Central and South America, our dangerous neighbors to the south." His solutions include expulsion and extermination: "So much for the blacks.

We must be purged of them. I do not care where they go, so long as they leave our great nation to flourish freed of their poisonous virus."[69] Heflock's vicious nativist demagoguery—as well as his proposals for expelling African Americans and Jews from the United States—sounds much like the political race-baiting prevalent throughout the twentieth and twenty-first centuries, and its language of contamination takes part in a long-standing American nativist discourse that produced strict immigration laws based on racial pseudoscience in the early twentieth century.

What is both impressive and prescient about Smith's take on the possibility of American fascism is that he locates the source of such a threat neither in populist economics (as does Lewis) nor in the realm of military force, but in the nativism already present in much of the mainstream American public. In Lewis's *It Can't Happen Here,* for example, Buzz Windrip rises to the presidency on the appeal of his promises to give every American a guaranteed income of a few thousand dollars—a generous sum in the depths of the Great Depression, and a policy doubtless inspired by left-leaning populist Louisiana Senator Huey Long's "Share Our Wealth" plan. Lewis's novel, on the one hand, imagines a kind of fascist bait and switch, in which largely disempowered working-class whites usher in an authoritarian regime under the assumption that they will receive a direct financial benefit. "The Black Stockings," on the other hand, imagines the rise of fascism as first and foremost rooted in racial animosity and American nativism—a fear and hatred of others that generates an irrational cycle of blame and resentment. In Smith's serial, in fact, the Black Stockings of the title are Heflock's informal militia, a group that has risen from the ashes of the Ku Klux Klan. They have given up the white hoods and now wear black stockings over their heads, ensuring anonymity as they terrorize nonwhite groups across the country, engaging in violent acts inspired by Heflock's campaign. In transformations like these, Smith alters the tropes of near-future dystopian fiction to offer an alternative explanation of fascist impulses. For Smith, the Black Stockings—and the Klan—are a form of fascism in miniature, and with his shrewd control of the media, presidential candidate Heflock taps into a kind of deep-seated American fascism that is ripe for development. This has far less to do with economic populism and charisma, and much more to do with the simmering politics of race in America. Members of the Black Stockings are not exclusively disenfranchised whites. Instead, as the serial says, "Under ordinary circumstances they would have passed for prosperous business men. And that is exactly what they were—well-to-do men who were high members of the Black Stocking organization."[70]

After introducing Heflock's white supremacist presidential campaign, "The Black Stockings" wrestles with a question vital to the newspaper's readership: Given the broad appeal of race-baiting and fearmongering in the campaign, how might the forces of antifascism and antiracism prevent the rise of fascism in the United States? For Smith, the answer to this lies in the generic conventions and narrative pleasures of adventure fiction. The serial focuses on challenges to Heflock's fascist campaign offered by a complex multiethnic operation known as the Sons of Light. Formed by a group of African American leaders and intellectuals—including Dr. Hagaran Du Lunt (a thinly veiled version of W. E. B. Du Bois); Dr. Brighton Carter, a "world famous Tuskegee scientist"; and others—this resistance campaign overcomes a timid and skeptical political class and fights fascism directly, deploying a variety of techniques in an effort to organize against the violent reign of terror sewn by the Black Stockings during the presidential campaign.[71] These methods—like those depicted in Schuyler's serials—draw heavily on the conventions of early science fiction, including a nimble air squadron and advanced weaponry. This multiracial coalition of "Fusionists"—a name that recalls multiracial political coalitions like the one overthrown by white supremacists in Wilmington, North Carolina, in 1898—uses both conventional and imagined military technology, with violent but effective results.[72]

Instrumental in Heflock's political rise is his savvy use of the media—a radio station owned and controlled by the politician himself—as a means of stirring up race hatred and resentment and inspiring violence against his enemies. Radio plays a major role in It Can't Happen Here, as it did in the rise of Hitler in Germany, but Smith takes the critique of modern mass media further. Lewis—and antifascist cultural critics like Theodor Adorno—place the blame on the medium itself, an alienating form that, in Horkheimer and Adorno's words, "makes everyone equally into listeners, in order to expose them in authoritarian fashion to the same programs put out by different stations."[73] Radio, the

Frankfurt School critics argue, "takes on the deceptive form of a disinterested, impartial authority, which fits fascism like a glove."[74] Smith, on the other hand, emphasizes the ownership of that medium: When white supremacists own the media, the message delivered is white supremacy. Heflock's message accrues an almost viral quality, something Smith emphasizes by opening the serial with a radio broadcast. Late in the serial (and the presidential campaign), Smith details this: "Heflock took to his privately owned radio station several times a week, blasting forth in venomous terms his concepts of a true American nation—one free from the dangerous threat of domination, by the colored race. . . . Thousands of white people who did not seek actual violence against colored people did discharge them from their jobs."[75] Despite this emphasis on the modern mass media's potential for inciting race hatred throughout "The Black Stockings," radio technology does not appear as inherently destructive; indeed, it plays an instrumental role in the fight against Heflock's fascist movement.

In contrast to Heflock's powerful radio station, the Sons of Light opt for advanced and encrypted radio technology—just one of many technical advances produced by Black scientists. Dr. Carter describes his invention as "an ultra-short wave radio which is an improvement on any that now exist—and I've designed an apparatus to so distort its messages that nobody else can understand them."[76] These radios, as one character notes, allow the Sons of Light to "know when another lynching or outrage is being perpetrated against our race. The squadron in the nearest zone to the scene will proceed there at once and will, if necessary, wipe that place off the map!"[77] This radio technology facilitates a power of response that can match—or at least counter—Heflock's power over the airwaves. In addition to the developments in radio technology, the Sons of Light also develop weapons technology that can be adapted to different forms of combat with the Black Stockings. Dr. Carter designs "tiny tritilium bombs," which are effective both as aerial devices and detonated in close quarters, and de facto protagonist Kent Johnson has lined up manufacturers—"young chemistry[,] physics and mathematics instructors in a hundred different schools"—to produce these in different locations across the country.[78]

The narrative's focal point is Kent Johnson, a pilot and romantic hero in the mode of adventure fiction. Passionate about the cause throughout the serial, Johnson consistently remains at the forefront of the action (often featured in the large illustrations), organizing the logistics for producing the tritilium bombs, flying a squadron to destroy a town that has lynched a framed man, engaging members of the Black Stockings in hand-to-hand combat, and winning the heart of Shirley Watkins, daughter of Senator Walter Watkins, who is initially opposed to violent antifacist response to Heflock's Black Stockings and skeptical of the Sons of Light. In a feat of extraordinary bravery that serves as the serial's climax, Johnson parachutes into Heflock's castle-like compound to rescue Dr. Du Lunt, who has been kidnapped and imprisoned there. In one of the most suspenseful scenes of the serial, Johnson is brought before Heflock and stripped naked at Heflock's orders; this serves as the source for one of Frances Yancey's most arresting illustrations of the serial's action. As Heflock looks down from his "throne" on the "magnificent copper body" of Johnson, the hero sends Heflock into an "uncontrollable rage" by calling into question his masculinity and sexuality: "I had heard you were a sissy!"[79]

While Kent Johnson serves as the serial's pulp-like action hero, rescuing Du Lunt and marrying the romantic interest at the conclusion of "The Black Stockings," he does not actually vanquish the villainous Heflock. Instead, this falls to a character that draws together significant thematic elements of Smith's serial: Cabot Glick. This character appears in the very first installment of "The Black Stockings," as "Cabot Click, known about Harlem the past year as an intellectual interested in the advancement association for colored people, a dilettante of means."[80] Glick is described as "the embodiment of the popular conception of the pure Nordic type," and his presence in these early scenes helps to underscore the multiracial and multiethnic nature of the Sons of Light coalition, which also includes Jewish industrialist Samuel Bernstein, who provides the antifascist coalition with airplanes and weapons and is later assassinated by the Black Stockings.[81] It turns out, however, that Glick has been passing (to readers, at least) through the first part of the serial, and his involvement with racial justice resembles, in some degree, the work Walter White did investigating lynching for the NAACP in the 1920s.[82] Du Lunt expresses some surprise at the risk Glick has taken going undercover: "I've often wondered through the years we've known each other in racial work why you've always been so loyal to our race,

"I had heard you were a sissy."

Frances Yancey, "I had heard you were a sissy," illustration for William Thomas Smith, "The Black Stockings," chapter 11, *Baltimore Afro-American*, August 14, 1937. Courtesy of the AFRO Newspaper Archives.

why you've risked your neck countless times on investigations in the South when exposure of your purposes and your true racial identity would have meant death!"[83] Glick's rationale is simple, and it serves to explain his biracial past. His mother was raped in a cotton field by a white man she refused to identify, and his work for racial justice is motivated by revenge: "So I could discover who the fiend is who sired me!"

Glick's personal quest and the serial's larger political aims merge at the conclusion of "The Black Stockings," with spectacular results. Thanks to the efforts of the Sons of Light, Heflock's presidential campaign is defeated at the ballot box, but the man himself has contingency plans that mimic the lead-up to the U.S. Civil War. Before he can put these plans into motion, an extra edition of the newspaper suddenly delivers unexpected news: Heflock is "shot to death in the corridors of his State capitol five minutes after he had delivered an address in which he declared the intention of his State to secede from the Union." A radio commentator adds additional details that help bring together the serial's various strands. The assassin, immediately killed by Heflock's bodyguards after murdering the fascist leader, bears an uncanny similarity to Heflock himself. As a radio news report details, "The blonde, blue-eyed slayer of America's most tempestuous political figure, very closely resembled his victim. If it were not definitely known that Governor Heflock had no younger brothers or sons, his slayer could easily be taken for either."[84] This is, of course, Glick, whose final act is the murder of his rapist father, the fascist Heflock. The dramatic deaths of Heflock and Glick bear much of the symbolic weight of the serial's conclusion, with Glick, a living product of Heflock's racial and sexual violence, returning to wreak vengeance on the father.[85]

If Schuyler's "Black Empire" serials flirted with the seductive power of authoritarianism, then Smith's "The Black Stockings" envisions the fight against fascism as a question of life or death for African Americans. Week after week, in installment after installment, the serial offers a compelling argument for the necessity of such a fight, even in the face of possible extinction or genocide. In chapter 5, Dr. Du Lunt declares, "We are prepared to clinch with Heflock in a manner I am sure he does not dream of. It may lead to a carnival of blood—it may lead to the extinction of every black face in America—but that is a risk we must take."[86] The next installment finds another character channeling Claude

McKay's famous 1919 protest poem: "I've lived so far only to see slavery of our people continue, our rights nullified, our lives perpetualy [sic] in danger at the whim of the cheapest white man. And it will be better for every last one of us to die than to go on as we have. If we must die— then let us die like men!"[87] Intertextual echoes like these emphasize this speculative serial's connection to and criticism of the fascism that inhered within Jim Crow America,[88] for it is not merely in Smith's imagined future that these characters "see slavery of our people continue, our rights nullified, our lives perpetualy in danger." Smith's serial reflects, like the most compelling speculative fictions, the reality of the present—a world where, as Adam Clayton Powell noted, "Fascism is here and has been, as far as the Negro is concerned, for some time."

"The Black Stockings" was not the last time Smith would turn to a speculative mode to address the concerns of racism and white supremacy in his work. In letters he exchanged with Bradford Smith (no relation) in 1948, they discuss the manuscript (now lost) of William Thomas Smith's "Decision," which involved "a racial revolution in our fair land" and was ultimately rejected by Random House.[89] After the widely promoted "Black Stockings" in 1937, the *Baltimore Afro-American* largely abandoned the speculative fiction genre in favor of war stories and hero fiction over the next decade. This genre returned, however, in the early 1950s with the dawn of space exploration and the atomic age. Serials like James Hill's "Space Ship" (September 16–30, 1950), "From Outer Space" (February 12–26, 1955), and "The Orbit of Doom" (April 2–23, 1955) downplay racial dynamics in favor of presenting cautionary tales about Cold War technology and the specter of nuclear annihilation.[90] In this respect, they form a complicated bridge between the ambitious 1930s dystopian fiction of Schuyler and Smith and the earliest work of "first African-American science fiction writer" Samuel R. Delany, the postapocalyptic paperback original *The Jewels of Aptor* (1962).

Delany's complex fictions have historically represented the most visible African American contributions to speculative fiction; he remains a major figure in the so-called New Wave of science fiction that emerged in the late twentieth century and a pioneering voice in the emergence of what is now called Afrofuturism.[91] This tradition has remained alive and well through the work of writers Octavia Butler, N. K. Jemisin, and Nnedi Okorafor, among many others.[92] The work of Schuyler and Smith together deserve attention not merely because they extend this history back in time but also because they too serve as powerful examples of science fiction's Golden Age, tracking the shift from Gernsbackian technocracy to the construction of complex social worlds with real political implications for the present. The specter of fascism in Europe and the reality of Jim Crow at home provided these writers with the perfect opportunity to craft science fiction serials that spoke clearly and directly to the concerns and anxieties of African American readers, animated their imaginations, and activated their fantasies. With the arrival of World War II, the interests of readers, writers, and editors shifted, and speculative stories of racial justice were superseded by stories of Black soldiers serving with the U.S. military in Europe. However, the elements that animated speculative fiction—the inventions, the conspiracies, and the fight for a more just future—returned in a different form in the hero fiction that appeared widely across the 1940s and 1950s in the *Afro-American*. These stories—more individual than collective—allowed for direct and powerful confrontations with the horrors of white supremacy and dramatizations of triumphs over injustices that ranged from the global to the extremely local.

4

BATTLING WHITE SUPREMACY
A PREHISTORY OF THE BLACK SUPERHERO

THERE IS LITTLE DOUBT that recent return of prominent Black comic book heroes like Black Panther (in Ta-Nehisi Coates's comic series and the 2018 Marvel film) and Luke Cage (in the 2016–18 Netflix series) and the reimagining of Alan Moore's *Watchmen* around issues of racial justice in the 2019 HBO miniseries has rekindled an interest in the history of Black superheroes in American popular culture, especially in the wake of contemporary racial justice movements like Black Lives Matter. These characters, initially created by white comic book writers in the 1960s and 1970s and more recently repurposed by Black creators, spawned a host of African American hero characters into the 1980s and beyond, but they nevertheless raise a troubling question: Was it impossible to imagine Black heroes before the 1960s, and, even then, could only white comic writers and artists do so? The answer to this question is a resounding no, but little work has been done to recover the elements of Black popular print culture that would document this critical prehistory of Black superheroes. To do this, one might reach back into the African American literary tradition to unearth the heroic exploits of Madison Washington, the protagonist of Frederick Douglass's 1852 novella *The Heroic Slave;* Henry Blake, the Black revolutionary title character of Martin R. Delany's 1861–62 serial "Blake; or the Huts of America" or even Reuel Briggs, the mesmeric central character of Pauline Hopkins's 1902–3 serial "Of One Blood; or, The Hidden Self."

Indeed, the description of a trajectory between these early texts and the African American comic book heroes of the late twentieth century would essentially leap over the period in which series heroes, from pulp stars like Doc Savage to comic book superheroes like Superman, established a prominent place in American popular culture. As with other genres discussed in *Black Pulp,* this substantial gap in the heroic representation of African American characters is in reality no gap at all. The popular fiction published in the *Pittsburgh Courier* and the *Baltimore Afro-American* was full of adventurous heroes of all kinds, populating many different genres. These characters, like their white counterparts in the pulps, found ways to overcome adversity, rescue the innocent, and challenge corruption. But this fiction also found ways to interrogate the assumptions behind the dominant heroic white figure that appeared in pulps and comics while bending the heroic formula to the service of racial justice.

In fact, Black heroes and Black heroics abound across the period discussed in *Black Pulp,* and the representation of series characters—that is, characters who appeared in multiple, and not necessarily sequential, adventures over time—began in the late 1930s, shortly after the surge in pulp magazines devoted to individual heroic protagonists. These characters dominated the pages of the nationally distributed Black newspaper the *Baltimore Afro-American* in the 1940s and early 1950s, in the decade and a half before integration and the national civil rights movement. Traditional African American literary histories mark this period with the emergence and success of writers like Richard Wright, Chester Himes, Ann Petry, and Ralph Ellison. The work of these now-canonical figures, however, presents the world of Jim Crow America almost exclusively as a naturalistic machine, driving African American men and women alternatively to crime, madness, or despair. In the work of these writers, the forces of white supremacy are both omnipresent and omnipotent, and texts as various as *Native Son* (1940), *If He Hollers Let Him Go* (1945), *The Street* (1946), and *Invisible Man* (1952) show characters imprisoned, in flight, or driven insane by the experience of structural racism in the United States. The hero fiction that appeared in the *Afro-American* at this time, however, articulated itself to this canonical fiction by offering narratives of revolutionary agency in place of naturalistic tragedy. Though these series characters present the triumphs facilitated by individual characters, they do not wallow in an existential individualism; rather, they present these heroes engaging in imagined solutions to the social and political problems of Jim Crow and segregation.

Created by semiprofessional fiction writers James H. Hill and H. L. Faggett, these fictional heroes included the Senegalese flying ace Jacques Lenglet, whose exploits involve fighting Germans in Europe and American racists in the South; hard-boiled reporter Jiggs Bennett, who covers and assists antiracist organizations including the fictional Black Retribution and the very real Mau Mau; and Black Robin, who travels across the South righting the wrongs of white supremacy at the request of *Afro* readers. While none of these characters exhibits the superpowers of a Black Panther or a Luke Cage, they nevertheless engage in the heroic work of battling what one of these texts called "the most ugly facet in America's Hall of 'Shame'—Jim-Crowism!" Like the other genres discussed in *Black Pulp,* the adventure heroes described here offer a variety of utopian fantasies that imagine the possibility of ending the horrors of white supremacy through any number of methods, both violent and nonviolent. Here the narrative pleasures of action and adventure merge with the political and social pleasures of eradicating white supremacy in manifestations both small and large. These series also exploit the newspaper form to bring these antiracist heroes directly in contact with a host of current events covered by the *Afro-American,* aligning these characters' heroism with local, national, and international struggles against racism at home and abroad.

"BIG, BEEFY HE-MEN": THE PROBLEM WITH PULP HEROISM

The comic book superhero—most recognizably exemplified by D.C. Comics characters Superman (who debuted in 1938) and Batman (who debuted in 1939)—emerged at a critical point in the history of American popular culture. Heroes were nothing new at this time, but in the years before the debuts of these famous superheroes, pulp magazine publishers—many struggling in the depths of the Great Depression—tried out some new conventions: In addition to publishing magazines devoted to a single genre *(Love Story Magazine, Adventure),* they began to introduce titles devoted to a single, heroic character. These so-called hero pulps capitalized on the popularity of series characters from the earliest pulps but amplified this by devoting most of an issue to one character. They quickly proliferated in the early 1930s; titles like "The Shadow" (1931–49), "Doc Savage" (1933–49), "The Spider" (1933–43), "G-8 and His Battle Aces" (1933–44), and "Operator #5" (1934–39) were among the most popular. But as the periodical publishing market became more complex and younger pulp readers were drawn away from the pulps to the relatively new comic book format, comic publishers (some of whom also published pulps) soon discovered that this single-character hero model would translate well into this new publishing format.

It is important to understand the publishing context of the pulps and comics in order to grapple with the complexity and politically radical genre revision that was the hallmark of Black newspaper fiction. Black heroes—almost always male characters—abound in the newspaper fiction of the twentieth century, especially the period I consider in *Black Pulp*. Heroes of this kind emerged quickly with the turn to popular genre fiction in the *Illustrated Feature Section*. These stories included a host of adventurous crimefighters, including the boxer turned crime fighter of William Thomas Smith's "The Dark Knight" (March 8–May 24, 1930), the preacher turned crimefighter of Nick Lewis's "The Clean Up" (August 20–September 24, 1932), and the quasi–secret identity tale of Monte King's "Questionmark" (published only in the *Pittsburgh Courier*, March 5–April 30, 1932), along with scores of other serials and short stories featuring protagonists protecting Black communities from threats both internal and external. In these early stories and serials, the emphasis remains rather firmly on the heroic protagonist. These texts—following the conventions of the *Illustrated Feature Section*—take place almost exclusively within African American communities, and as such, they offer a more conventional replication of the heroic tropes that appeared across crime and adventure pulp fiction. In "Questionmark," for example, World War I veteran Russ King goes in search of his mother, who was kicked out into the street by King's father. His journey takes him through the underworld, rescuing prostitutes from exploitation by the crime syndicate in Pittsburgh. Russ makes his universalist heroic intentions clear when he claims, "I am fighting humanity's battles."[1] With this universalist claim, "Questionmark" follows in the footsteps of the *Illustrated Feature Section*, which generally avoided depictions of interracial conflict in its genre fiction.

A couple of years later, after the surge in hero pulps like Doc Savage had made the hearty white adventurer a well-worn pulp adventure trope, George Schuyler raised serious questions about the structural and racial dynamics of the heroic adventure in his 1934 serial "Strange Valley" (August 18–November 10, 1934), an African adventure that prefigured the Black Empire serials discussed in chapter 3. "Strange Valley" follows Virginia Coleman and her father on a planned safari with their rugged guide, Bill Atwater, and their African American maid, Stella. Their plane crashes in the jungle, and they soon discover an international group of Black radicals planning to challenge white control of the continent. Like many Schuyler serials, "Strange Valley" features a prominent interracial union (in this case between Virginia and Sam Morgan, the general in the Black army). However, it also provides an explicit critique of the white hero at the heart of pulp adventure. The safari guide Bill Atwater is, on the surface at least, an adventure hero in the most stereotypical mode, a type that seems modeled on the ubiquitous cover images of a muscle-bound Doc Savage (or any number of other adventure heroes). Veteran pulp editor Harold Hersey's 1937 volume *The Pulpwood Editor: The Fabulous World of the Thriller Magazines Revealed by a Veteran Editor and Publisher* features one of the most succinct and revealing descriptions of the requirements for pulp heroism: "Just so long as he is handsome, a white man, brave, honest and sensitive about his honor to a fault—in other words, a true soldier of fortune, he is the hero for an adventure yarn."[2] Hersey emphasizes this point while lamenting the fact that western pulps have been unable to market "Indian stories" with Native American heroes, because, as he notes, "the white man in popular fiction must always triumph in his conquests."[3] Literary critics have seen this trend as part of a larger nativist project that underwrote much of the fiction published in pulp magazines, what Sean McCann has described as "a recurrent battle between insidious miscegenation and an imperiled, domestic homogeneity."[4]

Bill Atwater is in many ways is an excellent example of Hersey's "hero for an adventure yarn": "a true soldier of fortune." In a characteristic move, however, Schuyler inverts this convention so as to reveal its direct connection to white supremacist violence. Atwater's presence as the group's guide is actually a cover for his own selfish goal: the discovery of untold riches in the lost city of Kansa. This act of colonial looting is part of the hallmark of white adventure fiction. Ultimately, Atwater is far from the heroic figure common in adventure pulps; rather, he is lustful, violent, and selfish. After the group crashes in the jungle, Atwater plans to use their dire situation to take sexual advantage of Virginia Coleman, an otherwise unattainable white woman of the Southern aristocracy:

> Used to the ready acquiescence of easy women in a half dozen parts of the globe, Atwater was impatient with the indirectness of a woman of Virginia's class. He was a Georgian of the rough, straightforward, blustering, animal type; she was of an old family that had had money before the Civil War. He had been attracted to her by her father's money and by her fragile beauty. His animal magnetism and romantic, adventurous career had attracted Virginia to him. Even as he floated within the shadow of death, Atwater pondered ways and means of taking full advantage of their being marooned in the jungle.[5]

Atwater's "animal magnetism" and "rough, straightforward, blustering" exemplify Christopher Breu's argument that the "hard-boiled masculinity" of the pulps "borrowed in implicit ways from the iconography of black masculinity . . . find[ing] its shadowy double in the figure of the transgressive and primitivized black male."[6] Atwater, however, does not transform these characteristics into a pulp virtue and become "brave, honest, and sensitive about his honor," as Hersey described the white adventurer. Instead, he is a sexual predator, attempting to rape Virginia after she loses interest in him and seething over her rejection of him. As Atwater loses out to his Pan-African counterparts, the serial describes white figures like Atwater as "big beefy he-men whose true natures are always revealed by adversity."[7] Before the serial ends, Atwater pathetically and unsuccessfully attempts to bargain for his life, and Dr. Augustus Cranfield, leader of the Black revolutionary movement, mocks the typical pulp depiction of white heroics: "There's your white chivalry. . . . Ready to sell out and leave the others."[8]

Schuyler's "Strange Valley" offers a brutal critique of the white adventure hero, turning this "big, beefy he-man" into a petty and selfish figure, whose jealousy over Virginia enflames a murderous racism. Wrestling with the mental image of interracial sex between Virginia and

Cranfield's general, Sam Morgan, Atwater "was unable to understand how a Southern aristocratic girl like Virginia could yield to a Negro, even though he be the commander of the king's troops. It was just beyond his comprehension. His hands opened and closed and his jaw set belligerently as he conjured up again the memory of her pale white arms around Morgan's neck."[9] This underscores something vital in Schuyler's critique of pulp adventure; here he indicates that the fictions of white individualism and heroism are built on phantasmatic fears and white supremacist obsessions with interracial sex. Atwater's graphic imagination also inflames his murderous racism. He vows, "If I ever get out of here I'll fix that Morgan darky. Oh, it'll be a pleasure to lead an expedition of white men back here to wipe out these niggers."[10]

In confronting the ubiquity of the white hero trope, Schuyler would raise a variety of structural questions about the formulas and conventions that underwrote these fantasies. He would, on the one hand, provide counternarratives like those of Henry Belsidus (discussed in chapter 3), modeled on the criminal mastermind. But he would also deploy figures like Bill Atwater in an effort to expose the white supremacist underpinnings and the moral vacuity of these hero figures. In place of this, Schuyler's mid-1930s work would frequently celebrate the power of groups and associations, collective challenges to forms of white individuality. In other serials, Schuyler would often celebrate the power of the collective over the individualistic hero. Serials like "Georgia Terror" (July 8–September 23, 1933), "Mississippi Mud" (September 30–December 2, 1933), and "Down in the Delta" (May 18–September 28, 1935) feature prominent themes of labor organizing (especially of workers in the Mississippi Delta) and, in the case of "Georgia Terror," the interracial vigilante group the Merciless Avengers, which takes vengeance on the members of a lynch mob in the name of racial justice, with one prominent member declaring, "We shall go on fighting to banish hatred, bigotry, intolerance, exploitation and race prejudice from the South and from America. It will be difficult, dangerous, heartrending, bloody, but we shall go forward unafraid to our revolutionary goal."[11] Schuyler's 1930s challenges to heroic tropes offered compelling and radical responses to the idea of heroic white individuality, but Schuyler abandoned writing popular genre fiction by the end of the decade. In his place, writers for the *Baltimore Afro-American* would present Black heroes articulated differently to the mainstream hero fiction of pulp magazines and comic books.

RIPPED FROM THE HEADLINES: JAMES H. HILL AND THE BLACK ACTION HERO

If the *Baltimore Afro-American* had anything equivalent to the *Courier's* one-man fiction machine, George Schuyler, it was James H. Hill. Born in Baltimore in 1916, Hill published his first story in the pages of the *Afro-American* in 1935. He would go on to publish over three hundred stories and serial installments in the newspaper over the next twenty years. At times his fiction was virtually a regular feature in the newspaper's magazine section. Between 1948 and 1950, for example, his fiction appeared in 109 of the newspaper's 156 issues. The winner of a 1945 war story contest in the *Afro-American,* Hill received a brief profile, which highlighted his precocious writing talents (his "literary career began at the age of 13") and noted, "Mr. Hill holds a full-time job as organizer for a CIO union working in Baltimore and Philadelphia. He does his writing in his spare time and often stays up all night when he gets an inspiration."[12] In the late 1940s (and possibly earlier), Hill would correspond with *Afro-American* editor Carl Murphy, bouncing story ideas off him and asking for advice about subject matter, suggesting that Murphy played a significant role in editing and shaping fiction for the newspaper.[13]

Hill's contributions to the *Afro-American* ranged across every genre imaginable, including science fiction, westerns, romance, and crime fiction. His work received accolades, such as the 1945 "$300 War Story Contest" for a short short story, and three of his more conventional, realistic, stand-alone stories appeared in the 1950 volume *Best Short Stories by* Afro-American *Writers,* a long-forgotten anthology of stories originally published in the newspaper and edited by scholars Nick Aaron Ford and H. L. Faggett. But stories like the ones that this 1950 anthology—part of a strong uplift tradition in African American literature—represent the minority of Hill's output.[14] In truth, his specialty was sensational genre fiction, for which he created memorable, heroic characters that reappeared in serials over the years. With these series characters, Senegalese flying ace Jacques Lenglet and hard-boiled reporter

Jiggs Bennett, Hill developed his own response to the adventure and action hero conventions that traded on the repeated adventures of a character (like Doc Savage) with a recognizable name. Hill's genre signification would offer different kinds of vicarious pleasure for readers; rather than deconstructing the hero trope (as Schuyler had done in the mid-1930s), Hill would offer examples of African American protagonists confronting white supremacist violence head on and seeking justice by any means necessary. Further, rather than seeing such structures as all-powerful and inescapable—as many canonical texts of the period did—Hill's fiction imagined ways that African and African American characters could strategically and successfully challenge and triumph over specific manifestations of white supremacy.

While Hill published his first three short stories in 1935, his real breakthrough was the character of Senegalese flying ace Jacques Lenglet, who appeared in one story and seven short serials between 1938 and 1942. The stories of Lenglet—a talented fighter pilot—are articulated both to the hero pulps and to another niche genre, the aviation pulps, which featured stories of air warfare and daredevil stunts. Following the aviation pulps' obsession with air warfare, and especially World War I, Lenglet is a Senegalese pilot who enlists with the French army after the brutal German Eric von Brunen, known as the Red Scourge, kills his family in Dakar in the early days of the First World War. Moved to vengeance, Lenglet soon becomes an ace pilot, known as the Black Eagle. The early Lenglet stories, set during World War I, quite naturally feature German villains. Published in the late 1930s, however, such characterizations carry a different connotation. In contrast to this African American newspaper fiction, pulp magazines were slower to villainize the Nazis, as they had long trafficked in nativist politics of their own, often demonizing nonwhites (including African Americans and Asians). [15] Such conventions allowed white protagonists to play out the fantasies of white supremacy, often by saving white women from nonwhite natives in exotic locales. But genre fiction by Black authors like Hill offered no compromise with the genre's white supremacist formulas.

When Jacques Lenglet confronts his German enemy in "The Black Eagle Rides Again" (February 26–March 19, 1938), he discovers not a member of a physically or mentally superior race but rather a mangled body: "The man behind the green door was a physical atrocity.

"But M'sieur, I am a prisoner of war."

Frances Yancey, illustration for James H. Hill, "The Black Eagle Rides Again, Part 2,"
Baltimore Afro-American, March 5, 1938. Courtesy of the AFRO Newspaper
Archives.

A hunchback, he sat in a swivel chair, facing Jacques and his captors.
He wore a patch over an empty eye-socket, and his flesh had suffered
severe burns, having a strange, greenish caste. Jacques noted, too, with
revolting pangs, that the man wore a steel claw in the stump of his right
arm."[16] This character, Ludwig von Brunen (the Red Scourge's cousin),
represents the visual and bodily evidence of the lie of white supremacy;
he also serves as evidence of Lenglet's superior talents, as it is Jacques's
dogfighting skills that have destroyed the German's body. "I used to be

tall and straight like you, Lenglet," von Brunen says. "I had two good arms, two eyes, a straight back—like you. . . . But you robbed me of them!"[17] Such a symbolic destruction of the German—Lenglet kills him later in another dogfight—intersected vividly with the *Afro-American*'s news coverage of the Nazi rise and the impending war. For African American readers, this kind of victory represented a sophisticated act of signification: reimagining standard pulp scenarios to present not only stories of physical victory over the enemy but also victories over the very symbols of white supremacy, such as white fantasies of physical and biological racial superiority.

Lenglet soon follows in the footsteps of other globe-trotting popular culture heroes and demonstrates his wide-ranging talents, working first as a detective for the Paris police, then as an international agent uncovering sabotage in the United States during World War II. Lenglet's presence as a Senegalese hero already overturns the racial politics of hero pulps, but "The Land of the Free" (February 1–22, 1941) takes this inversion further by reversing the pulp binaries of civilized and savage in a critique of Jim Crow segregation. In this serial, Lenglet travels toward Savannah, Georgia, from Washington, D.C., with his wife and a journalist to investigate German espionage and sabotage in the docks of Savannah, but he is stopped on the way by a racist sheriff in a small South Carolina town. A remarkable upending of adventure hero conventions occurs when the globe-trotting protagonist is not a white he-man but a Senegalese flying ace, and when the uncivilized hordes he is fighting are not found in exotic, nonwhite locales but among the prejudiced whites of the American South. "The Land of the Free," then, takes a pulp genre—hero adventure—undergirded by the logic of white supremacy and turns that genre in on itself. Here, Jacques is the truly global figure, born in Senegal to a family known as the "Khartum Lenglets" (apparently with roots in the Sudan) and trained in Paris, while his wife, Carla, with her "Somaliland accent," comes from East Africa.[18] Together they represent a transnational, transcontinental, and cosmopolitan vision of Africa. When they encounter the realities of Jim Crow America, it resembles the incomprehensible savage backwater: "It was hard for these three—these people of color—to comprehend the dastardly limitations of segregation. They knew nothing of the resigned futility which engulfed the greater percentage of Americans of color. Why, to them, this was serfdom! The caste system being exercised for all its worth in the richest 'Democracy' of them all!"[19] Encountering the realities of the Jim Crow South, Lenglet responds with swift violence, mowing down the racist white mobs with military efficiency, and in a sense anticipating the "Double-V" campaign launched by the *Pittsburgh Courier* the following year by yoking the struggle in Europe to the struggle with racism on American soil. In the serial's didactic conclusion, after

"Oh, God! If they get the car, they will lynch us!"

Frances Yancey[?], illustration for James H. Hill, "Land of the Free, Part 3," *Baltimore Afro-American*, February 15, 1942. Courtesy of the AFRO Newspaper Archives.

Jacques's machine gun was taking its toll, as the mob pressed back.

Frances Yancey, illustration for James H. Hill, "Land of the Free, Part 2," *Baltimore Afro-American*, February 8, 1942. Courtesy of the AFRO Newspaper Archives.

Jacques and Carla's son, Jacques Jr., arrives to rescue his parents with an air attack, the elder Jacques declares, "If the Dies Committee is looking for un-American activities . . . it can hit at some of the jim-crowism and inject real Americanism for all. This 'One nation indivisible, with liberty and justice for all,' now, as in '61, is a 'House divided against itself.'"[20]

While Hill's Jacques Lenglet stories introduce the heroic series character into the pages of the *Afro-American,* his Jiggs Bennett serials use the hero form as a method for targeting more specific injustices and offering even more radical solutions. Jiggs Bennett, a hard-boiled reporter for the fictional New York newspaper the *Colored Journal,* appears in eleven short serials published between 1947 and 1955, and his investment in (and often support of) the causes he covers makes him a kind of idealized figure of the reporter for the Black press. A writer unsatisfied with merely covering the string of injustices faced by African Americans under Jim Crow, he becomes an advocate for and even a partner with radical organizations seeking to challenge white supremacy in all its forms. Stories featuring reporter protagonists were not uncommon in the fiction published in the *Afro-American,* but Jiggs Bennett was by far the most recognizable. An investigative reporter with the instincts of a private investigator, Jiggs Bennett centers Black journalists and the

Black press as active and aggressive protagonists in service of racial justice. Rather than being merely a witness to or victim of Jim Crow—as many of his canonical counterparts would be—Bennett embodies a powerful utopian fantasy: that writers and readers of the Black press can effectively challenge white supremacist power structures. The figure of the journalist-protagonist allows for a potent synchronicity within the pages of the *Afro-American;* Jiggs's assignments find him engaging directly with current events that appeared in the paper's news coverage. This moves far beyond the near-future faux-news angle that opens William Thomas Smith's "The Black Stockings," discussed in chapter 3, and instead offers a kind of internal call and response within the newspaper itself. The stories featuring Bennett—some explicitly called mysteries—typically feature the reporter's direct involvement in Black radical causes and put him at odds with various agents of the white supremacist order, from local law enforcement up to the House Un-American Activities Committee.

Hill introduced Jiggs in the five-part 1947 serial "Mysterious Bullets" (July 12–August 9, 1947) in a plot suggested to Hill by *Afro-American* editor Carl Murphy.[21] This serial opens as the hard-boiled reporter interviews an African American inmate on death row. This prisoner, a World War II veteran, has been convicted of "destroying the driver, bus, and twenty-two all-white passengers" in a "Whitehound Bus" in North Carolina. He tells Jiggs, "I'm only a small part of an organization pledged to destroy jim crow *[sic]* on the Whitehound Bus Line, segregating colored people, or refusing them altogether, depending on the number of white passengers. . . . Meanwhile, quote me as saying 'Disaster will follow Whitehound Buses with every revolution of their wheels until they cease to be Jim Crow.'"[22] This organization turns out to be the aptly named Black Retribution, which figures prominently in a number of other Jiggs Bennett serials. The organization terrorizes the Whitehound Buses, which have "flout[ed] the Federal edict outlawing segregation in interstate bus travel," an "edict" that stems from the Supreme Court ruling in *Morgan v. Virginia,* issued the previous June, about a year before the publication of "Mysterious Bullets."[23] In October 1946, the *Afro-American* reported on a Virginia bus company that refused to comply with the court's ruling, and the paper continued to report on cases like this into 1947 and beyond.[24] "Mysterious Bullets" imagines a radical response to bus companies that refuse to comply with the law of the land: violent resistance that amounts to a form of terrorism, with men shooting out bus tires as they travel the highways. Rather than use snipers—easy to identify and convict—the Black Retribution's terror depends on a small contraption mounted on the underside of the buses by "colored maintenance crews," and these "Mysterious Bullets" of the title simply confound authorities.[25] After the destruction of a number of buses, including one ridden by the owner of the Whitehound, the hospitalized owner relents and integrates his buses. "Mysterious Bullets" thus sanctions radical and violent opposition to white supremacy and the organizations that maintain it through the perpetuation of Jim Crow practices, even in the face of Supreme Court decisions. While the actions of the members of the Black Retribution may seem extreme, Hill writes, "Jiggs Bennett would rather look through the eyes of justice than of man-made law and envision the men as crusaders who knew that the price of liberty came high."[26]

After his introduction in "Mysterious Bullets," Jiggs Bennett's adventures range widely. Many of the later Bennett serials follow a more traditional crime fiction formula. For example, in "Ghost of a Chance" (September 4–25, 1954), Jiggs helps exonerate a Black jazz musician wrongfully arrested for a murder committed by a young white debutante. Others, however, confront a variety of early Cold War–era politics, dramatizing the intersection of geopolitics and Jim Crow in surprising and powerful ways. "Death Dust" (January 10–February 14, 1948), Hill's follow-up to "Mysterious Bullets," is more ambitious in its scope and ominous in its violent potential. This serial begins with the investigation of strange happenings in the fictional town of Eldington, New Jersey: "Some colored doctor was removed from a property by means of a covenant, and after his eviction, signs appeared on the house and property bearing the words: 'For Bigots Only.'" These new white residents receive warnings from the Black Retribution—in the form of recordings of the National Anthem and the song "'Atom and Evil' by the Golden Gates"—and soon after "the whole family is dead—from causes unknown—and nothing will grow on the place—or even live." [27] As Jiggs Bennett investigates the story, he discovers that the doctor evicted from the property "did some work for the government at Oak Ridge during the war," but during his investigations, Jiggs is soon knocked out and kidnapped by

Colonel Edward Javery, a Southern military man "working with the Un-American Activities Committee, ferreting out subversive groups, and," he tells Jiggs, "your Black Retribution is one of those groups."[28] The stakes become clear when Javery tells Jiggs, "We know that those vicious blacks are dabbling in nuclear research. The death radiations are positively gamma," and his driver, George, worries, "I'd hate to think what would happen to white supremacy here in the States if those people could make atomic bombs."[29]

It turns out that Black Retribution already has atomic capability, thanks to Bartholomew Gale, the "nuclear necromancer" who was evicted from his property in Eldington.[30] The Black Retribution has been using "death dust"—essentially the radioactive residue from their atomic tests—to poison the property of those actively seeking to inhibit the progress of racial justice. A group of black-robed horsemen rescue Jiggs from Colonel Javery's Southern plantation, cover it with death dust, and encourage him to do a story on it: "Say that Black Retribution has sterilized another American Monument to Bigotry—Javery Manse."[31] Jiggs's laudatory editorial about the Black Retribution gets him served with a summons to appear before the House Un-American Activities Committee at the behest of Southern senator Bartow. In front of the committee, Jiggs refuses to name names of Black Retribution members, instead telling those present, "You are anxious to find the identity of a group patently fighting for our rights. But you have never sought the identity of the thousands of lynching mobs who strung my people to the nearest tree and shot and slashed, and burned them—dragged their horribly mangled bodies through colored neighborhoods."[32] Jiggs emerges from the Capitol a hero, with a crowd regaling him with a triumphant rendition of "Lift Every Voice and Sing." Opposing the song widely known as the Negro national anthem to the racist double standards of the House Un-American Activities Committee provides a powerful example of how Black pulp stories like "Death Dust" could perform radical critiques of Jim Crow America.

"Death Dust" began its serialization days before arguments in front of the U.S. Supreme Court began in the case of *Shelley v. Kraemer,* which would ultimately find racially restrictive housing covenants unconstitutional in its May 3, 1948, decision. The *Afro-American* announced this with an enormous headline above the masthead reading, "Restrictive Covenants Outlawed."[33] Coverage of the Supreme Court case ran parallel with "Death Dust," with the news coverage featured on the paper's front page, while Hill's serial, imagining militant solutions to the problem of covenants, appeared prominently on the back page of the newspaper's magazine section. As if to emphasize their connection, both news coverage and fiction were accompanied by large illustrations by Francis Yancey.[34] The plot for "Death Dust"—like that of "Mysterious Bullets"— was suggested to Hill by *Afro* editor Carl Murphy in a letter dated November 21, 1947: "Would you like to do a story in which a young physicist, who worked on the manufacture of atomic bombs in Federal plants during the war, is forced to leave his newly purchased home because of a restrictive covenant?"[35] Murphy and the *Afro* were covering the issue of restrictive covenants intensely in the run-up to the *Shelley v. Kramer* case, and his suggestion to Hill shows the editor's interest in having the *Afro-American*'s fiction enact specific cultural work around these issues.

However, Hill's use of a form of weaponized fallout is intriguing, as it comes at a time before the public was widely aware of the dangers of a waste by-product (sometimes called atom dust) of nuclear testing. The immediate violence of an atomic blast was well known after the end of World War II, but the public was far less aware of the long-term violence of fallout. "Death dust" would make sites like Javery Manse "sterile for a thousand years. Not even germs will be able to live on it," Gale says.[36] Pulp editor John W. Campbell wrote about death dust in 1941, and Black journalist Charles Loeb detailed radiation dangers at the end of the war. However, real danger of fallout only began to enter the American consciousness after the late 1948 publication of David Bradley's *No Place to Hide*.[37] Hill may have gathered some additional information about this subject from his role as a Congress of Industrial Organizations (CIO) organizer. He was based in Philadelphia and Baltimore, but the CIO-affiliated United Gas, Coke, and Chemical Workers won the right to represent the workers at Oak Ridge, Tennessee, in early December 1947, and these workers nearly went on strike before winning a new contract on December 11.[38] The CIO had been organizing these workers for over a year, so it is conceivable that Hill had received more detail on the dangers of radiation through his union contacts.[39] Regardless, the idea of deploying the most modern forms of atomic weapons technology against white supremacy makes "Death Dust" an early Cold War form of Afrofuturist fantasy. By suturing ripped-from-the-headlines topics like *Shelley v. Kraemer* with anxieties about atomic weapons, "Death Dust" demonstrates the powerful potential of genre fiction to address a myriad of contemporary concerns, with the reporter Jiggs Bennett highlighting the role of the Black press in serving as an advocate for racial justice on a national—and even international—scale. The serial also maps out two key themes that would inform the best of the remaining Bennett serials: the fight against Jim Crow and the possibilities nuclear weapons might offer in the fight against worldwide white supremacy.

In the follow-up to "Death Dust," "Crime Wounds All Heels" (October 23–November 13, 1948), Jiggs acknowledges the outcome of *Shelley v. Kraemer* case but also recognizes that housing segregation remains the de facto condition across the South and that the threat of racial violence is ever present for African Americans. Here he travels to the small town of Simpkins, Georgia, where "scarcely more than 300 colored folk . . . live in a little sandy, run-down area called Sow-Belly Turn."[40] Jiggs arrives in town because the whites of Simpkins have lynched a World War II veteran who attempted to register to vote. The narrative hinges on a crucial misidentification early in the story. On the train south, Jiggs's coat and hat are stolen, and upon the train's arrival, the white locals—warned of the arrival of the famous African American activist reporter—kill a man at the station wearing clothes identified as those of Jiggs Bennett. The Black Retribution is on hand as well. When the Klan attempts to deposit what they think is the body of Jiggs Bennett on a doorstep in Sow-Belly Turn, they meet an empty town filled with booby traps, including fragmentation bombs and land mines that kill and maim the Klansmen. As the head of the Black Retribution puts it, "We've a long battle ahead before American whites will concede basic civil rights to their black brethren, Mr. Bennett. . . . But I'm sure prayer won't bring them around to it. Blood-letting is the only language they understand."[41] Once again, Jiggs discovers a Southern politician ("the candidate taking the President's place on the Party ticket—a Dixiecrat") is behind his attempted assassination. Jiggs, presumed dead, engineers a plan to "haunt" him from beyond the grave, and the terrified congressman leaps to his death from a twentieth-floor window.[42]

Bennett's concerns reach a more global level in two later serials, "Project W" (December 30, 1950–January 27, 1951) and "Big, Bad Boer" (January 23–February 13, 1954), both of which deal more explicitly with Cold War concerns. In "Project W," Jiggs finds himself working with the FBI after he accidentally comes in possession of Soviet plans to attack the United States. Here a communist front organization called the League of United Americans has hatched a plan to exploit racial tensions in the United States by "capitalizing on police brutality. First, the race-riots; then the A-bombs."[43] In its anticommunist focus, "Project W" suggests a wariness toward international efforts to exploit racism in the United States, suggesting that nationalism takes precedence in spite of Jim Crow. However, "Big, Bad Boer" returns the Jiggs Bennett series to a focus on global white supremacy and anticolonialism. In this serial, Jiggs, initially held hostage in his suburban home by a group of Boer spies, is drawn into intrigue over the ongoing colonial struggles in Kenya. The story hinges on the death of an exchange student from Liberia, a physics major who intended to share plans for an atomic weapon with the Mau Mau to assist their independence efforts. The serial's conclusion has the FBI apprehend Eritra Van Kaarlen, the leader of the Boer kidnappers, with Jiggs promising, "One day soon you'll be seeing a mushroom cloud rise from Kenya. The big, bad Boers will have to start another trek."[44] Here Jiggs once again sees violence—and the promise of the atomic age—as a potential deterrent against the global rule of colonial violence and white supremacy.

Throughout Jiggs's adventures, there is one other constant presence that links these stories to the romance fiction discussed in chapter 2: his white wife, Mae Bancroft. Mae appears at the outset of the series as the daughter of the segregationist owner of the Whitehound Bus Lines. Mae's sympathies, however, reside with Jiggs's efforts toward racial justice, and she soon falls deeply in love with him. Jiggs and Mae have an even longer history, as Jiggs's backstory notes that he had "grown up on the Bancroft truck farm near Columbia," and that "soon after he was twelve, his mother told him the score about racial equality and urged him to avoid Mae if he wanted to become an adult male."[45] However, after meeting again after many years, their romance develops as Jiggs investigates her father's bus company and the terrorist work of the Black Retribution. In the fourth installment—entitled merely "A New

Jiggs Bennett Detective Story" (April 2–3, 1949)—they get married after Jiggs helps Mae's father—now a reformed segregationist—out of a blackmail scheme. This prominent romantic subplot of the series generates much of the drama of the later serials, as Mae is routinely threatened or kidnapped and held for ransom by members of the Klan or other racist organizations. But Mae—like Jacques Lenglet's wife, Carla—takes an active role as well, donning a gas mask and returning fire on armed intruders in "Shoot Off Your Face" (July 22–August 5, 1950), a tale about racial discrimination, corruption, and murder in the Non-Ferrous Workers Union. By placing this interracial relationship at the center of the Jiggs Bennett series, Hill highlights the radical political component of interracial love in the 1940s and 1950s while hearkening back to the 1930s interracial romance stories in the *Afro-American* that also imagined utopian outcomes to these encounters typically rendered in the tragic mode in contemporaneous canonical fiction like Chester Himes's *If He Hollers Let Him Go* (1945) or Ann Petry's *The Narrows* (1953).

James H. Hill's heroic figures often resort to or endorse violence in their efforts to challenge racial injustice. It is important to remember that Martin Luther King Jr.'s entry into the national consciousness with the nonviolent 1955 Montgomery bus boycott was yet to happen. But it is also essential to note that the hero pulps of 1930s, and even the early superhero comics, showed no squeamishness about the use of violence. Indeed, retributive justice was built into many genres that features serial heroes, like adventures stories, crime fiction, and aviation fiction. The pulps of the 1930s and 1940s often featured extraordinary violence against people of color. Asians were frequently the target of early pulp science fiction, and pulp horror depended on racial otherness as a key ideological trope of its generic formula. Hill's serials were, if anything, signifying on the violence of these genres, presenting the repetitive pleasures of (violent) genres, but with, as Gates says, "a signal difference." In this case, that difference involved turning the violence of white supremacist generic formulas against the very structures and institutions of white supremacy. Whether Jacques Lenglet was firing a machine gun into a lynch mob or Jiggs Bennett was protecting members of a revolutionary group using terror to end Jim Crow, Hill was engaged in actively repurposing the familiar modes of generic pleasure in service of racial justice.

Every now and then Steiner would cry: "Ain't we got to Doc Hooker's yet?"

But Jiggs was preoccupied with still another thought now. What had happened to Eddie Bowden? Had Trask's men visited him tonight to find out about the expose

Frances Yancey[?], illustration for James H. Hill, "Shoot Off Your Face, Part 3," *Baltimore Afro-American,* August 5, 1950. Courtesy of the AFRO Newspaper Archives.

"HIS ADVENTURES MAY BE EXTENDED EVEN TO YOUR OWN COMMUNITY": H. L. FAGGETT'S BLACK ROBIN

While Hill's serials feature hard-hitting action, using themes that intersected directly with national and international news and starring increasingly hard-boiled protagonists, not all hero fiction published in the *Afro-American* operated in quite this way. Serials featuring Jacques Lenglet and especially those featuring Jiggs Bennett frequently received large illustrations and stylized titling; installments often took up a full page or more in the *Afro*'s magazine section. But another series character actually appeared more often than either of Hill's Black heroes, even if he was not granted quite the same amount of space. H. L. Faggett's John Robin, known as Black Robin, appeared in thirty-five short adventures between February 1949 and July 1953. Harry Lee Faggett himself was a fascinating figure; in 1947, two years before he began the "Black Robin" series, he completed his Ph.D. in English at Boston University, with a dissertation entitled "Attitudes Toward Foreigners Reflected in Elizabethan Drama." He published other work on writing instruction and Shakespeare, taught at a number of universities, and coedited the 1950 volume *Best Short Stories of* Afro-American *Writers* with fellow scholar Nick Aaron Ford.[46] This volume contained a couple of Faggett's own non–"Black Robin" contributions to the *Afro,* and his fiction in the newspaper ranged widely enough to include "Operations U.S.A." (March 4, 1950), a postapocalyptic story of nuclear disaster framed (like William Thomas Smith's "The Black Stockings") as a news story. Six years before his death in 2000, Faggett collected a number of the "Black Robin" tales (and other short fiction) in a volume published by Adams Press, a venue for self-publishing. This unassuming volume attracted no attention at the time of its appearance, and Faggett's name has been all but lost to scholars and historians despite his fascinating role as a midcentury Black scholar of early modern British literature and a writer and editor of popular Black newspaper fiction.

Faggett's "Black Robin" stories differed from Hill's hard-boiled serials in ways that highlight some of the possible variations within Black hero fiction in the *Afro.* Unlike Hill's serials, which ran anywhere from two long installments to five medium-length installments, Faggett's "Black Robin" stories were brief, single-shot adventures, designed to be consumed in one short sitting. They received smaller illustrations—sometimes none at all—and typically only occupied a half page in the newspaper's magazine section, while the other half of the page featured the newspaper's astrology column ("The Stars and You"), the "Lonesome Hearts" column, and/or "Looking for Someone," a missing persons column devoted to reuniting friends who had lost touch. Because of this, the "Black Robin" stories were more deeply embedded in the newspaper's interactive lifestyle content. Further, while Hill's stories sought to insert characters like Lenglet and Bennett into national and international headlines, the "Black Robin" series attested to the way that Black newspaper fiction spoke expressly to the local as well as the global. Featuring a witty vernacular narrator, and (initially, at least) with less emphasis on violence—early on, Robin claims, "I never wanted even a dog's death on my conscience"[47]—the "Black Robin" stories chronicle the adventures of John Robin, a crusader (and football star) who travels the South disguised as the chauffeur for "Mr. David Cargel, young millionaire-owner of the Brooklyn Bears, professional football team." Cargel has gone undercover to infiltrate the KKK "for his Dad's New York newspaper," once again foregrounding the role of the press in exposing and combatting the injustices of Jim Crow, though in this case it is the Northern white press that assumes this responsibility.[48] The focus of the series is not on this undercover white reporter, however, but on the undercover Black hero, masquerading as a chauffeur. Cargel ultimately takes on a sidekick role as the Black Robin takes center stage, traveling across the South in search of local injustices. In these stories, he encounters racial profiling by police, intimidation of Black landowners by the Klan, the abuse of African Americans in a Southern prison camp, and the sexual exploitation of Black women, among a host of other examples of racial injustice.

With a local and topical focus on small Southern towns, the "Black Robin" stories sought to connect directly with the readership of the *Afro-American,* which was distributed in multiple editions nationally and had a significant readership throughout the South. If the Lenglet and Bennett serials sought to highlight the agency of Black protagonists in national and global narratives, then the "Black Robin" reminded the *Afro*'s many small-town readers that their stories of the local experience of Jim Crow mattered and remained connected to larger struggles of racial justice. The placement of the "Black Robin" serials, alongside interactive lifestyle content that solicited readers' letters, reinforced this. In fact, during some of its run, the stories featured an inset announcement that both characterized the nature of the stories and presented them as possible solutions to real-life injustices: "Tan, terrific, and handsome John Robin, through his efforts to help his persecuted brothers, earns for himself the rather sinister title, BLACK ROBIN. To any victims of racial prejudice— John Robin may be contacted through the AFRO. He loves to travel, and his adventures may be extended even to your own community. Send information on 'New Ideas for the BLACK ROBIN,' in care of AFRO MAGAZINE, Baltimore 1, Md."[49] Here the newspaper's editors cannily anticipate the late twentieth-century theories of popular culture and fiction narrative that characterizes such narratives as "the imaginary resolution of a real contradiction," in the words of Fredric Jameson.[50] Elsewhere, Jameson accords popular culture a "utopian" dimension for precisely the same reason: It offers utopian solutions to the contradictions of the present, representing "our deepest fantasies about the nature of social life, both as we life it now, and as we feel in our bones it ought rather to be lived."[51] It can be difficult to find such utopian dimensions in the canon of African American literature, where the default mode of racial realism and the racial protocols of elite African American literature tend toward tragedy of one form or another. But in the "Black Robin" stories, the editors blur the boundaries between fiction and reality, encouraging readers to mail in story ideas based on the specific instances of racial prejudice "even [in] your own community," as if "Black Robin"'s narratives are journalism rather than fiction. As a result, Black Robin appears as a fictional hero responding directly to the concerns expressed by *Afro* readers, and Faggett's stories serve both to highlight the injustices of white supremacy across small towns in the South and to imagine the hero that the American South needs in the midst of Jim Crow.[52]

The sexual politics of Jim Crow represent one of the main currents that runs throughout Faggett's "Black Robin" series. Robin himself is a pretty serious playboy, and readers find him in the arms of a new girlfriend in essentially every story in the series—even those that fall in sequential issues of the newspaper. But while Robin's identity as a crimefighting lothario is central to his characterization, the series also demonstrates—via a wide variety of examples—a concern with the safety of Black women from sexual exploitation under a social order that trafficked in double standards about Black sexuality. Here the specter of inter-racial sexuality is not the utopian ideal it could be in the romance stories discussed in chapter 2. Instead, the realities of Jim Crow in the South mean that power dynamics put Black women in positions of extreme vulnerability, to be then easily exploited by powerful white men in any number of ways.

This first appears in "Dixie Masquerade" (July 9, 1949), one of the earliest and most intriguing of the "Black Robin" stories. This story opens with Robin's paean to the beauty of "the creole babes around Biloxi," but his local love interest, Antoinette, soon informs him that "it isn't safe for colored girls to walk the streets alone at night" because they are apt to be picked up (willingly or unwillingly) by prominent white men cruising around this small gulf town. In no uncertain terms, Robin illustrates the essential core of Jim Crow sexual politics in his characteristic vernacular: "Seems as if the Hoogies don't want any half-white babies unless they work the deal themselves."[53] Robin soon comes up with a "trick play" to punish the most egregious offender among the "Hoogies," the slang term Robin uses for these white racists across Faggett's stories.[54] They set the trap when Antoinette and her "new girl friend," Jane, go out as bait to attract "Moneybags," the worst offender in this small town. Of "Husky Jane," Robin notes, "I thought the new chick was right cute, too. She was a bit on the husky side, shoulders pretty wide like a football player's." The story develops in an intentionally confused and confusing third-to-first-person narration before Robin admits the obvious: He dressed in drag in order enact just vengeance on "Moneybags." When he and Antoinette are picked up and driven to a secluded spot by Moneybags and his friend, Jake, Robin gives them a sound beating before leaving them in the woods, driving their car back to Moneybags's house to leave a note for his wife: "PLEASE MAKE JAKE AND YOUR SPORTY OLD HUSBAND LEAVE US COLORED GIRLS ALONE."[55]

Stories like "Dixie Masquerade" feature some of the humor that characterizes the earliest installments of the "Black Robin" series. In contrast to the hard-boiled, serious tone of James Hill's work, Faggett's emphasis on first-person vernacular narration combines with occasionally comic resolutions to offer a different form of vicarious pleasure in the stories' challenge to white supremacy. Here solutions need not be tied to the development of atomic weapons or the organization of a nationwide resistance movement; instead, they can feature in the humorous come-uppance experienced by ignorant and incompetent racists. Without a doubt, "Dixie Masquerade" includes humor based on dated norms around gender and sexuality, and Robin's drag performance is supposed to elicit a laugh from Faggett's 1949 readers. But the (comic) pleasure of this queer performance is secondary to the comic retribution wrought on the two white men, whose lust for Black women's bodies is so intense that it initially blinds them to any sign of gender difference, even if Husky Jane's shoulders are obviously "wide like a football player's." The narration tantalizes with a queer backseat encounter that anticipates a famous (and famously homophobic) scene in Neil Jordan's 1992 film *The Crying Game:* "From her purse, the hefty one slipped a little black, heavy object, while in the dark the sporty Hoogie used his hands to get very, very chummy. Before he could speak his surprise at what he had found with his fumblin[g] fingers—the old Red Riding Hood line, I suppose, 'Oh Grandma, what large muscles you have'—the roof fell on him."[56] Faggett's slow reveal of detail here makes it easy for *Afro* readers to imagine that this "sporty Hoogie" has found something even more surprising than "large muscles" with his "fumbling fingers" before he is blackjacked by Robin.

The "Black Robin" series began in late February 1949 and included eighteen adventures in that year; by the second half of 1949, Robin's preference for comic humiliation over lethal violence as a solution to the problems of Jim Crow had started to weaken. In early 1950, he returned to the issues of sexual politics in two more stories, "We Got Justice" (January 7, 1950) and "Robin Sets Fire to a Hunting Lodge" (February 4, 1950). In "We Got Justice," Robin stakes out a prostitution ring in a small town in South Georgia. He first shoots the tires of the taxicabs that are bringing white men around; then he lures and beats up the African American pimp who has been hustling the young Black women for the white clientele. Robin deposits the unconscious pimp at the front door of the local newspaper, once again with an incriminating sign, this one reading "PUT ME AND THE Y———— TAXI CO. IN JAIL FOR SELLING COLORED WOMEN TO WHITE MEN."[57] The resolution here reads as far more serious than comic in its form of justice.

"Robin Sets Fire to a Hunting Lodge" highlights a similar form of sexual exploitation in terms that are considerably more violent. This installment opens with young Mae Parker telling Robin and Dave about her traumatic experience. Engaged as a domestic worker for what she believed would be "a regular social affair" organized by one Mr. Bradley, Mae is taken to a hunting lodge, where a group of white men ply her with alcohol and rape her.[58] In this Southern community, the courts are no help to Mae; as she tells Robin, "It was my word against that of three rich, white men. I had to admit going out there of my own free will; admit accepting drinks." Robin's girlfriend in this story, also present as Mae tells describes this crime, highlights how common this problem is: "This thing could have happened to any colored girl in town. Many of our best families allow their daughters to earn money by catering or serving parties." After Dave discovers when the men will be at the lodge again, Robin's plan goes into action. This time, the influential men have brought a number of young white women with them for what amounts to an orgy. After they all retire, Robin sets fire to the lodge, throwing rocks through the windows to ensure that everyone gets out before the structure burns to the ground. "Wearing practically nothing but their birthday suits," the group runs out into the cold night to find their gas tanks empty and their tires slashed. Robin speeds away with Dave, thinking about poetic justice: "Maybe they could keep each other warm—interesting sight, cuddled up close when their wives and newspaper photographers arrived on the scene. Oh, what a rescue! My boss David would lead the pack. Maybe I would drive him back there! I liked the idea."

As these stories of sexual exploitation demonstrate, the intensification of Black Robin's adventures moves the series away from its early comedy toward more combative and direct confrontations with the social order of Jim Crow. "Dixie Masquerade" offers a comic comeuppance to white men cruising for sex with Black women, "We Got Justice" tackles the economic exploitation of Black women's sexuality, and "Robin Sets Fire to a Hunting Lodge" exposes the unprosecuted gang rape of a young Black woman by white men who believe that Jim Crow law allows them to commit such acts with impunity. Each of these stories moves more deeply into the structural problems that allow threats to Black women to flourish in the Jim Crow south. Robin's response, too, becomes more intense. While a humiliating beating seems sufficient at the outset of these stories, by the time he seeks vengeance for Mae Parker's rape, he briefly fantasizes about a larger explosion that might kill them as they try to escape. No longer does Robin seem to ascribe to his early claim that "I never wanted even a dog's death on my conscience"; as the series explores more violent forms of structural injustice, Robin's solutions themselves become more radical.

This transformation appears in stories that tackle other topics as well. Another early story, "Black Robin in the Land of Lost Souls" (May 7, 1949), finds Robin investigating brutal conditions as a Georgia prison labor camp, where guards have killed nine Black inmates. Robin sneaks into the prison, drugs the guards' "corn liquor," and helps the remaining inmates escape.[59] Presented with an opportunity to kill the guards responsible, Robin simply cannot pull the trigger; instead, he hopes that the humiliation of the mass prison escape will mean that "the guards would have a hard time, now, proving they weren't just as drunk when they did the shooting. Perhaps they would even lose their jobs because nine colored men lost their lives." The mere possibility of the loss of a job seems a woefully small price to pay for the murders of nine inmates. In later stories, however, Robin's action is more direct and focused on structural and organizational injustices. In "Station KKK Signs Off" (January 28, 1950), Robin disrupts a Klan meeting in Atlanta. Working with the "colored janitor" of the hotel that is hosting the meeting, and the national radio broadcast that goes with it, Robin rigs up a remote microphone to interrupt the broadcast, cutting in with the words, "You're no American you d——— dirty rat! You're worse than Stalin or Hitler or any of the others, but you're not as big! You're not as good as the colored people and Jews you persecute! You're all sons of the tramps they shipped out of England years ago!"[60] Robin then threatens them with imminent destruction, giving them thirty seconds to clear the building, while the janitor, Jimson, sets off fireworks inside the hotel, resulting in a mad rush to the exit. In this installment, Robin understands the necessity for combating the message of violent racism and removing the voice of the Klan from the airwaves.

In other late stories, however, Robin encounters a vigilante group that works explicitly (and violently) to avenge the wrongs of the Klan and other racists. This group, known as the Men of Mystery, appears in a few of Faggett's later "Black Robin" stories, and it resembles both Schuyler's "Merciless Avengers" (from "Georgia Terror") and Hill's "Black Retribution" (from the Jiggs Bennett serials). The Men of Mystery first appear in "Alabama Bus Ride" (May 6, 1950), a story that features grue-some violence that far exceeds the comic justice from earlier stories. It opens with Robin and Dolly Oldham, a minister's daughter, stuck on a rural Alabama roadside with car trouble. After hitching a ride into a small town, they board a bus to get her home. There they watch as an African American "GI wearing the uniform of the U.S. Infantry" attempts to take a seat near the front of the bus, which upsets a white woman sitting nearby.[61] The driver grabs a pistol, chases the soldier off the bus, and murders him just outside the vehicle, within earshot of the wait-ing passengers. Expecting "Dolly's preacher daddy" to be upset with them for arriving so late, Robin discovers that her father shows far more interest in the murder and ultimately makes Robin an offer: "You have earned the right to become a regular member of the Grand Order of the Double M—the MEN OF MYSTERY. Vengeance is our purpose: to fight the KKK and the false doctrine of white supremacy. The old law of Moses is our creed: 'An eye for an eye and a . . . !'" Reverend Oldham details the international connections of the Men of Mystery and explains that the group has been responsible for some of the mysterious deaths that occurred in earlier "Black Robin" stories; they have been working in the background all along, it seems.[62] Robin helps capture the murderous bus driver, and the Men of Mystery take him on a helicopter to "a specially camouflaged field" in the Everglades. The story concludes, however, with Robin's deep ambivalence about the gruesome torture ritual he witnesses. First the guilty bus driver is blinded with "a red-hot steel rod," followed by "castration and life-at-labor in the mines of the MEN OF MYSTERY."

It is possible that this turn toward violence in the later "Black Robin" stories represents a response to reader demand or the influence of James Hill's hard-boiled Jiggs Bennett stories, which during 1950 appeared in issues between runs of "Black Robin" adventures. Regard-less, the presence of lethal violence offered new possibilities for just nar-rative resolution, but it also generated some self-conscious ambivalence about method in a manner similar to that of Carl Slater in Schuyler's "Black Empire" serials. In "Bombs in Alabama" (October 14, 1950), for example, Robin has little reservation about setting a trap for a group of racists that has firebombed a Black family living in a white neighbor-hood. Here he detonates radio-controlled bombs planted under the cars of the bombers, killing them all. "Just a Lost Victory" (July 19, 1952), one of the last "Black Robin" stories, published nearly two years later, sees Robin's relationship with the Men of Mystery falling apart. The intriguing title of this story evokes the problematic notions of justice and victory, and its content and lack of satisfying resolution run counter to the series' conventions. It opens with Robin on the run, with a surprising romantic companion: Audrey, a white girl who has been condemned to death by the Men of Mystery. Audrey's father has already been executed "for causing the death of two innocent, unoffending colored people," and the Men of Mystery have insisted that Robin bring Audrey back to be executed herself for knowing "information that can destroy our entire organization."[63] But Robin has fallen for Audrey: "A native of Louisiana, she had been an exchange student at my old CIAA Alma Mater; she had learned not to hate colored people there." Eventually they hole up in a cabin in the North Carolina mountains, pursued not only by the Men of Mystery but also by the FBI and a lynch mob. Robin's split allegiance generates some intensive self-reflection as he considers using force to defend Audrey's life: "To shoot down the men I'd sworn to work with—my own color—for a woman not of my race. My mind was a murky whirlpool with a gear for reverse spin. But I couldn't let 'em destroy that lovely creature who loved me—who was mine if half the things in this crazy world had ever been right." At the story's conclusion, however, Robin does not have to choose between these two allegiances; Audrey kills herself as the Men of Mystery close in. In a darkly ironic turn, the story's final words reveal that the head of the Double M might have let Audrey go, one of the Men of Mystery tells Robin, "if he'd known you were stuck on her."

While "Just a Lost Victory" is not the final installment of the "Black Robin" series—there would be two more to follow in the next year—its striking change in tone and focus suggests a conclusion of sorts.[64] With Robin completely broken after reading his white lover's suicide note, Faggett draws together a number of threads that appear throughout the literature discussed in *Black Pulp*. The power of education to make antiracists out of young Southerners echoes stories like "Red Love" (discussed in chapter 2) and the character of Mae Bancroft in Hill's Jiggs Bennett stories, while the Audrey's self-sacrifice resembles the devotion of Martha Gaskin of Schuyler's "Black Empire" serials. Appearing in 1952, "Just a Lost Victory" evokes the utopian fantasy of interracial romance—in that remote mountain cabin, far from society—but also crushes this dream with its concerns about the codes and conventions of Black collective action. The final two stories in the series would return to familiar formulas—one with a violent resolution, the other with a comic one—but "Just a Lost Victory" haunts the end of the series with something approaching an autocritique of the utopian fantasies of hero fiction, especially under the specter of Jim Crow. Although like all the "Black Robin" tales it is much shorter and simpler than many of the other tales discussed in *Black Pulp*, its "murky whirlpool"—the paradoxes of formula fiction, the contradictory intersections of different forms of narrative pleasure—lays bare some of the limitations and challenges faced by Black newspaper fiction and its authors in the middle of the twentieth century.

Forty years after the "Black Robin" series ended in 1953, Faggett collected thirteen of these stories, along with some of his other newspaper fiction, in a self-published volume, which appeared in 1994. In it, he suggested that the end of "Black Robin'"s run was due to readers' taking the character's exploits too seriously: "When black magazine editors were moved to print a number of readers' requests for Robin to intercede in cases of white folks' persecution of blacks, in several communities of the Southland, it was that time for Robin to exit—to disappear!"[65] Faggett's memory may have been a little hazy in this "Preface" (because the *Afro* explicitly solicited readers ideas early on), but the notion that the "Black Robin'"s adventures had struck too close to the realities of the racial injustices of the Jim Crow South merely demonstrates how successful Faggett's approach was, and how much it resonated with readers in search of the utopian catharsis of genre fiction. This 1994 publication was used as a fund raiser for Faggett's church. In the volume's preface, Mattie Ragin, the president of the Episcopal Church Women of St. Paul's, expressed an interesting hope: "There is the possibility (remote, of course) that a Mr. Spike Lee will notice our Black Robin Hood and want to make it into a TV series to match the million-dollar 'single' he made of the Malcolm X story."[66] Ragin's positioning of the "Black Robin" stories in the broader history of African American cultural production is canny, even prophetic. The through line extends not only from Faggett's Black pulp series to the prestige picture *Malcolm X* (1992) but also to Spike Lee's 2018 foray into antiracist pulp action, *BlacKkKlansman,* which combines the comic humiliation of what Robin would certainly call "Hoogies" with an exploration of justice and violence in an interracial buddy narrative that profoundly echoes the adventures of Black Robin and David Cargel, who would himself go undercover with the Klan during the "Black Robin" series.

While the fictional comeuppance of racists and white supremacists in these stories remains (in part, at least) in the realm of fantasy, the value of such pleasures should not be underestimated. During this period, the stories by James Hill and H. L. Faggett would have had a readership of over 120,000 nationwide, not including a considerable pass-along rate.[67] These stories also allow us to consider the ways in which serial heroes could serve as a cultural counterweight to the serial crimes of racial injustice. In a host of ways, they offer structural alternatives to the generic formulas of pulp magazines that routinely celebrated the triumph of white manhood over people of color. They also present pleasurable, utopian alternatives to the African American protest novel and to characters like Bigger Thomas, Bob Jones, and the nameless narrator of *Invisible Man,* who are more akin to objects shaped by white supremacy than they are subjects presenting a challenge to it, however fantastical that challenge might be. Whether in the guise of globe-trotting and cosmopolitan Jacques Lenglet, turning his machine gun on a horde of racist savages in the American South, hard-boiled Jiggs Bennett protecting and aiding groups seeking the end of Jim Crow by any means necessary, or the crafty Black Robin answering the call of injustices in individual communities, these serials expose the ideological workings of popular genre by engaging in a radical revision of the genres themselves, offering a version of Black hero fiction rich with revolutionary potential and the pleasures of genre for Black readers living under the violent shadow of Jim Crow.

Heroism in this Black pulp fiction was, however, not purely speculative in nature. If the characters described here imagined new ways of confronting racial injustice in the mid-twentieth century, other stories and serials published in the waning days of prominent Black newspaper fiction sought powerful ways of reinterpreting the African American past through the lens of historical heroes. This intersection of race, history, and genre translates the concerns of characters like Lenglet, Bennett, and Robin onto a powerful need to reimagine the Black past as a place filled with heroes as well as trauma, with powerful models of resistance as well as with the violent legacy of slavery. In this respect, these formulas offer new ways of conceptualizing African American history that can affect our own understanding of its literary counterpart.

CONCLUSION
WRITING NEW HISTORIES

THE FATE OF AFRICAN AMERICAN NEWSPAPER FICTION was to end—like the pulp magazines with which it was in constant dialogue—with a whimper rather than a bang. The first of the two major newspapers to reduce, then eventually eliminate, fiction was the *Pittsburgh Courier.* George Schuyler had served a one-man fiction-writing machine for the *Courier,* publishing a story or serial installment (sometimes both) in virtually every issue of the newspaper from March 25, 1933, through July 22, 1939. As Schuyler moved away from his popular fiction, some effort was made to attract other writers. In the late 1930s, the short-lived, irregularly published, and usually undated trade publication the *Negro Writer* printed a letter from Schuyler soliciting fiction for the *Courier* in an article highlighting markets for African American writers, but Schuyler's search for a successor would be unfruitful, and the *Courier* phased out regularly featured fictional content during World War II.[1] The *Baltimore Afro-American* published genre fiction well into the 1950s, bolstered by its larger stable of regular writers and the presence of prolific contributors like James H. Hill, who began publishing in the *Afro* in earnest in 1939, as Schuyler was leaving fiction behind and the *Courier* was phasing it out. After 1955, however, the fiction appearing in the *Afro* consisted almost entirely of reprints that had previously appeared in the newspaper and in the *Best Short Stories by* Afro-American *Writers* collection, published in 1950. In this respect, too, these newspapers tracked alongside the vagaries of the pulp magazine marketplace, with the *Courier* abandoning fiction in the wake of World War II paper rationing, many smaller independent pulp magazines failing, the *Afro-American* shifting away from fiction in the early 1950s, and the pulps finally succumbing to competition from comic books, television, and new paperback original novels—the latter a phenomenon that emerged in 1952 and eventually spawned publishers like Holloway House. Simultaneously, new venues for African American writing—often with more serious literary ambitions—began appearing regularly from the 1940s on.[2] Even as they phased out fictional content, both the *Courier* and the *Afro* continued to feature fascinating comic strips that took up many of the new generic formulas that developed in their popular fiction of the 1930s and 1940s.[3] During this time, the *Chicago Defender* published fiction irregularly, but it soon shifted toward publishing the work of more canonical figures (Langston Hughes's Simple stories, beginning in 1943) or second serializations of work by broadly popular white writers (like Erle Stanley Gardner).[4]

The *Afro-American* also did something rather curious in the later years of its foray into the publication of popular fiction: It began featuring more content by white writers. As early as 1936, the *Afro* had published fiction by Len Zinberg, a Jewish American leftist married to African American writer Esther Zinberg, who also wrote fiction for the *Afro* and other publications.[5] Len Zinberg published routinely in leftist publications, but he also wrote genre fiction, much of it featuring African American protagonists. He wrote first for the *Afro-American* and later in mass-market paperback novels under the pseudonym Ed Lacy, a name he also began using in the *Afro* beginning in 1940. His work as Lacy was quite popular, and his 1957 novel *Room to Swing* has a solid reputation as a midcentury hard-boiled novel with a strong and complex African American detective protagonist. But antiracist activist Zinberg was not alone. Longtime pulp writers like Richard Hill Wilkinson started appearing in the *Afro* in 1950, likely because so many pulp magazines had failed and the markets for pulp writers had simply disappeared. Wilkinson's work was more conventional genre fare, and without Zinberg's political and antiracist commitments, it paid little attention to the complex politics of race and genre that had developed in newspaper over the previous two decades. The regular presence of writers like Wilkinson in the early 1950s signaled, in effect, that Black pulp, with its social and political commitments and its radical revision of popular genre, was migrating away from newspapers to other publishing contexts. The end of this history of Black pulp, though, manifested a strong element of self-consciousness; its attention to its own history and to the history of African America represented a defining shift in the final years of Black pulp. Before the late 1940s, the genre fiction published in the *Illustrated Feature Section,* the *Pittsburgh Courier,* and the *Baltimore Afro-American* exhibited little historical sensibility. Indeed, the stories and serials published throughout the 1930s and 1940s exhibited a kind of urgent presentism, with a laser-like focus on contemporary conditions. To the extent that a story might reach back into the past, this past was— as in the early Jacques Lenglet stories, set in World War I—only about twenty years old. The legacy of a deeper past might loom large in the lives of characters, but the writers of Black pulp simply did not turn their attention to the depiction of historical scenes. Possible reasons for this are many. Newspaper editors may have preferred material that intersected more clearly with news coverage; writers and editors might have sought to avoid stories depicting the lives of enslaved African Americans; or the readership may have been more consistently interested in fiction that imagined solutions to the problems of contemporary life, rather than stories that rehearsed historical tragedies that were more likely to appear in canonical fiction.

While the writers of Black pulp chose to avoid explicit attention to history, other newspaper features embraced history wholeheartedly. Prominent among these is the work of J. A. Rogers, a crucial figure in Black popular history.[6] Rogers is reasonably well known among scholars for his many books that sought to correct the record of white supremacist history, but these volumes were often published by small presses with limited distribution. Many more African American readers likely encountered his work in the newspapers, published alongside this radical genre fiction. By the late 1920s, Rogers had already made a name for himself with publications like his novel of ideas *From "Superman" to Man* and historical articles in small-circulation intellectual journals like *Opportunity* and the *Messenger.* But as these venues disappeared or shifted focus, he too moved to the newspapers as a central venue for his own work. Two months into the life of the *Illustrated Feature Section,* Rogers contributed

"Dessalines the Terrible" ("The Dramatic Story of the Black Slave Who Rose to Be Emperor," January 19, 1929), and he continued to publish historical sketches through the end of the *IFS,* with his articles sometimes illustrated in a fashion similar to the fiction or, more often, appearing on the same page as a serial installment. After the failure of the *IFS,* Rogers continued to submit historical articles on a regular basis to the *Afro-American,* often alternating these with his reports from Europe. In late 1934, he started to produce "Your History" for the *Pittsburgh Courier.* Modeled in size and shape on the syndicated panel *Ripley's Believe It or Not* (begun in 1918), "Your History" distilled Rogers's lessons into a sharply focused and strikingly illustrated panel designed to popularize Black history among the many African American readers of the *Courier.* This popular feature ran from 1934 through Rogers's death in 1966. Rogers's regular contributions ensured that the legacy of Black history remained part of the content of these newspapers, even if the fiction presented in them retained a focus on the present and future. However, in the late 1940s, a couple of the regular *Afro* fiction writers suddenly turned attention to narrativizing and fictionalizing the exploits of both historical figures and fictional protagonists placed in real historical settings. In bringing the radical concerns of racial justice to their historical fiction, Elizabeth O. Hood and James H. Hill offered a powerful revision to historical narratives that emphasized trauma and tragedy. In its place, they offered stories of revolutionary agency, tales in which their Black protagonists could maintain dignity while offering challenges to white supremacist structures.

This late historical turn in Black newspaper fiction emerged in the summer of 1948 alongside a second critical—and biographically oriented—intervention in popular African American history. On Sunday, June 27, 1948, Richard Durham's weekly radio program *Destination Freedom* began its two-year run.[7] This program, featured on Chicago's WMAQ radio station, broadcast short historical sketches of prominent African American figures across American (and world) history, from Crispus Attucks to Joe Louis. These ninety-one dramatized historical radio plays, penned by Durham, featured African American voice actors—a radical move in radio at the time—and the series was briefly sponsored by the

Chicago Defender.[8] While *Destination Freedom* represents a watershed moment in African American radio, its initial reach was limited to the broadcast area of WMAQ, and its Sunday morning airtime was, in the words of one critic "a virtual graveyard for any dramatic programming."[9] Its legacy, however, remains important. Ryan Ellet, writing when the Library of Congress added Durham's work to the National Recording Registry in 2015, notes that *Destination Freedom,* "ironically, may have reached a wider audience in the last 35 years than it did while on the air thanks to the discovery of a large stash of the program's transcription discs found in the early 1980s."[10]

At virtually the same time that Durham began his now widely revered radio program, the *Baltimore Afro-American* started featuring its own historical fiction; among the first publications in this cycle was Elizabeth O. Hood's Black feminist retelling of global history, the series Sultry Sirens: Tan Beauties Who Changed Destinies of Nations. Sultry Sirens represents a conceptual and stylistic bridge between Rogers's histories and the historical fiction of James Hill, which appeared alongside Hood's series and ran for a few years after. Hood, later known as Elizabeth Murphy Oliver Abney, was the granddaughter of *Afro* founder John H. Murphy Sr. and ultimately the author of *The Black Mother Goose Book* (1969). She joined the staff of the *Afro* in 1941, and during that year she contributed her first piece of fiction, a Christmas story entitled "It's Some Jive."[11] She resumed publishing fiction in the *Afro* in 1948, at which point many of her publications straddled the line between fiction and nonfiction, with stories like "Was Justice Done in This Case?" (April 17, 1948) and "I Was His Other Wife" (June 12, 1948) drawing on documentary and confessional modes, and other stories falling into more conventional crime fiction rubrics, occasionally with a true crime angle. With this experience blending fact and fiction, Hood's series of Black women's histories offered her a way of redefining familiar historical narratives in a way that placed these women at the center of global history.

Lavishly illustrated by Francis Yancey and given a full page in the magazine section after the fashion of the *Afro*'s most prominent fictional content, Sultry Sirens takes up the stories of three women of color—Hagar, Cleopatra, and Josephine—and offers readers a vision of world history in which these women, as the subtitle of the series proclaims, "changed destinies of nations." While the stories of Cleopatra and Jose-phine follow the formulas of a more conventional historical sketch, the story of Hagar (July 10, 1948) represents Hood's most interesting revi-sion. Like Rogers's historical articles, Hood's sketch of Hagar features no imagined dialogue. However, it moves beyond Rogers as it imbues its historical retelling with a host of psychological motivations and com-plex characterizations, along with a radical reinterpretation that trans-forms Hagar into an agent of her own, a figure of dignity and power despite her enslavement and mistreatment by Sarah. This shifts the focus of the story away from Hagar's role as a vessel for the realization of God's plan and provides her with self-determination. In Hood's story, Hagar's "brown skin was the texture of transparent velvet and her eyes sparkled like stars," and her beauty shines through "the cast-off garments and fine cloth from the women in Pharaoh's court."[12] Meanwhile, Sarah arrives in Egypt as a foreigner. Her "skin was pale and fair. Her har was golden and her eyes were light." Hood imagines Hagar taking part in her own destiny, managing her own story, "decid[ing] to offer herself as maid to the woman with the fair skin whom they called Sarah." Once installed as a servant, Hagar learns of Sarah's inability to bear the children that "Abraham's God had promised," and she comes "upon a plan which, if it worked well, would place her high in Abraham's future court." Hagar then proposes her idea to Sarah, who accepts but then begins to mistreat Hagar after Ishmael is born. Hood's story ends with Hagar's triumph: Banished by Sarah and Abraham, she and Ishmael "received aid from heaven," and Ishmael "became the father of the great Ishmaelites who were princes, heroes and warriors." The concluding words of this sketch emphasize Hagar as the protagonist of this history: "Hagar's dream had come true."

Hood uses Hagar's story to explore historical parallels with the conditions of slavery in the United States. Hagar the Egyptian is clearly marked as Black; Sarah's "pale and fair" skin mark her as white; Hood's story takes up the traumatic legacy of sexual slavery that many African American women endured. But Hood reconfigures this story to give Hagar the ability to serve as the protagonist in her own history: Hagar herself schemes to offer her services as a maid to Sarah and Abraham, and it is Hagar's own idea to try and bear Abraham's child because of the advantages it may offer her in the future. Hagar looks skeptically on the things that "Abraham's God had promised" and decides to leverage her own power in this situation to better her position and ultimately realize her dreams at the story's conclusion. In this compelling revision, the story of Abraham, Sarah, and Hagar is not guided by divine intervention. Instead, it is Hagar herself who guides this process, using her proximity to the family and her powers of persuasion to determine her own outcome: the realization of her own dream or vision.

Hood's story of Hagar resembles, in a number of respects, the genre that has come to be defined as the neo–slave narrative. While it does not take up the voice of its protagonist, it nonetheless wrestles with a number of that genre's concerns. In the introduction to a recent issue of *Callaloo* devoted to the neo–slave narrative, Joan Anim-Addo and Maria Helena Lima describe the genre in broad terms: "Neo–slave narratives . . . not only demand that we re-evaluate a vexed history of trauma and violence but also urge us to re-consider the modern history of the representation of black bodies and selves."[13] Early considerations, like Ashraf H. A. Rushdy's seminal *Neo–Slave Narratives* (1999), located the genre's origins in "the social, intellectual, and racial formations of the sixties" and a new left that "began to appreciate how 'history' was made not solely by the imperial powers of a nation but also by those without any discernible institutional power."[14] Hood's Hagar sketch demonstrates how popular African American fiction writers of the 1940s were already engaged in a form of revisionist social history, interrogating the narratives of institutional power and providing powerful alternatives that gave agency to characters marginalized in both history and narrative form. By casting Hagar—and not "Abraham's God"—as the agent in this story, Hood provides readers of the *Afro-American* with a tale that does not define an enslaved woman by her trauma but instead imagines her as a protagonist able to change the course of world history from the most marginal of positions.

Like Hood, prolific *Afro-American* contributor James H. Hill also turned his attention in the late 1940s and early 1950s to an historical fiction that recast disempowered figures, both historical and fictional, as agents of social change. In part, this new interest in historical dramas may have stemmed from the success of the African American novelist Frank Yerby's historical melodrama *The Foxes of Harrow* (1946), a phenomenal best seller that rewrote some of the conventions of the plantation romance. The *Afro-American* featured prominent coverage of Yerby, including "the first press interview" with the author, but Yerby sought to distance himself from his role (or responsibilities) as an African American writer.[15] Correspondence preserved in the *Afro-American* records attest to the fact that Hill and *Afro* editor Carl Murphy had an ongoing conversation about historical fiction and the importance (and scarcity) of historical material on African Americans in the late 1940s. In early 1948, Hill proposed a serial on Nat Turner, which would become "The Black Valhalla" (June 5–26, 1948), and he corresponded with Murphy about possible subjects for his historical fiction. Later that year, he complained about his struggles to find source material for this work, writing to Murphy,

> Some time ago I mentioned the extreme difficulty I experience getting books by and about Negroes . . . here in Philadelphia. Last night I went through the card index of the Central Library at Logan Square and the only thing by Roi Ottley was his "New World A-Coming." Many of the books you mention in your letters from time to time, really belong in my own library, but my circumstances do not permit of my buying books at this time.[16]

The fact that Hill—a part-time writer based in a major U.S. city—found it difficult to access "books by and about Negroes" in 1948 testifies to the importance of the fiction—and especially the historical fiction—published by the *Afro-American* during this time. For many readers, these stories may have been the only African American fiction available to them; indeed, the work published in African American newspapers may have described the boundaries of African American literary production for the vast majority of middle- and working-class African American readers.

Between mid-1948 and mid-1951, Hill published eight serials and one long story that sought to use his experience and talents in writing sensational fiction to explore the Black past and invest marginalized figures with dignity and purpose. Virtually all of these stories involve resistance to slavery in one form or another. The first of these, "Black Valhalla," tells the story of Nat Turner's rebellion. "Tiger Man" (August 14–September 4, 1948) and its sequel, "Rouse the Tiger" (March 26, 1949), present a compelling form of Black Atlantic resistance set in the early nineteenth century. In "Tiger Man," South Carolina slaver Japeth Adams encounters a slave revolt led by the "Khangi Prince," Babol, whose sister Adams had enslaved years earlier.[17] Babol and his sister, Noona, work from opposite vantage points to foils the slaver's plans while securing a promise to return their brother from North America by holding Adams's new bride hostage. Stories like "Tiger Man" highlight the active resistance to slavery and global white supremacy in ways analogous to Hill's hero fiction. However, by setting these stories in the early nineteenth century, Hill insists on seeing enslaved Africans not solely as victims or tragic figures but also as heroes in the face of structural violence. This vision of the past does not erase the trauma of slavery, but it complicates it by adding new narratives that show an historical challenge to white supremacy.

In addition to producing narratives that (like Hood's) seem to anticipate the revisionism of the neo–slave narrative, Hill's historical fiction of this period also highlights a wide variety of interracial collaboration and interaction that offered *Afro-American* readers a broader and more complex vision of their own history. In "Custer's Last Stand" (September 18–October 2, 1948), Hill uses elements of the western to place his protagonist, the freedman Isaiah Dorman, in a legendary moment in American history. While this serial ends with Dorman's death during the Battle of the Little Bighorn, its first two installments concern Dorman's Cheyenne lover, Little Fawn, who has committed suicide rather than submit to the violent sexual demands of a white frontiersman. "Custer's Last Stand" offers a host of contradictions. It begins by connecting the struggles of African Americans and Native Americans under U.S. imperialism, but its conclusion finds Dorman and Custer's aptly named native scout, "White Man Runs Him," as active—though conflicted and less than enthusiastic—participants in Custer's failed efforts.[18] As Dorman's "bullet-riddle[d] body" falls to the ground, he sees a vision of Little Fawn running toward him, suggesting an afterlife where these two can be free of U.S. imperialism and racial violence.

In other historical serials, Hill mixes western tropes with the conventions of the fugitive slave narrative to remind readers that these two fictional forms occupy the same temporal and spatial place in American history. "Red Trail" (November 26–December 10, 1949) follows the escape of enslaved cook Genesis Reed, who abandons his enslaver's wagon train on a homesteading trip from Alabama to the west. On the run, he encounters a young white woman, Jane Caldwell, from an anti-slavery Kansas family. She too is on the run from a group of proslavery vigilantes. In the serial's wild conclusion, the group seeking Genesis, the proslavery vigilantes seeking Jane, and a group of Comanches arrive. A bloodbath ensues. Meanwhile, Jane and Genesis leave to start a life together on land from the Homestead Act, another nod to the utopian possibilities offered by interracial romance across African American newspaper fiction. Another Hill western, "Big Yellow" (December 31, 1949–January 14, 1950), presents a complex Civil War–era Arkansas inheritance story centered around Juan Martinez, the mixed-race son of the "pure Castillian" "Widow Wyatt" and what one aggrieved white character calls "that Barbados black that ran amuck and murdered most of the Wyatts back in Natchez some twenty-odd years ago. Poor Widder Wyatt! Wonder what she ever saw in Iron Rim, that black killer!"[19] Known as "El Amarillo Grande," or "Big Yellow," Martinez is working as a cowboy on the Texas border with Mexico and courting Tina Rodriguez. Despite the violent scheming of the white men from Arkansas, Big Yellow retains his inheritance and marries Tina at the serial's end. Again, in "Big Yellow" Hill seeks to transform familiar western formulas with a broad depiction of interracial and interethnic collaboration. From the interracial romance of Iron Rim and the Widow Wyatt (née Martinez) to Big Yellow's courtship of the Mexican Tina Rodriguez, Hill's work insists on the racial and ethnic complexity of the west in the face of generic formulas that usually celebrate white masculinity, manifest destiny, and imperial conquest. By showing Big Yellow's triumph over the greedy Arkansas Confederates, he turns these generic formulas upside down, presenting the West not solely as a theater for the fantasies of white supremacy but also as a complex multiracial space where African American, Native American, and Mexican characters also have lives to lead and stories to tell.

Through mid-1951, Hill continued to produce occasional historical fiction, including "The Lion of Devil Mountain" (March 18–April 1, 1950), the story of a "Negro-Indian" rebelling against slavery on Hispaniola; "The Mutineer" (June 3–24, 1950), a story of a revolt on a slave ship; and "The Hostile Brothers" (June 16–July 7, 1951), a melodrama about two half-brothers (one white, one mixed race) during the Civil War. After this brief moment, Hill largely returned to writing his crime-fighting serials featuring Jiggs Bennett, but he did produce one more historical serial in 1955, the last year he published new work in the *Afro-American*. This story, "Market for Murder" (January 8–29, 1955), concerns the common practice of body snatching for medical school anatomy classes. A young doctor in Norfolk, Virginia, uses Black labor to unearth recently deceased bodies from the cemetery, but he also stoops to murdering young African Americans for fresh bodies. Initially presented as a piece of forgotten history, the story becomes one of revenge, with an ending fit for a horror tale when the doctor discovers his own wife on the dissecting table, placed there by the men he sought to murder for the white medical establishment. Throughout these tales, Hill seeks to rewrite the dominant narratives of American and global history, allowing characters of color to strike back at the structures of white supremacy and even to find comfort and joy in a broadly multiethnic and multiracial vision of the past.

A brief survey of the historical fiction of Hood and Hill reveals that, well before the political revolutions of the 1960s, African American writers of popular fiction were engaged in a complex process of historical recovery and revision. That these efforts have gone unnoticed speaks to the profound need of our own recovery and revision of African American literary history. If Hood and Hill look to the Black past to unearth and imagine stories that can offer a fuller and more dignified vision of Black history, then we must follow their lead and look to the broader literary historical record—not only to give dignity to the many forgotten African American writers that produced vast quantities of popular reading material in unexpected places but also to give credit to the vast majority of African American readers of the middle of the twentieth century. Our accepted histories of African American literature—particularly of literature before the 1960s—write out all but the most elite readers of African American literary production. This dismissal falls in line with the "extraordinary expectation" carried by Black literacy in what Kinohi Nishikawa has described in his essay "Merely Reading."[20] But as the consideration across *Black Pulp* has shown, the popular genre fiction discussed here entails far more than "merely reading": it offers a laboratory for experimenting with imagined solutions to the real problems of racial injustice and white supremacy. Like Hood and Hill, we too need new histories to grant a fuller picture to the story of African American literature and popular culture, and to give African American readers their own kind of justice as active collaborators in the radical practice of genre revision.

It is this kind of new history that *Black Pulp* has sought to encourage. In the process of developing this project, two critical questions have remained central to my inquiry. In 2011, Kenneth Warren asked *What Was African American Literature?* and gave a controversial answer, asserting that "African American literature was a postemancipation phenomenon that gained its coherence as an undertaking in the social world defined by the system of Jim Crow segregation" and that "with the legal demise of Jim Crow, the coherence of African American literature has been correspondingly, if sometimes imperceptibly, eroded as well."[21] Warren's claims—debatable as they are—complement, in his timeline at least, the story I have been outlining in *Black Pulp*.[22] However, some of his central assumptions vary widely from the concerns of Black pulp. He argues that African American literature is defined by "having responded creatively to the imperatives that derived from the establishment of a social order on the basis of assumed black inferiority, and not in any transcendence of these imperatives."[23] Following Jarrett's racial realism and Tate's racial protocols, Warren's notion of imperatives suggests that African American writers had no choice but to address racial injustice and to find characters unable to transcend these realities. However, transcendence and transformation are the hallmarks of the work discussed in *Black Pulp*, and the writers discussed here sought, over a nearly thirty-year period, to imagine fiction that celebrated Black excellence and offered narrative pleasure to readers who found in this literature stories that rejected the idea of Black inferiority from the outset. For the canonical writers who were read by James Weldon Johnson's divided audience, Warren's clam that "black writers made black literature only and precisely because they encountered circumstances they would not themselves have chosen" may ring true. But for the writers of Black pulp, who addressed an almost entirely Black audience of middle- and working-class African Americans in the pages of nationally distributed weekly newspapers, these circumstances were vastly different. This readership, a truly popular Black readership, created the kind of conditions where the writers of Black pulp could imagine a past, present, and future where racial justice was possible.

Warren does acknowledge some of the limitations of his critique, especially around the concept of the popular. He notes that "black critics did not have to contend that the term 'popular literature' referred to works that were widely read by blacks (in part because they could argue that black popular literary taste had been corrupted by sellout black elites)" and that "none of the works championed by vernacular critics were or are popular," which has resulted in the transformation of "'elite' and 'popular' into formal categories—instead of assessments of actual readership."[24] Warren's invocation of the vernacular turn in African American literary studies is telling; this emphasis on vernacular form has influenced countless critics, who now take for granted the smooth and easy transition from folk cultural forms to elite literary productions. The influence of these critical approaches has, in its leaping from the blues to the canon, occluded the vast majority of Black readers—indeed, the very readers whose reading preferences and practices *Black Pulp* has sought to recover.

The idea of the vernacular as a kind of critical fetish also informs the second question, asked by Stuart Hall in his 1992 essay "What Is This 'Black' in Black Popular Culture?" Hall's essay, written at the height of the vernacular turn, situates the critical interest in "black American popular vernacular traditions" in a host of postmodern contexts.[25] Hall warns against an easy reliance on essentializing the signifier "Black" "because it naturalizes and dehistoricizes difference, mistaking what is historical and cultural for what is natural, biological, and genetic."[26] Returning to his ideas about articulation, he insists that "in black popular culture, strictly speaking, ethnographically speaking, there are no pure forms at all. Always these forms are the product of partial synchronization, of engagement across cultural boundaries, of the confluence of more than one cultural tradition, of the negotiations of dominant and subordinate positions, of the subterranean strategies of recoding and transcoding, of critical signification, of signifying."[27] For Hall, then, seeking a vernacular essence that somehow defines Black popular culture is at best a dead end and at worst a form of ahistorical essentialism that reinforces the very structures of white supremacy.

Despite the fact that Hall emphasizes an inquiry into Blackness in his title, his essay closes with a compelling consideration of the popular, as if in the process of concluding the essay it has surreptitiously become "What Is This 'Popular' In Black Popular Culture?" Here Hall seeks to underscore the difference between what critics have called the vernacular and the theater of true popular culture, which, as Warren rightly claimed, has been summarily dismissed by scholars of African American literature. As Hall writes,

> Popular culture, commodified and stereotyped as it often is, is not at all, as we sometimes think of it, the arena where we find who we really are, the truth of our experience. It is an arena that is *profoundly* mythic. It is a theater of popular desires, a theater of popular fantasies. It is where we discover and play with the identifications of ourselves, where we are imagined, where we are represented, not only to the audiences out there who do not get the message, but to ourselves for the first time.[28]

The "theater of popular desires," the "theater of popular fantasies"—this better than anything describes the function of the fiction I have been considering throughout *Black Pulp*. The stories and serials considered across this book do not represent the truth of any experience but rather act as a place where desire and fantasy could be acted out and where a great audience of African American readers could discover, play, and imagine themselves, even while struggling under the shadow of Jim Crow. This kind of pleasure, too, is vital to survival and selfhood, and the radical transformation of popular genres—the recoding, the articulation, the signifyin(g)—by a host of long-forgotten writers made this possible.

Like the historical fictions offered by Hood and Hill, *Black Pulp* has sought to retell (literary) history from a new vantage point. Across this work, I have attempted to bracket the received wisdom and dominant narratives that have established and propped up a canon of African American literature that spoke—in the early twentieth century at least—to a small minority of African American readers. This canonical fiction remains without a doubt one of the points of articulation for the writers of Black pulp. But in this story—like that of Hagar or Big Yellow—those narratives must be revised and complicated with a rich legacy of marginalized voices. In this case, those marginalized voices happen to represent a widely distributed and widely read body of literature that has never had a chance at its own history. It is my hope that the story of this history is only beginning.

ACKNOWLEDGMENTS

The research for *Black Pulp* began in 2013 and 2014 in the wake of the murders of Trayvon Martin, Michael Brown, and Eric Garner and the emergence of the Black Lives Matter movement. Too many names have followed these in the years since. This project was guided by a desire to recover and celebrate texts that gave dignity to Black lives and offered the pleasures and escape of genre fiction to Black readers living under the shadow of Jim Crow.

Black Pulp would have been impossible without the generous assistance of many individuals and institutions. I made extensive use of the archives at the Schomburg Center for the Study of Black Culture, the Moorland-Spingarn Research Center at Howard University, and the *Afro-American* Archives. The staff at these institutions during my visits there—including Steven Fullwood, Joellen El Bashir, and Sheila Scott—facilitated access to valuable archival material that was instrumental in completing this project. Support from the libraries at James Madison University—including the assistance of English librarian Brian Flota and the intrepid interlibrary loan staff—was also crucial for this work. JMU provided additional support in the form of English department funding, a College of Arts and Letters summer research grant, and the opportunity to present work in progress at the inaugural event of the JMU Africana Literatures and Cultures Workshop. My participation in the 2015 National Endowment for the Humanities institute City of Print, run by Mark Noonan, helped me shape this project into something more far reaching.

A number of scholars paved the way for the discoveries here, and they generously shared research and advice with me. These include Kim Gallon, Mark J. Madigan, Kimberley Mangun, Martha H. Patterson, and Laurie Powers. I'm also grateful for an illuminating telephone conversation with Anne Wilhelen Smith, the daughter of William Thomas Smith, who helped me better understand her father's writing career.

I shared this research at a number of conferences, in conversations, and in draft form with many colleagues who made valuable suggestions for revision and improvement and offered all kinds of encouragement. To them I am very grateful. These include Lauren Alleyne, Jim Casey, Darryl Dickson-Carr, Anna Mae Duane, David Earle, John Ernest, Allison Fagan, Eric Gardner, Mollie Godfrey, Sean Grattan, Gary Holcomb, Jessica Ingram, Catherine Keyser, Adam McKible, Erin Lee Mock, Kristin Moriah, Besi Muhonja, John Ott, Matthew Rebhorn, Sarah Salter, Sofia Samatar, Derrick Spires, and Andreá Williams, among many others. Tyler Fleming first suggested I read Schuyler's pulp writing. Casey Howard kept me grounded. Without the help of Joost Burgers, I would have struggled to access vital digital resources. Completing a book project in the midst of a pandemic only intensifies the feeling that without rich networks of generous readers and interlocutors, research is simply impossible.

I also want to thank two undergraduate research assistants who helped me work through this vast archive: Chris Hughes and Marina Shafik. Marina was so invested in the material that she insisted on doing an independent study on this subject after her time as a research assistant ended. I did my most valuable and focused thinking on this project during the semesters I spent in conversation with Marina about these texts. Her thoughtful engagement with the material had no small influence on my own.

If there is a soundtrack to *Black Pulp*, it is the work of Prince, whose music was my first master class in genre, its pleasures, and its transformations.

My final and deepest thanks go to my partner, Bethany Hurley, whose commitment to justice never ceases to inspire.

NOTES

INTRODUCTION

    1. Ridley Scott's *The Martian* (2015) was also submitted under this category in a controversial nomination.

    2. Mike Fleming Jr., "*Get Out*'s Jordan Peele Responds to Golden Globes Category," Deadline, November 17, 2017, https://deadline.com/.

    3. Yohana Desta, "Is *Get Out* Really a Comedy? Don't Ask Jordan Peele," *Vanity Fair,* November 16, 2017, https://www.vanityfair.com/.

    4. Lloyd Osbourne and Henry E. Baker, "Daggancourt," *Crisis,* March 1911, 26–27. I am indebted to William Reed Quinn, whose "Readerly Revisions: Letters to the Editor in the *Crisis,*" *American Literature* 92, no. 2 (June 2020): 257–80, alerted me to this exchange.

    5. Brooks E. Hefner, "Pulp Magazines," in *American Literature in Transition, 1920–1930,* ed. Ichiro Takayoshi (Cambridge: Cambridge University Press, 2017), 439–41. *Manuscript Market Guide,* April–June 1929, 76.

    6. "Harlem's Theatrical Life Brought to Broadway in New Magazine," *Baltimore Afro-American,* April 23, 1932, 19.

    7. David M. Earle, "New York City: Pulp Mecca or Pulp Hell?," lecture, City of Print (Brooklyn, N.Y., National Endowment for the Humanities Institute), June 15, 2015.

    8. Erin A. Smith, *Hard-Boiled: Working-Class Readers and Pulp Magazines* (Philadelphia, Pa.: Temple University Press, 2000), 27.

    9. Will Thomas, "Negro Writers of Pulp Fiction," *Negro Digest,* July 1950, 81. Thomas lays out the conditions that form the premise for the *Star Trek:*

Deep Space Nine episode "Far Beyond the Stars" (season 6, episode 13, 1998). I am grateful to Casey Howard for introducing this episode to me.

10. Thomas, "Negro Writers of Pulp Fiction," 82.

11. Shawn Anthony Christian, *The Harlem Renaissance and the Idea of a New Negro Reader* (Amherst: University of Massachusetts Press, 2016), 11. The citation is from Amy Jacques Garvey, "Read, Think, Then Talk," *Negro World*, July 17, 1926, 7.

12. Quentin Reynolds, *The Fiction Factory; or, From Pulp Row to Quality Street* (New York: Random House, 1955), 257.

13. John Cheng, *Astounding Wonder: Imagining Science and Science Fiction in Interwar America* (Philadelphia: University of Pennsylvania Press, 2012), 147–78. John Rieder, *Colonialism and the Emergence of Science Fiction* (Middletown, Conn.: Wesleyan University Press, 2012).

14. Harold Brainerd Hersey, *Pulpwood Editor: The Fabulous World of the Thriller Magazines Revealed by a Veteran Editor and Publisher* (New York: Frederick A. Stokes, 1937), 193.

15. Mark C. Jerng, *Racial Worldmaking: The Power of Popular Fiction* (New York: Fordham University Press, 2018), 2.

16. Jerng, *Racial Worldmaking*, 22.

17. E. Franklin Frazier, *Black Bourgeoisie* (New York: Free Press, 1957), 174. Other early historians of the Black press were more generous. See Eugene Gordon, "The Negro Press," *American Mercury*, June 1926, 207–15; and Eugene Gordon, "The Negro Press," *Annals of the American Academy of Political and Social Science* 140 (November 1928): 248–56.

18. Andrew Buni, *Robert L. Vann of the* Pittsburgh Courier: *Politics and Black Journalism* (Pittsburgh, Pa.: University of Pittsburgh Press, 1974). Hayward Farrar, *The Baltimore* Afro-American, *1892–1950* (Westport, Conn.: Greenwood Press, 1998).

19. Armistead S. Pride and Clint C. Wilson II, *A History of the Black Press* (Washington, D.C.: Howard University Press, 1997). Patrick S. Washburn, *The African American Newspaper: Voice of Freedom* (Evanston, Ill.: Northwestern University Press, 2006).

20. Todd Vogel, ed., *The Black Press: New Literary and Historical Essays* (New Brunswick, N.J.: Rutgers University Press, 2001). Only one of these two essays in this collection—Michael Thurston's essay on Langston Hughes's coverage of the Spanish civil war (140–58)—actually takes up the Black newspapers of this period.

21. See, for example, John Ernest, *Liberation Historiography: African American Writers and the Challenge of History, 1794–1861* (Chapel Hill: University of North Carolina Press, 2004); P. Gabrielle Foreman, *Activist Sentiments:*

Reading Black Women in the Nineteenth Century (Urbana: University of Illinois Press, 2009); Frances Smith Foster, *'Til Death Do Us Part: Love and Marriage in Early African America* (Oxford: Oxford University Press, 2010); Eric Gardner, *Black Print Unbound: The* Christian Recorder, *African American Literature, and Periodical Culture* (Oxford: Oxford University Press, 2015); Elizabeth McHenry, *Forgotten Readers: Recovering the Lost History of African American Literary Societies* (Durham, N.C.: Duke University Press, 2002); Carla L. Peterson, *"Doers of the Word": African-American Women Speakers and Writers in the North (1830–1880)* (New Brunswick, N.J.: Rutgers University Press, 1998); Benjamin Fagan, *The Black Newspaper and the Chosen Nation* (Athens: University of Georgia Press, 2016); Katherine Capshaw Smith and Anna Mae Duane, eds., *Who Writes for Black Children? African American Children's Literature before 1900* (Minneapolis: University of Minnesota Press, 2017); Derrick R. Spires, *The Practice of Citizenship: Black Politics and Print Culture in the Early United States* (Philadelphia: University of Pennsylvania Press, 2019); Nazera Sadiq Wright, *Black Girlhood in the Nineteenth Century* (Urbana: University of Illinois Press, 2017).

22. Justin Gifford, *Pimping Fictions: African American Crime Literature and the Untold Story of Black Pulp Publishing* (Philadelphia: Temple University Press, 2013), 3. Kinohi Nishikawa, *Street Players: Black Pulp Fiction and the Making of a Literary Underground* (Chicago: University of Chicago Press, 2018), 6, 10.

23. For an early and influential history of paperbacks in the United States, see Kenneth C. Davis, *Two-Bit Culture: The Paperbacking of America* (Boston: Houghton Mifflin, 1984).

24. Hans Robert Jauss, *Toward an Aesthetic of Reception* (Minneapolis: University of Minnesota Press, 1982), 22–23.

25. Steve Neale, "Questions of Genre," *Screen* 31, no. 1 (Spring 1990): 56.

26. Neale, "Questions of Genre," 56.

27. Henry Louis Gates Jr., *The Signifying Monkey: A Theory of African-American Literary Criticism* (Oxford: Oxford University Press, 1988), xxiv. When using this term as a conceptual noun, I will adopt Gates's orthographic formulation "signifyin(g)"; when using it as a verb or adjective, I will use the more conventional "signifying."

28. Gates, *Signifying Monkey,* 124.

29. Gates, *Signifying Monkey,* xxiv.

30. Other important works include Houston A. Baker Jr., *Blues, Ideology, and Afro-American Literature* (Chicago: University of Chicago Press, 1984) and Houston A. Baker Jr., *Modernism and the Harlem Renaissance* (Chicago: University of Chicago Press, 1988).

31. Gates, *Signifying Monkey,* 110.

32. V. N. Vološinov, *Marxism and the Philosophy of Language,* trans. Ladislav Matejka and I. R. Titunik (Cambridge, Mass.: Harvard University Press, 1973), 23.

33. Jurij Tynjanov, "On Literary Evolution," in *Readings in Russian Poetics: Formalist and Structuralist Views,* ed. Ladislav Matejka and Krystyna Pomorska (Chicago: Dalkey Archive, 2002), 72.

34. Vološinov, *Marxism and the Philosophy of Language,* 23.

35. Stuart Hall, "On Postmodernism and Articulation: An Interview with Stuart Hall," ed. Lawrence Grossberg, *Journal of Communication Inquiry* 10, no. 2 (June 1986): 53.

36. John Clarke, Stuart Hall, Tony Jefferson, and Brian Roberts, "Subcultures, Cultures and Class," in *Resistance through Rituals: Youth Subcultures in Post-war Britain,* 2nd ed., ed. Stuart Hall and Tony Jefferson (New York: Routledge, 1993), 8. John Clarke, Stuart Hall, Tony Jefferson, and Brian Roberts, "Subcultures, Cultures and Class: A Theoretical Overview," *Working Papers in Cultural Studies* 7/8 (1975): 15.

37. John Clarke, Stuart Hall, Tony Jefferson, and Brian Roberts, "Subcultures, Cultures and Class," in Hall and Jefferson, *Resistance through Rituals,* 6. Clarke et al., "Subcultures, Cultures and Class," 12.

38. This is similar to what Houston A. Baker Jr. calls "the discursive strategies . . . [of] 'the mastery of form' and 'the deformation of mastery.'" See Baker, *Modernism and the Harlem Renaissance,* xvi.

39. Andreas Huyssen, *After the Great Divide: Modernism: Mass Culture, Postmodernism* (Bloomington: Indiana University Press, 1986).

40. Gene Andrew Jarrett, *Deans and Truants: Race and Realism in African American Literature* (Philadelphia: University of Pennsylvania Press, 2011), 8.

41. Thomas, "Negro Writers of Pulp Fiction," 82.

42. James Weldon Johnson, "The Dilemma of the Negro Author," in *The New Negro: Readings on Race, Representation, and African American Culture, 1892–1938,* ed. Henry Louis Gates Jr. and Gene Andrew Jarrett (Princeton, N.J.: Princeton University Press, 2007), 378.

43. One canonical figure who published fiction in the newspapers is Langston Hughes, whose Simple stories were featured in the *Chicago Defender* over a more than twenty-year period from 1943 to 1965. As I note in chapter 1, the *Defender* never really embraced the genre fiction I term "Black pulp," and Hughes's presence in the *Defender* owed more to his literary celebrity than to the newspaper's commitment to literary entertainment.

44. Anna L. Petry, "Dancer from Harlem," *Baltimore Afro-American,* November 12, 1938, 14. This recalls Boots Smith's "shiny, expensive" car, "the

kind of car you see in the movies." Ann Petry, *The Street* (Boston: Houghton Mifflin, 1946), 155.

45. In his introduction to the republication of "Marie of the Cabin Club," Gene Jarrett notes that scholars might dismiss this story because of "Petry's artistic immaturity," but he still advocates for its inclusion in her body of work. See Gene Jarrett, "Introduction: African American Noms de Plume," *PMLA* 121, no. 1 (January 2006): 247.

46. Fredric Jameson, "Reification and Utopia in Mass Culture," *Social Text* 1 (Winter 1979): 140, 145, 147.

47. Huyssen, *After the Great Divide.*

48. Laura Frost, *The Problem with Pleasure: Modernism and Its Discontents* (New York: Columbia University Press, 2013), 11–12.

49. Q. D. Leavis, *Fiction and the Reading Public* (London: Chatto & Windus, 1939), 7, 19, 225.

50. Max Horkheimer and Theodor W. Adorno, *Dialectic of Enlightenment: Philosophical Fragments,* trans. Edmund Jephcott (Stanford, Calif.: Stanford University Press, 2002), 106.

51. "Announcement," *Colored American,* February 1900, 1

52. "Editorial," *Crisis,* November 1910, 10.

53. "Editorials," *Opportunity,* February 1923, 3.

54. Christian, *Harlem Renaissance,* 9.

55. Christian, *Harlem Renaissance,* 1.

56. Kevin K. Gaines, *Uplifting the Race: Black Leadership, Politics, and Culture in the Twentieth Century* (Chapel Hill: University of North Carolina Press, 1996), 14.

57. Gaines, *Uplifting the Race,* 17.

58. McHenry notes that "some black Americans participated actively in the activities sponsored by African American literary societies without ever acquiring the ability to read or write for themselves," but these participants certainly encountered texts—and the concomitant uplift ideology—through connections with more educated readers. See McHenry, *Forgotten Readers,* 13.

59. William J. Collins and Robert A. Margo, "Historical Perspectives on Racial Differences in Schooling in the United States," *Handbook of the Economics of Education,* vol. 1, ed. Eric A. Hanushek and Finis Welch (Amsterdam: North-Holland, 2006), 112.

60. Raw census figures are from Campbell Gibson and Kay Jung, "Historical Census Statistic on Population Totals by Race, 1790 to 1990, and by Hispanic Origin, 1970 to 1990, for the United States, Regions, Divisions, and States," Population Division Working Paper No. 56, U.S. Census Bureau, 2002.

61. Kim Gallon, *Pleasure in the News: African American Readership and Sexuality in the Black Press* (Urbana: University of Illinois Press, 2020), 40–43.

62. Gallon, *Pleasure in the News,* 43.

63. Ishmael Reed, "Introduction: Black Pleasure—An Oxymoron," in *Soul: Black Power, Politics, and Pleasure,* ed. Monique Guillory and Richard C. Green (New York: New York University Press, 1998), 169.

64. Reed, "Introduction," 169.

65. Claudia Tate, *Psychoanalysis and Black Novels: Desire and the Protocols of Race* (Oxford: Oxford University Press, 1998), 3.

66. Jarrett, *Deans and Truants,* 8.

67. Zora Neale Hurston, "What White Publishers Won't Print," *Folklore, Memoirs, and Other Writings* (New York: Library of America, 1995), 953.

68. Michael Denning, *Mechanic Accents: Dime Novels and Working-Class Culture in America* (London: Verso, 1987), 81.

69. "Backstage," *Ebony,* November 1945, 2, qtd. in Adam Green, *Selling the Race: Culture, Community, and Black Chicago, 1940–1955* (Chicago: University of Chicago Press, 2007), 130.

70. The closest thing the 1920s had to a publication like this was the *Inter-state Tattler,* a gossipy newspaper published about (and for) New York's Black elite.

71. *Manuscript Market Guide,* April–June 1929, 200. *The Editor,* May 21, 1932, 154.

72. James Hill, "Land of the Free," part 1, *Baltimore Afro-American,* February 1, 1941, 7.

1. BENEATH THE HARLEM RENAISSANCE

1. See W. E. B. Du Bois, "The Talented Tenth," *The Negro Problem* (New York: James Pott, 1903), 33–75.

2. Cary D. Wintz, *Black Culture and the Harlem Renaissance* (Houston, Tex.: Rice University Press, 1988), 164.

3. Langston Hughes, *The Big Sea* (1940, reprint, New York: Hill & Wang, 1964), 228.

4. An advertisement for the novel asks, "Would you like to read an interesting story of the day when the Negro race will lead civilization?" and quotes Du Bois as saying, "I have read this book with interest and recommend it to my friends. It has a fine lesson in its breast which is voiced in the concluding lines: 'The white man's burden is himself.'" *Crisis,* February 1916, 204.

5. "The Vamp and the Virgin" was credited to Parke Reed in the *Baltimore Afro-American,* the *Dallas Express,* and the *Washington Bee* but to Aubrey

Bowser in the *New York Amsterdam News* and the *Norfolk Journal and Guide*. In *The Rainbow* (1919–20), it is titled "The Iron Altar" and credited to Parke Reed. "The Man Who Would Be White" is credited to Jane La Mott in *The Rainbow* (1919) but to Bowser elsewhere, and it was the basis of the now-lost six-reel feature film *The Call of His People* (1921), produced by Reol Pictures. Most of the fiction published in *The Rainbow* appears to have been written by Bowser, whether under his own name or under pseudonyms. On the history of Reol Pictures and the marketing of *The Call of His People*, see Christina Petersen, "The 'Reol' Story: Race Authorship and Consciousness in Robert Levy's Reol Productions, 1921–1926," *Film History* 20, no. 3 (2008): 308–24.

6. Bowser's papers at the Schomburg Center for the Study of Black culture include an intriguing typescript for an unpublished novel entitled *Black Pilgrim: A Novel of Harlem's Early Life*.

7. John C. Moore, "Fiction in the Afro-American Press," *Washington Sun*, February 19, 1915, 2. Quoted in Marya Annette McQuirter, "Claiming the City: African Americans, Urbanization, and Leisure in Washington, D.C., 1902–1957" (Ph.D. diss., University of Michigan, 2000), 67n109.

8. On the concept of distinction, see Pierre Bourdieu, *Distinction: A Social Critique of the Judgment of Taste*, trans. Richard Nice (Cambridge, Mass.: Harvard University Press, 1984).

9. In the aftermath of the end of *Abbott's Monthly* in late 1933, the *Defender* featured fiction only sporadically between March and December 1934. Much of this was written by regular *Abbott's Monthly* contributors, which suggests that these stories were originally intended for *Abbott's* before it folded. On the history of the *Defender*, see Ethan Michaeli, *The Defender: How the Legendary Black Newspaper Changed America* (New York: Houghton Mifflin, 2016).

10. On Ziff's role as an advertising agent for African American newspapers, see Pride and Wilson, *History of the Black Press*, 240–42.

11. George S. Schuyler, autobiographical note to "Some Unsweet Truths about Race Prejudice," *Behold America!*, ed. Samuel D. Schmalhausen (New York: Farrar & Rinehart, 1931), 88.

12. "A New Forward Step in Negro Journalism," advertisement, *Houston Informer*, October 13, 1928, 3.

13. Advertisement, *Norfolk Journal and Guide*, October 20, 1928, 1. "Chocolate Baby," advertisement, *Baltimore Afro-American*, October 13, 1928, 18.

14. *Manuscript Market Guide*, April–June 1929, 200. *The Editor*, May 21, 1932, 154.

15. Eurie Dahn, *Jim Crow Networks: African American Periodical Cultures* (Amherst, Mass.: University of Massachusetts Press, 2021), 31, 45. Dahn's

text highlights how the magazine's 1919–20 serialization of James Weldon Johnson's *The Autobiography of an Ex-Colored Man* complicates its identity as a middlebrow publication with a focus on domesticity.

16. The average monthly circulation of the *Half-Century* for 1920 was 46,754. See *Nelson Chesman & Co.'s Newspaper Rate Book* (St. Louis, Mo.: Nelson Chesman, 1922), 42. In earlier years, the magazine used the subtitle "A Colored Monthly for the Business Man and the Home Maker" (1917–21). Most studies of the *Half-Century* highlight its connection to the fashion and beauty industries, as the magazine was funded by Anthony Overton, a personal care product magnate. See, for example, Nowlie M. Rooks, *Ladies' Pages: African American Women's Magazines and the Culture that Made Them* (New Brunswick, N.J.: Rutgers University Press, 2004), 65–88; Robert E. Weems Jr., "A Man in a Woman's World: Anthony Overton's Rise to Prominence in the African American Personal Care Products Industry," *Journal of African American History* 101, no. 4 (Fall 2016): 407–35; Robert E. Weems Jr., *The Merchant Prince of Black Chicago: Anthony Overton and the Building of a Financial Empire* (Urbana: University of Illinois Press, 2020), 62–78; and Dahn, *Jim Crow Networks,* 29–64.

17. George S. Schuyler to Walter F. White, January 11, 1929, National Association for the Advancement of Colored People Records, Library of Congress, Washington, D.C., C97. Schuyler's letterhead does not include the *Atlanta World* (which started in late 1928), the *Kansas City Call,* or the *Portland Advocate.*

18. The 1929 circulation figures for fourteen of these were taken from *N. W. Ayer & Son's Directory of Newspapers and Periodicals* (Philadelphia: N. W. Ayer & Son, 1930), 1348–50. The Ayer & Son's volume records the following average circulation figures for 1929: *Arkansas Survey,* 1,200; *Atlanta Independent,* 30,000; *Baltimore Afro-American,* 24,300; *Detroit Independent,* 8,100; *Gary Sun,* 12,310; *Houston Informer,* 10,890; *Iowa Bystander,* 1,620; *Kansas City Call,* 16,661; *Nashville Clarion,* 900; *New York News,* 12,000; *Norfolk Journal & Guide,* 17,000; *Pittsburgh Courier,* 38,760; *Portland Advocate,* 4,500; *Washington Tribune,* 8,055. Ayer did not list circulation for the following: *Atlanta World, Birmingham Truth, Cincinnati Union, Cleveland Call-Post, Dallas Express, Dayton Forum, Galveston Eagle, Hartford Pilot, Louisiana Weekly, Memphis Triangle, Newark Herald, Omaha Guide,* and [?] *Register.* By contrast, David Levering Lewis notes that National Urban League journal "*Opportunity* sold a mere eleven thousand copies a month during its peak circulation period—1928—and 40 percent of these were to whites. This was a far cry from the sixty thousand copies monthly of *The Crisis.*" David Levering Lewis, *When Harlem Was in Vogue* (1981; reprint, Oxford: Oxford University Press, 1989), 199.

19. Farrar, *Baltimore* Afro-American, 6. Current pass-along rates are estimated at 2.5 readers per copy, although this would likely be a conservative estimate for the Black press of the first half of the twentieth century.

20. Kim Gallon, *Pleasure in the News; African American Readership and Sexuality in the Black Press* (Urbana: University of Illinois Press, 2020), 31. The citation is from Melissa Mae Elliot, "News in the Negro Press," (M.A. thesis, University of Chicago, 1931), 33.

21. George S. Schuyler, "Views and Reviews," *Pittsburgh Courier,* April 6, 1929, 12.

22. Schuyler, "Views and Reviews," 12.

23. "Tilts and Attack on Press Feature Durham Fact-Finding Conference," *Baltimore Afro-American,* April 27, 1929, 3.

24. "Misinformation," *Norfolk Journal and Guide,* May 4, 1929, § 2, p. 8.

25. "Notice, Readers!," *Pittsburgh Courier,* April 19, 1930, § 2, p. 1.

26. On Ziff and the Black press, see Jason Chambers, *Madison Avenue and the Color Line: African Americans in the Advertising Industry* (Philadelphia: University of Pennsylvania Press, 2008), 31–39.

27. *The Negro Market: Published in the Interest of the Negro Press* (Chicago: W. B. Ziff, 1932), 38.

28. Buni, *Robert L. Vann,* 223.

29. Robert L. Vann to C. A. Franklin, August 21, 1933 (copy), *Baltimore Afro American* Records, Box 67, Manuscript Division, Moorland-Spingarn Research Center, Howard University, Washington, D.C.

30. For a recent history of the ANP, see Gerald Horne, *The Rise and Fall of the Associated Negro Press: Claude Barnett's Pan-African News and the Jim Crow Paradox* (Urbana: University of Illinois Press, 2017).

31. Benjamin J. Davis, *Communist Councilman from Harlem: Autobiographical Notes Written in a Federal Penitentiary* (New York: International, 1969), 43.

32. On Boone as editor, see "Editor's Secretary Becomes Editor," *New York Amsterdam News,* July 22, 1931, 9. On Davis's resignation, see Benjamin J. Davis, *Communist Councilman from Harlem,* 43–44. This also hints at Carl Murphy's interest and involvement in editing fictional content, which I discuss in chapter 4.

33. Eugene Gordon, "Negro Fictionist in America," *Saturday Evening Quill,* April 1929, 20.

34. Gordon, "Negro Fictionist in America," 20.

35. Gates, *Signifying Monkey,* 179–80.

36. The most influential of these arguments is Huyssen, *After the Great Divide.*

37. Hurston's other *Courier* publications include "The Back Room" (February 19, 1927), "Monkey Junk" (March 5, 1927), "The Country in the Woman" (March 26, 1927), and "She Rock" (August 5, 1933).

38. "Common Meter" appeared on February 8 and February 15, 1930. On Fisher as a vernacular writer, see Brooks E. Hefner, *The Word on the Streets: The American Language of Vernacular Modernism* (Charlottesville: University of Virginia Press, 2017), 92–102.

39. Curiously, the *IFS* continued to advertise in the *Manuscript Market Guide* into 1937, using as its editorial contact the address of the *Afro-American* offices on Eutaw Street in Baltimore. The editorial offices of the *IFS* moved there when Davis was editor in 1930. I have been unable to locate any evidence of the *IFS* after December 1932, and Schuyler referred to it as the "ill-starred Illustrated Feature Section" in early 1935, suggesting that it had failed some time earlier. Perhaps the continued inclusion of the *IFS* in the *Manuscript Market Guide* was an oversight, or perhaps the *Afro-American* used this to solicit submissions for its own fiction. See George S. Schuyler, "News and Reviews," *Pittsburgh Courier,* February 16, 1935, § 1, p. 10.

40. Lawson's "Pigskin Brown," which was published in the *Baltimore Afro-American* after the *Illustrated Feature Section* ceased publication, also appeared in the *All-America Sports Magazine* in March 1934, one of the only stories I have discovered that crossed over in this way.

41. Cora Jean Moten, "The Creeping Thing," pt. 1, *Baltimore Afro-American,* June 22, 1929, § 2, p. 11.

42. Cora Jean Moten, "The Creeping Thing," pt. 5, *Baltimore Afro-American,* July 20. 1929, § 2, p. 11. Cora Jean Moten, "The Creeping Thing," pt. 8, *Baltimore Afro-America*n, August 10, 1929, § 2, p. 11.

43. Cora Jean Moten, "The Creeping Thing," pt. 8, *Baltimore Afro-American,* August 10, 1929, § 2, p. 11.

44. On one example of this in Dashiell Hammett's *The Dain Curse,* serialized in the crime fiction pulp *Black Mask* about six months before "The Creeping Thing" appeared in the *Illustrated Feature Section,* see Brooks E. Hefner, "Weird Investigations and Nativist Semiotics in H. P. Lovecraft and Dashiell Hammett," *Modern Fiction Studies* 60, no. 4 (Winter 2014): 651–76.

45. Reprinted in S. S. Van Dine, *I Used to Be a Highbrow but Look at Me Now* (New York: Scribner, 1929), 32–33.

46. Cora Jean Moten, "The Creeping Thing," pt. 12, *Pittsburgh Courier,* September 7, 1929, § 2, p. 7.

47. Stephen F. Soitos, *The Blues Detective: A Study of African American Detective Fiction* (Amherst: University of Massachusetts Press, 1996), 42.

48. As Moten's intriguing serial indicates, the "curse of firsts," as Rafia Zafar has described it, remains an issue within African American literary history even into the twentieth century. See Rafia Zafar, "Of Print and Primogeniture, or, The Curse of Firsts," *African American Review* 40, no. 4 (Winter 2006): 619–21.

49. Sarah Juliet Lauro, *The Transatlantic Zombie: Slavery, Rebellion, and Living Death* (New Brunswick, N.J.: Rutgers University Press, 2015), 78.

50. William Seabrook, *The Magic Island* (1929; reprint, Mineola, N.Y.: Dover, 2016), 93.

51. Jeffrey Shanks, "Introduction: Dawn of the Zombie Genre," in *Zombies from the Pulps! Twenty Classic Stories of the Walking Dead* (n.p.: Skelos Press, 2014), 7.

52. Cora Jean Moten, "The Creeping Thing," pt. 4, *Baltimore Afro-American,* July 13, 1929, 11.

53. "Sentinel's South L.A. Deadlines, Aims Told," *Los Angeles Sentinel,* January 10, 1946, 9. "Services for Mrs. Cora B. Moten Mon." *Los Angeles Sentinel,* July 19, 1956, 1.

54. "Ziff Candidate for Congress," *Pittsburgh Courier,* February 27, 1932, § 1, p. 6.

55. Chambers, *Madison Avenue,* 31.

56. George S. Schuyler, "Views and Reviews," *Pittsburgh Courier,* February 16, 1935, § 1, p. 10.

57. Eric Gardner, *Unexpected Places: Relocating Nineteenth-Century African American Literature* (Jackson: University Press of Mississippi, 2009), 13.

58. Gardner, *Unexpected Places,* 12. Emily Lutenski's *West of Harlem: African American Writers in the Borderlands* (Lawrence: University Press of Kansas, 2015) is typical in this respect; it addresses spaces outside Harlem, but only as they connect to well-known Harlem Renaissance figures like Langston Hughes, Jean Toomer, and Wallace Thurman. Notable exceptions that do bring attention to literary and cultural life of African Americans outside the major metropolises during this period include Kimberley Mangun, *A Force for Change: Beatrice Morrow Cannady and the Struggle for Civil Rights in Oregon, 1912–1936* (Corvallis: Oregon State University Press, 2010), a study of the editor of the Portland *Advocate;* and Bruce A. Glasrud and Cary D. Wintz, eds., *The Harlem Renaissance in the American West: The New Negro's Western Experience* (New York: Routledge, 2012). Richard M. Breaux's contribution to this volume, "The New Negro Renaissance in Omaha and Lincoln, 1910–1940" (121–39), mentions the *Illustrated Feature Section.* See also Andreá N. Williams, "Cultivating Black Visuality: The Controversy over Cartoons in the Indianapolis *Freeman,*" *American Periodicals* 25, no. 2 (2015): 124–38.

59. "In 1940, for example, the total circulation of the Black press was 1,265,000. By 1947 it was 2,120,000. Of that circulation, 812,700 was gathered by just four newspapers, the Pittsburgh *Courier* (277,900), the *Afro-American* (235,600), the Chicago *Defender* (193,900), and the New York *Amsterdam News* (105,300). Along with the Norfolk *Journal & Guide,* these were the 'big five' of the Black press during the 1940s and as such were the leading media representatives of America's black community." See Farrar, *Baltimore* Afro-American, *1892–1950,* 19. For visualizations depicting the circulation of the biggest three weeklies through 1945, see "Early 20th Century National Black Newspaper Circulation," *Black Press Research Collective.* http://blackpressresearchcollective .org/united-states-black-press-circulation-1920-1945/.

60. "Schuyler Is Visitor at World Plant," *Atlanta Daily World,* July 29, 1932, 1.

61. Joseph Stafford, "Atlanta after Dark," chap. 1, *Atlanta Daily World,* May 20, 1935, 3. In a notice advertising the serial on page 1 of this issue, Stafford is described as a "talented young Fort Benning, Ga., Officer."

62. Monte King's "Questionmark" appeared in the *Courier,* March 5–April 30, 1930. Edward Lawson's "Miss Norfolk" appeared in the *Norfolk Journal and Guide* September 15–October 13, 1934.

63. Marjorie Tucker Brown, "The Call of the Blood," *Indianapolis Recorder,* July 11, 1931, 1. Jeanette Bunn, "For Better, for Worse," *Indianapolis Recorder,* November 28, 1931, 1.

64. Hopkins's work appeared in the *Colored American,* one of the uplift journals described in the introduction. Micheaux sold his western autobiographical fiction door to door, and many of his films—some uplift-oriented adaptations of writers like Charles Chesnutt, others more standard genre fare—were beset by problems with censorship and distribution. See Patrick McGilligan, *Oscar Micheaux: The Great and Only* (New York: Harper, 2008).

65. The *New York Amsterdam News*'s magazine section represented part of the newspaper's rebranding after its sale in 1935. The magazine section did not survive long. See "Bigger and Better! Amsterdam News Enters New Phase of Growth Next Week," *New York Amsterdam News,* May 18, 1935, 9.

2. ROMANCING THE RACE

1. For statistics on these genres, see Jess Nevins, *The Pulps: A History* (n.p.: Jess Nevins, 2016).

2. Samuel I. Brooks [George S. Schuyler], "Chocolate Baby," pt. 1, *Baltimore Afro-American,* November 3, 1928, § 2, p. 1. This was one of Schuyler's first examples of published fiction, along with the story "Woof," which appeared

in Wallace Thurman's single issue of the literary journal *Harlem: A Forum of Negro Life,* which also bore the date November 1928. Martha H. Patterson has written on this early Schuyler serial and images of a modern, New Negro womanhood in the *Pittsburgh Courier.* See Martha H. Patterson, "'Chocolate Baby, a Story of Ambition, Deception, and Success': Refiguring the New Negro Woman in the *Pittsburgh Courier,*" in *The New Woman International: Representations in Photography and Film from the 1870s through the 1960s,* ed. Elizabeth Otto and Vanessa Ross (Ann Arbor: University of Michigan Press, 2011), 193–211.

3. Examples of these include Louise Camper's twenty-one-part serial, "Passion's Price," in the *Afro-American* (December 17, 1927–May 5, 1928), Blanche Taylor Dickinson's four-part serial "Nellie Marie from Tennessee" in the *Pittsburgh Courier* (January 22–February 12, 1927), and Marjorie Damsey Wilson's ten-part serial "Vagrant Love" in the *Chicago Defender* (July 14–September 22, 1928).

4. Janice A. Radway, *Reading the Romance: Women, Patriarchy, and Popular Literature* (Chapel Hill: University of North Carolina Press, 1984).

5. Tania Modleski, *Loving with a Vengeance: Mass-Produced Fantasies for Women* (New York: Methuen, 1984).

6. Lauren Berlant, *The Female Complaint: The Unfinished Business of Sentimentality in American Culture* (Durham, N.C.: Duke University Press, 2008). See also, for example, Nina Baym, *Woman's Fiction: A Guide to Novels by and about Women in America, 1820–70,* 2nd ed. (Urbana: University of Illinois Press, 1993); Jane Tompkins, *Sensational Designs: The Cultural Work of American Fiction, 1790–1860* (Oxford: Oxford University Press, 1985), 122–46; and Marianne Noble, *The Masochistic Pleasures of Sentimental Literature* (Princeton, N.J.: Princeton University Press, 2000).

7. For a well-needed recent corrective to this problem, see Laurie Powers, *Queen of the Pulps: The Reign of Daisy Bacon and* Love Story Magazine (Jefferson, N.C.: McFarland, 2019).

8. Stuart Hall and Paddy Whannel, *The Popular Arts* (New York: Pantheon, 1965), 180.

9. David Earle and Georgia Clarkson Smith, "'True Stories from Real Life': Hearst's *Smart Set,* Macfadden's Confessional Form, and Selective Reading," *Journal of Modern Periodical Studies* 4, no. 1 (2013): 30–54.

10. Hersey, *Pulpwood Editor,* 174.

11. Powers, *Queen of the Pulps,* 112.

12. Stuart Hall and Paddy Whannel, *The Popular Arts* (New York: Pantheon, 1965), 185.

13. See Christine M. Rudisel, "'A Lack of Acquiescence': The Women Writers and Uncanonized Texts of the Harlem Renaissance" (Ph.D. diss., City University of New York, 2004), 148–86; and Amber Harris Leichner, "'To Bend without Breaking': American Women's Authorship and the New Woman, 1900–1935" (Ph.D. diss., University of Nebraska, 2012), 144–56.

14. Her publications in the *Saturday Evening Quill* include "Black Madness" (1928) and "The Red Quill" (April 1929).

15. For a discussion of Schalk's work in the *Quill*, see Lorraine Elena Roses, *Black Bostonians and the Politics of Culture, 1920–1940* (Amherst: University of Massachusetts Press, 2018), 117–18, 120–21.

16. Information on Schalk's sales of stories to *Love Story Magazine* is from Box M-107, Street & Smith Records, Special Collections Research Center, Syracuse University Libraries. I am grateful to Laurie Powers for supplying this information.

17. In 1954, she wrote of her pulp writing, "Eventually in 1930 I sold my first manuscript. From then until I left Boston to come to Pittsburgh to become women's editor of the *Courier,* I made my living in the writing field. During those years I went to Europe twice, cruised the Caribbean, and lived a charmed life." See Toki Schalk Johnson, "Faith Came . . . When I Needed It Most," *Message Magazine,* February 1954, 17.

18. Gertrude Schalk to Bernice Dutrieuille Shelton, n.d. [December 1933], Bernice Dutrieuille Shelton Papers, Box 9, Folder 7, Historical Society of Pennsylvania.

19. Daisy Bacon, *Love Story Writer* (New York: Hermitage House, 1954), 12.

20. Gertrude Schalk to Bernice Dutrieuille, n.d. [late 1930], Bernice Dutrieuille Shelton Papers, Box 4, Folder 2, Historical Society of Pennsylvania.

21. "Modern Miss Doesn't Want the Old Hokum," *Boston Sunday Globe,* May 31, 1931, 62. The piece is unsigned, but Schalk mentions it in a letter to a friend. See Gertrude Schalk to Bernice Dutrieuille Shelton, n.d. [June 1931], Bernice Dutrieuille Shelton Papers, Box 5, Folder 6, Historical Society of Pennsylvania.

22. Gertrude Schalk to Bernice Dutrieuille Shelton, n.d. [June 5, 1931], Bernice Dutrieuille Shelton Papers, Box 5, Folder 6, Historical Society of Pennsylvania. Gertrude Schalk to Bernice Dutrieuille Shelton, January 5, 1933, Bernice Dutrieuille Shelton Papers, Box 8, Folder 3, Historical Society of Pennsylvania.

23. "My Stars!" *Ainslee's,* July 1935, 51.

24. "George S. Schuyler is editing a new weekly called the National News and he wrote asking me for stories." Gertrude Schalk to Bernice Dutrieuille

Shelton, n.d. [late 1931?], Bernice Dutrieuille Shelton Papers, Box 10, Folder 2, Historical Society of Pennsylvania.

25. Gertrude Schalk, "Night-club Romance," *Street & Smith's Love Story Magazine*, March 31, 1934, 72.

26. Schalk, "Night-club Romance," 76.

27. The resolution of these dangerous potentialities in Schalk's pulp stories can veer in a direction that is, in a word, disturbing. For example, in "Divorce You? Never" (*All Story Love Stories*, May 1, 1932), the protagonist is expecting to marry a young doctor. The doctor, who realizes he can make a better match, hires a man to kidnap her and put her in a compromising situation so he can break the engagement. Once she discovers that her fiancé is a cad, she falls in love with her kidnapper.

28. Jayna Brown, *Babylon Girls: Black Women Performers and the Shaping of the Modern* (Durham, N.C.: Duke University Press, 2008), 10.

29. Gertrude Schalk, "The Sprung Trap," *Baltimore Afro-American*, January 19, 1929, § 2, pp. 1, 4.

30. Schalk, "Sprung Trap," § 2, p. 7.

31. Hersey, *Pulpwood Editor*, 174.

32. Laurie Powers, "Love on the Newsstands," in *The Art of the Pulps: An Illustrated History*, ed. Douglas Ellis, Ed Hulse, and Robert Weinberg (San Diego, Calif.: IDW, 2017), 120. Minna Bardon, "Love Is in Style," *Writer's Digest*, January 1934, 26. Love pulps with smaller circulations and shorter lifespans—especially those that were more often characterized as sex pulps—did demonstrate some boundary crossing. For a brief description of the market, see Bardon, "Love Is in Style."

33. Jayna Brown also emphasizes the fact that "the sleek-haired girls of the chorus line remained public figures of black mobility" (*Babylon Girls*, 237). Shane Vogel's *The Scene of Harlem Cabaret* (Chicago: University of Chicago Press, 2009) details the complex and queer politics of Harlem cabaret culture.

34. Brown, *Babylon Girls*, 233.

35. Gertrude Schalk, "The Yellow Parrot: The Kid from Richmond," *National News*, March 3, 1932, 3.

36. Schalk, "Yellow Parrot: The Kid from Richmond," 3.

37. Schalk, "Yellow Parrot: The Kid from Richmond," 4.

38. One might compare this to the narrative structure of one of the most famous romances of the early twentieth century, Edith Maude Hull's *The Sheik* (1919), made into an even more popular film (1921) directed by George Melford. In this story, the independent-minded protagonist is captured by an Arab sheik, with whom she soon falls in love during her captivity. The novel's

conclusion addresses any fears about racial mixing by revealing that the supposedly Arab sheik is actually white after all.

39. Roses, *Black Bostonians,* 118.

40. Gertrude Schalk, "The Yellow Parrot: The California Lemon," *National News,* March 31, 1932, 11.

41. Gertrude Schalk, "The Yellow Parrot: The Bronx Baby," *National News,* April 14, 1932, 11.

42. Gertrude Schalk, "The Yellow Parrot: The Chicago Kid," *National News,* March 24, 1932, 11.

43. Schalk, "Yellow Parrot: Chicago Kid," 11.

44. Schalk, "Yellow Parrot: Chicago Kid," 14.

45. Schalk, "Yellow Parrot: Chicago Kid," 14.

46. Eugene Gordon, "Negro Fictionist in America," *Saturday Evening Quill,* April 1929, 20.

47. "Love of English Woman Costs Singer $12,000," *Baltimore Afro-American,* March 17, 1934, 13.

48. Kim Gallon, "'How Much Can You Read about Interracial Love and Sex without Getting Sore?' Readers' Debate over Interracial Relationships in the *Baltimore Afro-American,*" *Journalism History* 39, no. 2 (Summer 2013): 112. See also Gallon, *Pleasure in the News,* 118–29.

49. Gallon, "How Much Can You Read," 105.

50. Gallon, "How Much Can You Read," 110. For Gallon's statistical analysis of the responses, see 105–6.

51. "Where Is Your Boiling Point on the Race Question?" advertisement, *Baltimore Afro-American,* April 7, 1934, 13.

52. This was especially common in weird fiction and science fiction titles. For an excellent discussion of how dedicated readers helped to shape the early history of pulp science fiction, see Cheng, *Astounding Wonder,* 51–78. For a reading of letters pages as a kind of social and cultural serial form, see Carey Snyder and Leif Sorensen, "Letters to the Editor as a Serial Form," *Journal of Modern Periodical Studies* 9, no. 1 (2018): 123–46.

53. The *Afro-American* included some coverage of the debate on this. See "Annapolis Plans Fight on Issue of Intermarriage," *Baltimore Afro-American,* March 2, 1935, 6. The *Baltimore Sun,* on the other hand, merely listed it in a summary titled "Legislative Bills Which Took Governor Six Hours to Sign," *Baltimore Sun,* May 18, 1935, 4.

54. Robert Anderson, "Empress," *Baltimore Afro-American,* April 28, 1934, 24. Such tropes were even used by African American romance novelist Frank Yerby, who is briefly discussed in the conclusion. On Yerby's engagement with this, see Jerng, *Racial Worldmaking,* 89–100.

55. Robert Anderson, "Brown Love," pt. 1, *Baltimore Afro-American,* May 5, 1934, 24.

56. Robert Anderson, "Brown Love," pt. 2, *Baltimore Afro-American,* May 12, 1934, 24.

57. Bernard Braxton, "Red Love," pt. 1, *Baltimore Afro-American,* June 9, 1934, 24.

58. Bernard Braxton, "Red Love," pt. 2, *Baltimore Afro-American,* June 16, 1934, 24.

59. Farrar, *Baltimore* Afro-American, 91, 117.

60. As Gallon notes, the opposition to these stories was due in part to the concerns that even with white narrators, these stories represented a kind of white exploitation. See Gallon, "How Much Can You Read," 110.

61. Tate, *Psychoanalysis and Black Novels,* 9. Stephanie Li, *Playing in the White: Black Writers, White Subjects* (Oxford: Oxford University Press, 2015), 95–128.

62. Gene Davis, "Dusky Flower," *Baltimore Afro-American,* August 25, 1934, 24.

63. Quoted in George S. Schuyler, Afterword to *Black Empire,* ed. Robert A. Hill and R. Kent Rasmussen (Boston: Northeastern University Press, 1991), 282.

64. The majority of Schuyler's serials have, at the very least, romantic subplots. Of the *Courier* serials of the 1930s, "Midsummer Madness" (July 10–September 11, 1937) is his only other romance serial. He used this genre, however, in other contexts, including the early serial "Chocolate Baby" (*Pittsburgh Courier,* November 3–December 10, 1928) and "Summer School Idyll" (*New York Amsterdam News,* July 20–August 17, 1935).

65. Samuel I. Brooks [George S. Schuyler], "Black Mistress," chap. 5, *Pittsburgh Courier,* December 15, 1934, § 2, p. 1.

66. There are some basic similarities between "Forbidden Romance" and Harriet Wilson's "Ebony Poet," one of the series published in the *Afro-American;* the protagonist of "Forbidden Romance" is an African American poet named Andrew Richards. But "Ebony Poet" takes places in northern Minnesota and follows the story of a love triangle that could just as easily be told without any racial distinction between characters.

67. Concepción de León, "Racism Dispute Roils Romance Writers Group," *New York Times,* December 30, 2019, https://www.nytimes.com/.

68. Ralph Matthews, "She Wolf," pt. 2, *Baltimore Afro-American,* November 24, 1934, 24.

69. Kim Gallon, "'No Tears for Alden': Black Female Impersonators as 'Outsiders Within' in the *Baltimore Afro-American,*" *Journal of the History of Sexuality* 27, no. 3 (September 2018): 368. Elsewhere, however, Gallon has

charted Matthews's negative attitude toward "same-sex relationships between women." See *Pleasure in the News,* 98–101.

70. James H. Hill, "Kitty Lane," pt. 4, *Baltimore Afro-American,* September 20, 1947), M7.

3. NEWS FROM ELSEWHERE

1. Samuel R. Delany, "Racism and Science Fiction," in *Dark Matter: A Century of Speculative Fiction from the African Diaspora,* ed. Sheree R. Thomas (New York: Warner Books, 2000), 383.

2. Delany, "Racism and Science Fiction," 384.

3. Although these texts are closer to novel-length serials, I will mark them with quotations to eliminate confusion with the volume *Black Empire,* which collected both texts between covers in 1991.

4. W. G. Nunn to George S. Schuyler, January 11, 1937, Box 1, Folder 1, George S. Schuyler Papers, Special Collections Research Center, Syracuse University Libraries.

5. This era, beginning sometime in the late 1930s, is often called the Golden Age of Science Fiction and is associated with John W. Campbell, editor of *Astounding Stories.* Others have imagined this as the beginning of what might be termed social science fiction. On the Golden Age and the shift from Gernsback to Campbell as the dominant influence in science fiction, see Adam Roberts, *The History of Science Fiction* (New York: Palgrave Macmillan, 2006), 195–229; and Gary Westfahl, "The Mightiest Machine: The Development of American Science Fiction from the 1920s to the 1960s," in *The Cambridge Companion to American Science Fiction,* ed. Gerry Canavan (Cambridge: Cambridge University Press, 2015), 17–30. On the concept of social science fiction, see Neil Gerlach and Sheryl N. Hamilton, eds., "Social Science Fiction," special issue of *Science Fiction Studies* 30, no. 2 (July 2003); and Christopher S. Leslie, "Social Science Fiction" (Ph.D. diss., City University of New York, 2007).

6. T. Shirby Hodge [Robert Sherman Tracy], *The White Man's Burden: A Satirical Forecast* (Boston: Gorham, 1915), 43.

7. Advertisements, *Crisis,* October 1915, inside cover, 266. For a brief notice revealing the identity of Hodge, see "Men of the Month," *Crisis,* May 1916, 16–18.

8. John P. Moore, "The Hidden Kingdom," pt. 1, *Baltimore Afro-American,* November 15, 1930, 11. "The Shot into Space" appeared October 4 and 11, 1930; "The Hidden Kingdom" November 15 and 22, 1930; and "Love on Mars" December 13 and 20, 1930.

9. Moore, "The Hidden Kingdom," pt. 1. John P. Moore, "Love on Mars," pt. 1, *Baltimore Afro-American,* December 13, 1930, 11.

10. John P. Moore, "Love on Mars," pt. 2, *Baltimore Afro-American,* December 20, 1930, 11.

11. Burroughs's novel, first serialized in *All-Story Magazine* in 1912, opens with Confederate soldier John Carter fleeing hostile Native Americans, hiding in a cave, and then being unexpectedly transported to Mars.

12. Philip Francis Nowlan, "The Airlords of Han," *Amazing Stories,* March 1929, 1106.

13. Cheng, *Astounding Wonder,* 176.

14. See R. D. Mullen, "The Black Mencken (and Black David H. Keller)," review of *Black Empire,* by George Schuyler, *Science Fiction Studies* 19, no. 2 (July 1992): 267–69.

15. David H. Keller, "The Menace," *Amazing Stories Quarterly,* Summer 1928, 389.

16. Keller, "Menace," 389, 390.

17. Edward James, "Yellow, Black, Metal, and Tentacled: The Race Question in American Science Fiction," in *Science Fiction, Social Conflict, and War,* ed. Philip Davies (Manchester: Manchester University Press, 1990), 26–49. On this tradition, see also Isiah Lavender III, *Race in American Science Fiction* (Bloomington: Indiana University Press, 2011).

18. "The Insect War" (n.d.), Box 17, Folder 1, Manuscripts, Schuyler (Philippa, George, and Josephine) Family Papers, Archives and Rare Books Division, Schomburg Center for Research in Black Culture, The New York Public Library.

19. R. Jere Black Jr., "The Pseudo-Scientific Field," *Author and Journalist,* May 1930, 8. The others are "The Interplanetary Tale," "The Tale of the Future," and "The Fourth Dimension Tale."

20. Black, "Pseudo-Scientific Field," 9.

21. "The Sinister Physician" (n.d.), Box 17, Folder 1, Manuscripts, Schuyler (Philippa, George, and Josephine) Family Papers, Archives and Rare Books Division, Schomburg Center for Research in Black Culture, The New York Public Library.

22. "The Land under the Ice" (n.d.), Box 17, Folder 1, Manuscripts, Schuyler (Philippa, George, and Josephine) Family Papers, Archives and Rare Books Division, Schomburg Center for Research in Black Culture, The New York Public Library.

23. "The Last White Man" (n.d.), Box 17, Folder 1, Manuscripts, Schuyler (Philippa, George, and Josephine) Family Papers, Archives and Rare Books Division, Schomburg Center for Research in Black Culture, The New York Public Library.

24. Samuel I. Brooks [George S. Schuyler], "The Beast of Bradhurst Avenue," chap. 12, *Pittsburgh Courier*, May 19, 1934, § 2, p. 1.

25. In "The Baron of Harlem," rival gang bosses, one Black and one white, each end up taking advantage of "a secret process that will change the color of any man's skin, make it either very much lighter or very much darker" and effectively end up swapping identities, so closely do they resemble one another in every feature except skin tone. Nick Lewis, "The Baron of Harlem," pt. 1, *Baltimore Afro American*, June 10, 1933, 24.

26. For a discussion of "Ape Carver," see my article "Signifying Genre: George S. Schuyler and the Vagaries of Black Pulp," *Modernism/Modernity* 26, no. 3 (September 2019): 483–504.

27. Henry Louis Gates Jr., "A Fragmented Man: George Schuyler and the Claims of Race," *New York Times Book Review*, September 20, 1992, 31, 42–43. For readings emphasizing Schuyler's satire, see Fritz Gysin, "Black Pulp Fiction: George Schuyler's Caustic Vision of a Panafrican Empire," *Empire: American Studies; Selected Papers from the Bi-national Conference of the Swiss and Austrian Associations for American Studies at the Salzburg Seminar, November 1996*, ed. John G. Blair (Tübingen: G. Narr, 1997), 167–79; Alexander M. Bain, "*Shocks Americana!* George Schuyler Serializes Black Internationalism," *American Literary History* 19, no. 4 (Winter 2007): 937–63; Martha H. Patterson, "Fascist Parody and Wish Fulfillment: George Schuyler's Periodical Fiction of the 1930s," *Journal of Modern Periodical Studies* 4, no. 1 (2013): 76–99; and Yogita Goyal, "Black Nationalist Hokum: George Schuyler's Transnational Critique," *African American Review* 47, no. 1 (Spring 2014): 21–36. For readings emphasizing science fiction contexts, see Benjamin S. Lawson, "George S. Schuyler and the Fate of Early African-American Science Fiction," in *Impossibility Fiction: Alternativity, Extrapolation, Speculation*, ed. Derek Littlewood and Peter Stockwell (Amsterdam: Rodopi, 1996), 87–105; Jeffrey A. Tucker, "'Can Science Succeed Where the Civil War Failed?' George S. Schuyler and Race," in *Race Consciousness: African-American Studies for the New Century*, ed. Judith Jackson Fossett and Jeffrey A. Tucker (New York: New York University Press, 1997), 136–52; Kali Tal, "'That Just Kills Me': Black Militant Near-Future Fiction," *Social Text* 20, no. 2 (Summer 2002), 66–91; Amor Kohli, "But That's Just Mad! Reading the Utopian Impulse in *Dark Princess* and *Black Empire*," *African Identities* 7, no. 2 (May 2009): 161–75; and Pavla Veselá, "Neither Black nor White: The Critical Utopias of Sutton E. Griggs and George S. Schuyler," *Science Fiction Studies* 38, no. (July 2011): 270–87.

28. Ruth Mayer, *Serial Fu Manchu: The Chinese Supervillain and the Spread of Yellow Peril Ideology* (Philadelphia: Temple University Press, 2014), 23, 4. On the ways in which Fu Manchu represents a nexus of racial and species

difference, see Mel Y. Chen, *Animacies: Biopolitics, Racial Mattering, and Queer Affect* (Durham, N.C.: Duke University Press, 2012), 115–21.

29. George S. Schuyler, *Black Empire*, ed. Robert A. Hill and R. Kent Rasmussen (Boston: Northeastern University Press, 1991), 53.

30. Schuyler, *Black Empire*, 46.

31. Hugo Gernsback, "A New Sort of Magazine," *Amazing Stories*, April 1926, 3.

32. Cheng, *Astounding Wonder*, 85

33. John Cheng notes, "Later critics and fans describe, often pejoratively, stories of the interwar era as clunky, clumsy, simplistic, and more concerned with discourses on the operation of their science than development of character or theme" (*Astounding Wonder*, 93).

34. Schuyler, *Black Empire*, 17, 49.

35. Catherine Keyser, *Artificial Color: Modern Food and Racial Fictions* (Oxford: Oxford University Press, 2018), 43–44.

36. Schuyler, *Black Empire*, 17. This too recalls Hodge's 1915 *White Man's Burden*.

37. Schuyler, *Black Empire*, 53.

38. Cheng, *Astounding Wonder*, 93.

39. George S. Schuyler, "Georgia Terror," pt. 12, *Pittsburgh Courier*, September 23, 1933, § 2, p. 1.

40. Schuyler, *Black Empire*, 69, 70.

41. Schuyler, *Black Empire*, 37.

42. Schuyler, *Black Empire*, 47.

43. George S. Schuyler to Percival Prattis, April 4, 1937, Percival Leroy Prattis Papers, Box 144-12, Folder 20, Manuscript Division, Moorland-Spingarn Research Center, Howard University, Washington, D.C.

44. Schuyler to Prattis, April 4, 1937.

45. Harry Louis Cannady, letter to the editor, *Pittsburgh Courier*, May 8, 1937, p. 14. Reader Matilda Howell asked for "the address of the Temple of Love in the Black Internationale" (March 27, 1937, p. 14).

46. Lena Walker, letter to the editor, *Pittsburgh Courier*, June 19, 1937, p. 14.

47. Schuyler, *Black Empire*, 3.

48. Chester L. Washington to George S. Schuyler, January 28, 1937, Box 1, Folder 1, George S. Schuyler Papers, Special Collections Research Center, Syracuse University Libraries.

49. "The Black Internationale" promotional insert, Box 1, Folder 1, George S. Schuyler Papers, Special Collections Research Center, Syracuse University Libraries.

50. Schuyler, *Black Empire,* 202, 242, 245.

51. Schuyler, *Black Empire,* 189–90.

52. Schuyler, *Black Empire,* 229, 230.

53. Schuyler, *Black Empire,* 111.

54. Delany, "Racism and Science Fiction," 386.

55. Schuyler, *Black Empire,* 255, 254.

56. Schuyler, *Black Empire,* 257–58.

57. Schuyler, *Black Empire,* 258.

58. I thank my student, Marina Shafik, whose interest in and focus on this final image helped highlight its complexity to me.

59. These two serials are collected in George S. Schuyler, *Ethiopian Stories,* ed. Robert A. Hill (Boston: Northeastern University Press, 1994).

60. William Thomas Smith, "The Black Stockings," chap. 1, *Baltimore Afro-American,* June 5, 1937, 24.

61. "The Black Stockings," advertisement, *Baltimore Afro-American,* May 29, 1937, 13. Each installment of "The Black Stockings" covered nearly the full back page of the *Afro-American,* and each featured a large illustration in the center. In anticipation of the serial's publication, the newspaper featured a number of teasers, hinting at the sensational content of Smith's narrative.

62. Will Thomas, *The Seeking* (1953; reprint, Boston: Northeastern University Press, 2013), 73. The only pulp publication I have been able to locate was one Thomas published under his own name: "The Corpse that Walked" (*Hollywood Detective,* October 1949).

63. He published the serials "The Dark Knight" (as William Smith, March 8–May 24, 1930) and "White Laughter" (as William T. Smith, September 6–November 29, 1930) in the *IFS,* as well as a single story, "Snake Eye" (as William Thomas Smith, February 3, 1934), in the *Afro-American.*

64. "The Best-Selling Books of 1935," *New York Times Book Review,* January 5, 1936, 13. "Best Sellers of the Week, Here and Elsewhere," *New York Times,* June 8, 1936, 17.

65. W. E. B. Du Bois, "Forum of Fact and Opinion," *Pittsburgh Courier,* March 4, 1936, § 2, p. 2. Ted Poston, "About Books," *New York Amsterdam News,* January 25, 1936, 9.

66. A. Clayton Powell Jr., "The Soapbox," *New York Amsterdam News,* June 13, 1936, 12.

67. Will Thomas to Bradford Smith, June 26, 1948, Papers of Bradford Smith, 1926–75, Special Collections, Bailey/Howe Library, University of Vermont, Burlington.

68. Thomas, *Seeking,* 284.

69. William Thomas Smith, "The Black Stockings," chap. 1, *Baltimore Afro-American,* June 5, 1937, 24.

70. William Thomas Smith, "The Black Stockings," chap. 4, *Baltimore Afro-American*, June 26, 1937, 24.

71. William Thomas Smith, "The Black Stockings," chap. 1, *Baltimore Afro-American*, June 5, 1937, 24.

72. William Thomas Smith, "The Black Stockings," chap. 8, *Baltimore Afro-American*, July 24, 1937, 24.

73. Max Horkheimer and Theodor Adorno, *Dialectic of Enlightenment: Philosophical Fragments*, trans. Edmund Jephcott (Stanford, Calif.: Stanford University Press, 2002), 95–96.

74. Horkheimer and Adorno, *Dialectic of Enlightenment*, 129.

75. William Thomas Smith, "The Black Stockings," chap. 8, *Baltimore Afro-American*, July 24, 1937, 24.

76. William Thomas Smith, "The Black Stockings," chap. 1, *Baltimore Afro-American*, June 5, 1937, 24.

77. William Thomas Smith, "The Black Stockings," chap. 1, *Baltimore Afro-American*, June 5, 1937, 24.

78. William Thomas Smith, "The Black Stockings," chap. 1, *Baltimore Afro-American*, June 5, 1937, 24.

79. William Thomas Smith, "The Black Stockings," chap. 11, *Baltimore Afro-American*, August 14, 1937, 24. The intersection of homophobic and antifascist rhetoric here anticipates some of the same problematic connections in Wilhelm Reich's *The Mass Psychology of Fascism* (1933, English translation 1970) and Theodor Adorno's *The Authoritarian Personality* (1950). I am indebted to Rosa Hamilton's essay "The Very Quintessence of Persecution: Queer Antifascism in 1970s Western Europe," *Radical History Review* 138 (2020): 60–81, for these references.

80. William Thomas Smith, "The Black Stockings," chap. 1, *Baltimore Afro-American*, June 5, 1937, 24.

81. William Thomas Smith, "The Black Stockings," chap. 1, 24.

82. On White's undercover work in the 1920s, see Walter White, *Rope and Faggot: A Biography of Judge Lynch* (New York: Knopf, 1929).

83. William Thomas Smith, "The Black Stockings," chap. 5, *Baltimore Afro-American*, July 3, 1937, 24.

84. William Thomas Smith, "The Black Stockings," chap. 12, *Baltimore Afro-American*, August 21, 1937, 24.

85. Heflock's lack of legitimate children—along with the homophobic slur Johnson directs at him—might suggest a deeper psychosexual dynamic at work here: a simultaneous desire and hatred for Blackness that informs his politics.

86. William Thomas Smith, "The Black Stockings," chap. 5, *Baltimore Afro-American*, July 3, 1937, 24.

87. William Thomas Smith, "The Black Stockings," chap. 6, *Baltimore Afro-American,* July 10, 1937, 24.

88. In another intriguing example of this, one of the towns punished by the Sons of Light's Black Squadron of Death is Tulsa, Oklahoma, site of a 1921 racial massacre and the destruction of its Black Wall Street. William Thomas Smith, "The Black Stockings," chap. 7, *Baltimore Afro-American,* July 17, 1937, 24.

89. Will Thomas to Bradford Smith, June 6, 1948, Papers of Bradford Smith, 1926–75, Special Collections, Bailey/Howe Library, University of Vermont, Burlington.

90. The *Afro-American* also reprinted W. E. B. Du Bois's "The Comet" (as "Comet's Tail") in 1953 and featured another, very brief postapocalyptic story by H. L. Faggett ("Operations U.S.A.") in 1950.

91. Delany himself raised questions about the term "new wave" and the historical periodization of science fiction. See Samuel R. Delany, "Reflections on Historical Models in Modern English Language Science Fiction," *Science Fiction Studies* 7, no. 2 (July 1980): 135–49.

92. For a compelling argument about the prehistory of Afrofuturism, see Isiah Lavender III, *Afrofuturism Rising: The Literary Prehistory of a Movement* (Columbus: Ohio State University Press, 2019).

4. BATTLING WHITE SUPREMACY

1. Monte King, "Questionmark," *Pittsburgh Courier,* April 23, 1932, § 2, p. 3.

2. Hersey, *Pulpwood Editor,* 180.

3. Hersey, *Pulpwood Editor,* 193.

4. Sean McCann, *Gumshoe America: Hard-Boiled Crime Fiction and the Rise and Fall of New Deal Liberalism* (Durham, N.C.: Duke University Press, 2000), 65.

5. George S. Schuyler, "Strange Valley," chap. 2, *Pittsburgh Courier,* August 25, 1934, § 2, p. 1.

6. Christopher Breu, *Hard-Boiled Masculinities* (Minneapolis: University of Minnesota Press, 2005), 36.

7. George S. Schuyler, "Strange Valley," chap. 4, *Pittsburgh Courier,* September 8, 1934, § 2, p. 1.

8. George S. Schuyler, "Strange Valley," chap. 6, *Pittsburgh Courier,* September 29, 1934, § 2, p. 1.

9. George S. Schuyler, "Strange Valley," chap. 7, *Pittsburgh Courier,* October 6, 1934, § 2, p. 1.

10. George S. Schuyler, "Strange Valley," chap. 8, *Pittsburgh Courier,* October 13, 1934, § 2, p. 1.

11. George S. Schuyler, "Georgia Terror," chap. 12, *Pittsburgh Courier,* September 23, 1933, § 2, p. 1. For more on Schuyler's serials, see Hefner, "Signifying Genre," 483–504.

12. "Winner Was Writing at Tender Age of 13," *Baltimore Afro-American,* August 4, 1945, 5.

13. Correspondence between Murphy and Hill is in the *Afro-American* Records collection. I consulted this resource at the Moorland-Spingarn Research Center at Howard University before it was returned to the *Afro-American* archives.

14. The introductory material to this volume states, "These stories show that the Negro shares the ambition of the majority of all mankind—he simply wants to be happy." Nick Aaron Ford and H. L. Faggett, "Content," in *Best Short Stories by Afro-American Writers* (Boston: Meador, 1950), 13.

15. One prominent antifascist pulp was the hero title *Operator #5,* which imagined a fascist invasion of the United States in its Purple Invasion story arc, which lasted from June 1936 to March 1938. However, much of the rest of the title's run (1934–39) features villainous anti-Asian and anti-Mexican stereotypes.

16. James H. Hill, "The Black Eagle Rides Again," pt. 2, *Baltimore Afro-American,* March 19, 1938, 6.

17. Hill, "Black Eagle Rides Again," pt. 2, 6.

18. James H. Hill, "The Ace from Senegal," *Baltimore Afro-American,* January 22, 1938, 15. James H. Hill, "The Black Eagle Rides Again," pt. 1, *Baltimore Afro-American,* February 26, 1938, 15.

19. James Hill, "The Land of the Free," pt. 2, *Baltimore Afro-American,* February 8, 1941, 7.

20. James Hill, "The Land of the Free," pt. 4, *Baltimore Afro-American,* February 22, 1941, 7.

21. James H. Hill to Carl Murphy, April 22, 1947, Box 50, *Baltimore Afro-American* Records, Moorland-Spingarn Research Center, Howard University, Washington, D.C.

22. James H. Hill, "Mysterious Bullets, Part 1: The Hounds of Hate," *Baltimore Afro-American,* July 12, 1947, M8.

23. The *Afro-American* reported the news in a flash headline above the masthead: "Interstate Bus Jim Crow Outlawed by Supreme Court." *Baltimore Afro-American,* June 8, 1946, 1, 19.

24. Ralph Matthews, "Bus Company Defiance of U.S. Headed for Court," *Baltimore Afro-American,* October 19, 1946, 3.

25. James H. Hill, "Mysterious Bullets, Part 4: Where Angels Fear to Re-tread," *Baltimore Afro-American,* August 2, 1947, M8.

26. James H. Hill, "Mysterious Bullets, Part 3: Assignment—Dixie," *Baltimore Afro-American,* July 26, 1947, M8.

27. James H. Hill, "Death Dust," pt. 1, *Baltimore Afro-American,* January 10, 1948, M12.

28. James H. Hill, "Death Dust," pt. 2, *Baltimore Afro-American,* January 17, 1948, M12. James H. Hill, "Death Dust," pt. 4, *Baltimore Afro-American,* January 31, 1948, M12.

29. James H. Hill, "Death Dust," pt. 3, *Baltimore Afro-American,* January 24, 1948, M12.

30. James H. Hill, "Death Dust," pt. 5, *Baltimore Afro-American,* February 7, 1948, M11.

31. James H. Hill, "Death Dust," pt. 4, *Baltimore Afro-American,* January 31, 1948, M12.

32. James H. Hill, "Death Dust," pt. 6, *Baltimore Afro-American,* February 14, 1948, M11.

33. "Restrictive Covenants Outlawed," *Baltimore Afro-American,* May 8, 1948, 1.

34. See, for example, Carl Murphy, "Right to Live Anywhere Debated in High Court," *Baltimore Afro-American,* January 24, 1948, 1.

35. Carl Murphy to James H. Hill, November 21, 1947, Box 50, *Baltimore Afro-American* Records, Moorland-Spingarn Research Center, Howard University, Washington, D.C.

36. James H. Hill, "Death Dust," pt. 5, *Baltimore Afro-American,* February 7, 1948, M11.

37. Alex Wellerstein, "Death Dust, 1941," Restricted Data: The Nuclear Secrecy Blog, March 7, 2014, http://blog.nuclearsecrecy.com/2014/03/07/death-dust-1941/. On Loeb, see William J. Broad, "The Black Reporter Who Exposes a Lie about the Atom Bomb," *New York Times,* August 9, 2021; Charles Loeb, "Loeb Reflects on Atomic Bombed Area," *Atlanta Daily World,* October 5, 1945, p. 1, 6; Charles Loeb, "Power of Atomic Bomb Awes War Correspondent," *Baltimore Afro-American,* October 13, 1945, p. 3. I am indebted to Justin McBrien for details around public perception of fallout during this period.

38. "CIO Union Wins Oak Ridge Poll," *New York Times,* December 5, 1947, 28. "Wage Pact Reached for Oak Ridge Plant," *New York Times,* December 11, 1947, 44.

39. "Unrest Reported among A-Bomb Plant Workers," *Los Angeles Times,* September 5, 1946, 11.

40. James H. Hill, "Crime Wounds All Heels," pt. 2, *Baltimore Afro-American,* October 30, 1948, § 2, p. 12.

41. Hill, "Crime Wounds All Heels," pt. 2, p. 12.

42. James H. Hill, "Crime Wounds All Heels," pt. 4, *Baltimore Afro-American,* November 13, 1948, § 2, p. 12.

43. James H. Hill, "Project W," pt. 5, *Baltimore Afro-American,* January 27, 1951, § 2, p. 4.

44. James H. Hill, "Big, Bad Boer, Pt. 4," *Baltimore Afro-American,* February 12, 1954, § 2, p. 5.

45. James H. Hill, "Mysterious Bullets," pt. 1, *Baltimore Afro-American,* July 12, 1947, M8.

46. "Obituaries," *Greensboro News and Record,* August 3, 2000, https://www.greensboro.com/obituaries/article_9e72f5ef-358a-522d-b3bd-9a1971c2 e983.html.

47. H. L. Faggett, "Land of Lost Souls," *Baltimore Afro-American,* May 7, 1949, § 2, p. 4.

48. H. L. Faggett, "Black Robin Goes South," *Baltimore Afro-American,* March 19, 1949, § 2, p. 4.

49. Notice in *Baltimore Afro-American,* May 28, 1949, 4. This notice appeared alongside seven installments in the "Black Robin" series between May 28, 1949, and September 3, 1949.

50. Fredric Jameson, *The Political Unconscious: Narrative as a Socially Symbolic Act* (Ithaca, N.Y.: Cornell University Press, 1981), 77.

51. Jameson, "Reification and Utopia," 140, 145, 147.

52. Readers often wrote to national papers like the *Afro-American* and the *Pittsburgh Courier* with tips on specific racial injustices in their towns in hopes of bringing national attention to such outrages; the use of such tips as raw material for "Black Robin" stories seems to be unique in the genre fiction that appeared in the *Afro-American.*

53. H. L. Faggett, "Dixie Masquerade," *Baltimore Afro-American,* July 9, 1949, § 2, p. 4.

54. According to Clarence Major, *hoogie* was a 1940–50s term for "white racist." See Clarence Major, *Juba to Jive: A Dictionary of African-American Slang* (New York: Penguin, 1994), 241.

55. H. L. Faggett, "Dixie Masquerade."

56. Faggett, "Dixie Masquerade."

57. H. L. Faggett, "Tales of Black Robin: We Got Justice," *Baltimore Afro-American,* January 1, 1950, § 2, p. 4.

58. H. L. Faggette [sic], "Robin Sets Fire to a Hunting Lodge," *Baltimore Afro-American,* February 4, 1950, § 2, p. 4.

59. H. L. Faggett, "Black Robin in the Land of Lost Souls," *Baltimore Afro-American,* May 7, 1949, § 2, p. 4.

60. H. L. Faggett, "Station KKK Signs Off," *Baltimore Afro-American,* January 28, 1950, § 2, p. 4.

61. H. L. Faggett, "Alabama Bus Ride," *Baltimore Afro-American,* May 6, 1950, § 2, p. 4.

62. The Men of Mystery claim responsibility for the deaths of a Klan leader, a Southern senator, and four taxi drivers. A couple of these appear in "Voodoo" (November 26, 1949), when an old woman's dolls seem to cause two deaths.

63. H. L. Faggett, "Just a Lost Victory," *Baltimore Afro-American,* July 19, 1952, § 2, p. 8.

64. One of the final two "Black Robin" stories, "Case of the Third Degree," appeared on July 26, 1952, the week after "Just a Lost Victory." The final "Black Robin" adventure, "Burial at Midnight," appeared almost exactly a year later (July 11, 1953).

65. Harry L. Faggett Sr., *Tales of the Black Robin (Adventures of a Black Robin Hood) and a Collection of Short Stories* (Chicago: Adams Press, 1994), v.

66. Mattie W. Ragin, foreword to Faggett's *Tales of the Black Robin,* vii.

67. *Afro-American* circulation in 1949, when both Jiggs Bennett and "Black Robin" were appearing in the pages of its newspapers, included the *Washington Afro-American* (33,945), the *Baltimore Afro-American* (63,207), the *New Jersey Afro-American* (14,031), and the *Philadelphia Afro-American* (18,369), totaling 129,552 copies nationwide. Data are from *N. W. Ayer & Son's Directory of Newspapers and Periodicals* (Philadelphia: N. W. Ayer, 1950), 1338–39.

CONCLUSION

1. "Market Veiws *[sic],*" *Negro Writer* 1, no. 3 (n.d.): 1.

2. Dorothy West and Harold Jackman's *Challenge* was active from 1934 to 1937, but other (often short-lived) literary and intellectual magazines appeared later. These included *Negro Digest* (1942–51), *Negro Digest* (1942–76), *Negro Story* (1944–46), and *Harlem Quarterly* (1949–50). Left-leaning journals also routinely published African American writers. This was also the era that saw the emergence of popular periodicals like the Johnson Publications' *Ebony* (est. 1945) and *Jet* (est. 1951), as well as other magazines with similar formats, like *Color* (est. 1944), *Our World* (est. 1946), *Sepia* (est. 1947), *Tan* (est. 1950), and *Bronze Thrills* (est. 1951).

3. See, for example, the discussion of Jackie Ormes in Deborah Elizabeth Whaley, *Black Women in Sequence: Re-inking Comics, Graphic Novels, and Anime* (Seattle: University of Washington Press, 2016), 28–66.

4. The *Defender* published Erle Stanley Gardner's *You Can Die Laughing* (December 4, 1957–February 5, 1958) and *Some Slips Don't Show* (June 12–August 16, 1958). Both were originally published under the pseudonym A. A. Fair, though the *Defender* identifies Gardner as the author. During the late 1950s, the *Defender* also published second serializations of novels by Maysie Greig, Archie Joscelyn, Elizabeth Seifert, Rae Foley, Wayne Roberts, John Keene, and William Fuller. Most of these were mysteries or westerns featuring primarily white characters.

5. For a serious consideration of Zinberg, see Alan M. Wald, *Trinity of Passion: The Literary Left and the Antifascist Crusade* (Chapel Hill: University of North Carolina Press, 2007), 1–15.

6. For a detailed survey of Rogers's role as a popular historian of global Black history, see Thabiti Asukile, "Joel Augustus Rogers: Black International Journalism, Archival Research, and Black Print Culture," *Journal of African American History* 95, no. 3–4 (Summer–Fall 2010): 322–47.

7. On Durham, see Sonja D. Williams, *Word Warrior: Richard Durham, Radio, and Freedom* (Urbana: University of Illinois Press, 2015). For Durham's scripts, see J. Fred MacDonald, ed., *Richard Durham's Destination Freedom: Scripts from Radio's Black Legacy, 1948–50* (New York: Praeger, 1989).

8. John Dunning, *On the Air: The Encyclopedia of Old-Time Radio* (Oxford: Oxford University Press, 1998), 197.

9. Ryan Ellet, "'Destination Freedom': 'A Garage in Gainesville' and 'Execution Awaited' (September 25; October 2, 1949)," Library of Congress, 2015, https://www.loc.gov/static/programs/national-recording-preservation-board/documents/DestinationFreedom.pdf.

10. Ellet, "'Destination Freedom': 'A Garage in Gainesville' and 'Execution Awaited.'"

11. "Elizabeth Murphy Oliver Abney, 85, Editor," obituary by Frederick N. Rasmussen, *Baltimore Sun*, August 18, 1999, https://www.baltimoresun.com/.

12. Elizabeth O. Hood, "Sultry Sirens," pt. 1, *Baltimore Afro-American*, July 10, 1948, § 2, p. 12.

13. Joan Anim-Addo and Maria Helena Lima, "The Power of the Neo–Slave Narrative Genre," *Callaloo* 40, no. 4 (Fall 2017): 5.

14. Ashraf H. A. Rushdy, *Neo–Slave Narratives: Studies in the Social Logic of a Literary Form* (Oxford: Oxford University Press, 1999), 3, 4.

15. Michael Cater, "Meet Frank 'Foxes of Harrow' Yerby," *Baltimore Afro-American*, March 2, 1946, 14. On Yerby's fraught relationship to race, see Gene Andrew Jarrett, "'For Endless Generations': Myth, Dynasty, and Frank Yerby's *The Foxes of Harrow*," *Southern Literary Journal* 39, no. 1 (Fall 2006): 54–70.

16. James H. Hill to Carl Murphy, November 16, 1948, Box 50, *Baltimore Afro-American* Records, Moorland-Spingarn Research Center, Howard University, Washington, D.C.

17. James H. Hill, "Tiger Man," pt. 4, *Baltimore Afro-American,* September 4, 1948, § 2, p. 3.

18. James H. Hill, "Custer's Last Stand," pt. 3, *Baltimore Afro-American,* October 2, 1948, § 2, p. 12.

19. James H. Hill, "Big Yellow," pt. 1, *Baltimore Afro-American,* December 31, 1949, § 2, p. 8.

20. Kinohi Nishikawa, "Merely Reading," *PMLA* 130, no. 3 (May 2015): 698.

21. Kenneth Warren, *What Was African American Literature?* (Cambridge, Mass.: Harvard University Press, 2011), 1, 2.

22. On the response to Warren, see the "MLA Roundtable: Assessing *What Was African American Literature?* or, The State of the Field in the New Millennium," *African American Review* 44, no. 4 (Winter 2011): 567–91.

23. Warren, *What Was African American Literature?,* 18.

24. Warren, *What Was African American Literature?,* 65.

25. Stuart Hall, "What Is This 'Black' in Black Popular Culture," in *Essential Essays, Vol. 2: Identity and Diaspora,* ed. David Morley (Durham, N.C.: Duke University Press, 2019), 84.

26. Hall, "What Is This 'Black,'" 91.

27. Hall, "What Is This 'Black,'" 90.

28. Hall, "What Is This 'Black,'" 93.

INDEX

Brooks E. Hefner is professor of English at James Madison University. He is author of *The Word on the Streets: The American Language of Vernacular Modernism* and codirector of the digital humanities project Circulating American Magazines.

CPSIA information can be obtained
at www.ICGtesting.com
Printed in the USA
LVHW080719110322
712859LV00009B/76

9 781517 911577